PEACE ACTION IN THE EIGHTIES

PEACE ACTION IN THE EIGHTIES

SOCIAL SCIENCE PERSPECTIVES

edited by Sam Marullo and John Lofland

RUTGERS UNIVERSITY PRESS
New Brunswick and London

Library of Congress Cataloging-in-Publication Data

Peace action in the Eighties : social science perspectives / edited by
    Sam Marullo and John Lofland.
        p.   cm.
    Includes bibliographical references.
    ISBN 0-8135-1560-2 (cloth)   ISBN 0-8135-1561-0 (pbk.)
    1. Peace movements—United States.   2. Antinuclear movement—
United States.   I. Marullo, Sam, 1954–   . II. Lofland, John.
JX1961.U6P43   1990
327.1′72′0973—dc20   89-49216
                                                                  CIP

British Cataloging-in-Publication information available

Copyright © 1990 by Rutgers, The State University
All Rights Reserved
Manufactured in the United States of America

Contents

List of Tables and Figures

Acknowledgments

The studies contained in this volume describe and analyze the U.S. peace movement of the Eighties. As analysts and contributors, we maintain a professional detachment from the peace activists being studied. Yet as concerned citizens and human beings, we acknowledge the importance of their efforts and admire the fortitude of those most committed to the cause of peace. It is the efforts of these peace activists that inspired this work.

We appreciate the cooperation of our contributors, sticking to the numerous deadlines for revisions through the several iterations of this volume. The original work of twenty-one social scientists is contained in the seventeen articles found in this volume, so one can imagine the amount of accommodation and cooperation required to assemble their works on a common timeline to produce a collective product. We are grateful to the authors for their goodwill in complying. Of course, each of the articles retains its own distinctive point of view. We have not imposed our own perspectives on their analyses, even when we have disagreed.

We would like to acknowledge the support of the editorial staff at Rutgers University Press. Our editor, Marlie Wasserman, provided commitment, enthusiasm, and support throughout the project. Copy editor Elizabeth A. Martin made this a cleaner, tighter book. The anonymous reviewer provided insightful comments and words of support when they were crucial. We also acknowledge the material and staff support provided by the Georgetown University Department of Sociology, and financial support from the Institute on Global Conflict and Cooperation.

Finally, we would like to thank our spouses who provided support and encouragement throughout the project. From Sam to Sue, words cannot express the love and appreciation I have for you. From John to Lyn, this book marks twenty-five years of fretting and discovering on more than three score books and articles we have written together and separately. Does this mean we have a relationship?

List of Contributors

Robert D. Benford is working on a monograph on the nuclear disarmament movement. An Assistant Professor of Sociology at the University of Nebraska, Lincoln, he has coauthored articles on social movement theory and the nuclear arms race which have appeared in the *American Sociological Review* and the *Journal of Applied Behavioral Science*. His research on the peace movement is based on active participation in several peace associations, including United Campuses to Prevent Nuclear War, Texas Mobilization for Survival, and the Austin Peace and Justice Coalition.

Elise Boulding, Professor Emeritus of Sociology, Dartmouth College, is author or editor of numerous works on questions of world peace and justice, including *The Understanding of History: A View of Women Through Time, Bibliography on World Peace and Conflict, Women: the Fifth World*, and *Children's Rights and the Wheel of Life*. The Women's International League for Peace and Freedom, the International Peace Research Association, the Institute for World Order, and the Consortium for Peace Research, Education and Development are among the many peace associations in which she is active.

William Brigham is an Instructor of Sociology at National University, San Diego. He is completing his Ph.D. in Sociology at the University of California, San Diego, where he is analyzing the relationships among scientists, journalists, and the resultant public image of science. He first undertook a field study of Beyond War in the early 1980s under the direction of John Lofland.

Mary Anna Colwell, Adjunct Research Professor at the University of San Francisco, has been active in nonprofit organizations and peace groups for three decades. A consultant on organization, management, and fund raising for public interest groups, her publications include *Pluralism Beyond the Frontier, Guide to California Foundations*, and articles on peace movement organizations and philanthropy. She has served as Chair of the International Conflict and Cooperation Division of the Society for the Study of Social Problems.

Barbara Epstein, Associate Professor of History, University of California, Santa Cruz, is the author of *The Politics of Domesticity: Women, Evangelism and Temperance in the Nineteenth Century*. Her forthcoming book on the nonviolent direct action movement is based on her participation in the Livermore Action Group and other peace and progressive organizations. She is currently researching the transformation of the conception of democracy as it relates to foreign policy in postwar America.

James Hannon, Visiting Assistant Professor of Sociology at Clark University, has been an activist in several branches of the peace movement including the sanctuary and Central America solidarity movements. A member of the Peace Studies program at Clark, he is also a student at Harvard Divinity School where he is preparing for the Unitarian Universalist ministry. Other of his publications focus on religion as a force for social change, decision making in religious organizations, and fatherhood.

Bradley D. Harper is a student of sociology at the University of Minnesota. His involvement on the Core Group of the Honeywell Project led to his research with Leah Rogne on the meaning of civil disobedience. He has also been active in the Fight Military Contractors Committee and People Against Military Madness. He is developing a social change model based upon dialectics and social ecology, and is a National Science Foundation Fellow.

Victoria Johnson is a doctoral student in Sociology at the University of California, Davis, and Research Assistant on a study of the American peace movement funded by the University of California Institute on Global Conflict and Cooperation. She is coauthor or coeditor of several publications on the peace movement, including "Peace Movement Organizations and Activists: An Analytic Bibliography," in the *Behavioral and Social Science Librarian*.

Carmen Knudson-Ptacek's chapter is derived from a larger study of the life histories of peace activists. An Assistant Professor of Health and Human Development at Montana State University, her research is concerned with the reciprocal influences of self, family, and society with a special focus on the impact of the nuclear age on family interaction. She has been an active participant in Beyond War and is involved in a variety of peace education efforts.

John Lofland's publications on social movements include *Protest: Studies of Collective Behavior and Social Movements* and *Doomsday Cult*. A Professor of Sociology at the University of California, Davis, he has served as Chair of the Section on the Sociology of Peace and War of the American Sociological Association and as a member of the Steering Committee of the University of California Institute on Global Conflict and Cooperation.

John MacDougall, Professor of Sociology at the University of Lowell and coordinator of the Peace and Conflict Studies progam there, is active in, among other groups, the Institute for Peace and International Security, American-Soviet Cultural Exchange, and the Massachusetts 5th District Disarmament Caucus. His current research focuses on the congressional impact of the antinuclear movement. His publications include *Land or Religion? Social Movements among the Tribal of Bihar India*.

Sam Marullo is completing a monograph on the nuclear freeze campagn, focusing on its grassroots nature. He was a board member of the Cleveland Freeze Campaign when he conducted the field research reported on in this volume. He is an Assistant Professor of Sociology at Georgetown University, and served as an arms-control Fellow in Congress in 1989–1990. Other of his arms race related articles have appeared in *The Sociological Quarterly*, *Sociological Focus*, and *Teaching Sociology*.

David S. Meyer is the author of *A Winter of Discontent: The Nuclear Freeze and American Politics*. He worked at the Institute for Defense and Disarmament Studies and has been involved in a number of peace movement activities. Currently, he teaches political science at Tufts University.

Earl A. Molander, Executive Director of Ground Zero and the Ground Zero Pairing Project, was a leader in organizing the anti-nuclear movement of the early 1980s and coauthor of the widely selling *Nuclear War: What's In It For You?* and *What About the Russians— and Nuclear War?* An Associate Professor of Management at Portland State University, he is author of several papers on aspects of the antinuclear movement and publications on the social and political environment in business, including *Responsive Capitalism: Case Studies in Corporate Social Conduct*.

Roger C. Molander is currently a research analyst at the Rand Corporation. Along with Early Molander, he cofounded Ground Zero and served as its executive director from 1981–1983. After leaving Ground Zero, Roger served as president of the Roosevelt Center for American Policy Studies until 1989. During the 1970s, he worked as a defense analyst in several government agencies, including the National Security Council from 1974–1981.

Mary Neal holds a Ph.D. in Medical Anthropology from the University of California, San Francisco, and is currently researching the cultural dynamics of environmental dispute resolution. She has been active in peace organizations since 1980, including Physicians for Social Responsibility, the UCSF Program on Health Science and Human Survival, and the Commission on the Study of Peace of the International Union of Anthropological and Ethnological Sciences. Her forthcoming book documents the organizing strategies of PSR in the early 1980s.

Michael R. Nusbaumer's scholarly interest in the peace movement comes from a long-term personal commitment to peace activities and an interest in the study of social problems. His research in this area has been published in *Peace and Change* and *Teaching Sociology*. He is currently Associate Professor of Sociology at Indiana University-Purdue University at Fort Wayne and co-coordinator of the Program for the Study of Peace and Conflict Resolution.

H. Edward Price, Jr., has served on the boards of the North Carolina and national SANE/Freeze and is coordinator of the Jackson County, North Carolina, Peace Network. An Associate Professor of Sociology at Western Carolina University, his scholarly work on social movements has included studies of voter support for George Wallace for President and the strategies and tactics of revolutionary terrorism.

Leah Rogne is a student of Sociology at the University of Minnesota. Her involvement on the Core Group of the Honeywell Project led to her research with Brad Harper on the meaning of civil disobedience. She has also been active in the Fight Military Contractors Committee and People Against Military Madness. She is a Pre-doctoral Fellow with the Midwest Council for Social Research on Aging, and is exploring pathways to lifelong resistance among World War II war resistors.

D. R. Wernette is a sociologist at Argonne National Laboratory, where he conducts a wide variety of applied sociological studies. He is also Professor of Sociology at Lewis University, where he teaches courses on war, social conflict, and race relations.

Louis A. Zurcher, former Professor of Sociology and Social Work at the University of Texas at Austin, was a prolific scholar of collective behavior and social movements. Many of his more than ninety journal articles and book chapters and sixteen monographs addressed collective action dynamics. Just prior to his untimely death in December 1987 he was examining social change agents, including peace activists.

PEACE ACTION IN THE EIGHTIES

CHAPTER 1

Introduction:
Social Science and Peace
Action in the Eighties

JOHN LOFLAND AND SAM MARULLO

In the United States during the Eighties, on the order of ten million citizen activists attempted to turn American national security policies in directions they perceived to be more peaceful. The social science studies assembled here analyze key aspects of this immense upwelling and the enduring structure of peace-oriented institutions these citizens built.

This groundswell of peace activism was a "social movement"—a collective effort to resist or achieve social change that was marked by conflict and acrimony. When a social scientist characterizes something as a social movement, a complex template of salient matters to describe, questions to pose, and debates to address is triggered. The social scientists whose analyses we present here have examined the peace movement from the several angles supplied by social science theories of social movements.

These studies address the interests of social movement analysts, but we believe that they are also of great interest to wider audiences. We have in mind, in particular, people active in the peace movement (as well as in other movements), although we think any citizen involved in war and peace issues can find much of interest. We present here an overview of these studies. We begin with a brief characterization of social science as a form of analysis and of one of its prime justifying functions.

The Social Science Vantage Point

Social science is, in our view, set off by three features. First and most fundamentally, it is about social organization—about the ways in which people aggregate themselves as collective actors, the effects that individuals have on such formations, and the effects these formations have on individuals.

Second, it is about concepts, which capture the flux of social reality in terms of "freezing" labels that allow us to inspect various forms of social organization with clarity and in detail. The application of concepts takes social science beyond description, history, and journalism.

Third, social scientific studies are based on elaborate procedures of collecting information and of ordering it theoretically. The most important reason the studies assembled in this volume are being published several years after the events have concluded is that the authors have needed time to carefully analyze their data so as to achieve a thorough understanding of them and their relationship to social scientific questions.

A Key Aim of Social Science Analysis

Aside from the sheer pleasure of "doing" social science, of what value is this vantage point? The answer is that clearly phrased social science questions and answers are not merely theoretical or academic but, if taken seriously, supremely practical. The phrase "if taken seriously" is the critical qualifier in this assertion! For, although social analyses can tell a great deal, what social analysts say is often not easy to act upon. The questions and answers provided by social science offer few "quick fixes" to pro- or antimovement concerns. And in their concern for the quick fix, activists and citizens alike tend to focus on questions and answers that deflect attention away from more fundamental or critical matters.

Movement activists, especially (and in tandem with their most ardent opponents), tend to be enmeshed in devising activities that are responsive to immediate exigencies. They tend to be so immersed in the day-to-day activities of "doing" a social movement that they are unable to reflect on the larger questions surrounding their work. Even when such questions do arise, the perceived constraints of activists do not enable them to systematically gather and disinterestedly analyze the data needed to address them. In other words, "the requirement of acting vitiates, nay cripples, the capacity . . . to reflect" (Lofland 1985:281).

The need to act and to accommodate crystallizes into collective self-deceptions that form the ideological logjams of all ordinary life. The central task of social analysis is set exactly against the rush of ordinary life. Instead of the hasty collection and analysis of data, social scientists carefully and systematically gather and analyze their data, offering only generalizations that have been reflected upon and carefully qualified. Their examination of causes and consequences go beyond the immediate circumstances and attempt to be comparative and historical. In the end, they shed light on perhaps currently unfeasible but not totally impossible ways of thinking about and acting toward any matter at hand. One of the optimistic aims of social analyses, then, is to provide "transcending" or "liberating" visions that help enmeshed actors reframe their situations.

One sad corollary is that practical people sometimes cannot or will not allow themselves (for psychic, financial, practical, or other reasons) to take social science analyses seriously. However, peace movement activists have shown a pronounced willingness to think again and to think broadly, which are among their more endearing tendencies.

Four Social Science Aspects of Social Movements

To understand the American peace movement of the Eighties, we may think of this fluid and rapidly changing collective effort as consisting of four main aspects: stages, structures, campaigns, and participants. These aspects proceed from the macrosocial to the microsocial: from considerations of movementwide processes of change and societal factors that bear on movement stages, scale, and impact over time; through internal structure and organization of the movement itself; to the campaigns it mounts; to the intimate dynamics of participants' memberships. These four form the four major parts of this volume.

Part I: Stages—Rise, Decline, Effects

One of the most dramatic aspects of social movements is that they commonly exhibit very rapid rises to a peak of participation and social reaction and then decline into a state of quiescence over a period of only five to seven years. The peace movement of the Eighties displayed this pattern.

Key parts of the "rising" phase in the early Eighties are very clearly documented in chapter 2 by Elise Boulding, who uses survey data on organizational foundings in that period to show quite pronounced growth in what Lofland, Colwell, and Johnson, in chapter 6, term the "educator" constituencies of the peace movement.

Hows and Whys of Rise and Decline

The tasks of social analysts addressing the rise and decline of social movements include trying to capture the dynamics of these processes. Although few would deny that movements rise and decline in the pattern just described, there is disagreement on exactly why this is so. We offer two accounts that provide two different emphases. The first, by Earl A. Molander and Roger C. Molander in chapter 3, focuses on what they regard as inadequate educational preparation in the peace movement before direct political engagement. Because of that deficit, the movement failed to pass a critical threshold and stalled. The second, by David S. Meyer, in chapter 4, stresses the importance of political constraints in "demobilization," arguing that the movement entered into direct political struggle before it had built a sufficiently strong political organization, base, and constituency. Lacking in such resources, and failing to exploit its grass-roots strengths, it was outmaneuvered in the legislative fray (cf. Solo 1988).

The nature of historical analysis of unique cases makes it impossible to fully adduce the empirical contrasts needed for convincing evidence. In debates like that between the Molanders and Meyer, the reader must form his or her own judgment, bearing in mind that both accounts might be true.

Effects

One of the most difficult and, therefore, avoided questions in movement analysis asks: What effects do movements have on their host societies? With regard to the peace movement of the 1980s, a crucial version of this question is: What effect did the movement have on U.S. government foreign policy, on national security concerns, and on orientations to war and peace? Although many divergent answers to this question have been propounded, social science wisdom cautions that, when dealing with unique historical situations, universally convincing causal arguments are virtually impossible. Given the inevitably ambiguous and incomplete character of the evidence, we achieve little more than claims about effects that are skewed by proponents' political sympathies. Deterred by the irresolvability of questions regarding effect, few sociologists pursue them. Fortunately, John MacDougall and Michael Nusbaumer are among the exceptions.

MacDougall's exploratory analysis, in chapter 12, attempts to address the problem of irresolvability by examining the relationship between movement-lobbying tactics and congressional votes on the MX missile. With the limited nature of his case study, it is not possible for him to assess the larger question of how the movement affected the decision to limit the deployment of the MX to only fifty missiles. Instead, he focuses on the various lobbying strategies employed by the peace movement to influence a number of swing members of Congress to vote against the MX. He presents evidence suggesting that an indirect lobbying strategy may have indeed been effective in influencing members' votes.

Nusbaumer (chapter 5) addresses the question of the longer-term impact of the movement on educational institutions. Selecting the discipline of sociology for detailed study, he compiled trend statistics on the degree to which teaching and research on war-peace questions increased. He finds, surprisingly (to us at least), that teaching seemed to have been quite discernibly affected, but research was not.

Part II:
Structures—Movement-wide, Cluster, Local

In Part I—questions of a movement's stages—we have viewed the peace movement as an on-going process. This is particularly appropriate in the study of social movements because of the rapidity with which they change. However, complementary to a process view, we need also to conceptualize a movement as a structure, as a constellation of features that are always changing, but not fast enough to make it unreasonable to depict relatively enduring aspects. Structure itself may be thought of on three levels of scale: movement-wide, "cluster," and local.

MOVEMENT-WIDE

At the movement-wide level, analysts describe features of the movement as a whole and its relationship to its encompassing society. The focus is on the anatomy of the movement, so to speak, as well as on relevant features of U.S. society.

One approach to such analysis is presented in chapter 6 by John Lofland, Mary Anna Colwell, and Victoria Johnson, who begin by explicating the variety of beliefs found in the peace movement regarding how to achieve desired social changes. In their view, there were six main change-theories:

Transcender—belief in rapid shifts of consciousness
Educator—belief in communicating facts and reasoning
Intellectual—belief in new facts and reasoning
Politician—belief in parliamentarianism
Protest—belief in forcing by noncooperation and disruption
Prophet—belief in deep moral regeneration

The organizations and more informal associations making up the peace movement did not have a random relationship to one another. Instead, peace movement organizations and participants selectively interacted and cooperated with one another in terms of preference for one or a few of the six change-theories. Composited at the movement-wide level, these selective interactions produced what Lofland et al. call clusters of movement organizations. These clusters constituted the movement-wide structure of the peace movement.

We believe that it is critically important to bear these six clusters in mind when reading all the studies in this volume. Almost all are using data from only one, or at most two, clusters. Therefore, the generalizations developed in each study are likely not applicable to the movement as a whole. Each of the phenomena documented may have occurred within one cluster or between two or a few clusters, alerting us to the necessity to take great care when generalizing about "the movement."

CLUSTER

Knowledge of the six change-theory clusters allows us to identify with some clarity how the various studies in this volume focus selectively on one or two clusters rather than on the movement as a whole and how structural changes in them—such as in number of participants—did not occur evenly.

The great surge of peace activism taking place in the early Eighties, described by Elise Boulding in chapter 2, seemed to have occurred in all six of the clusters, but perhaps not evenly. Although all grew, the educator and politician clusters appeared to have grown most rapidly. These are the two clusters Boulding focuses on in her analysis of the new peak and plateau of the movement that was established in the early Eighties. In her analysis of the dates of founding of a variety of educator-theory organizations, we see a stunningly clear upwelling. Of critical significance is that during this period the movement-wide structure of the peace movement was decisively altered: peace constituencies expanded to include, on a new scale, members of the liberal professions.

Viewed in change-structure context, this volume's chapters are focused in this fashion:

Transcenders: Brigham, chapter 10; Knudson-Ptacek, chapter 16.
Educators: Molander and Molander, chapter 3; Neal, chapter 11.
Intellectuals: Nusbaumer, chapter 5.
Politicians: Molander and Molander, chapter 3; Meyer, chapter 4; Benford and Zurcher, chapter 8; Wernette, chapter 9; McDougall, chapter 12; Price, chapter 14; Marullo, chapter 17.
Protesters: Benford and Zurcher, chapter 8; Rogne and Harper, chapter 13; Hannon, chapter 15.
Prophets: Epstein, chapter 7; Rogne and Harper, chapter 13; Hannon, chapter 15.

In the spectrum of all six clusters of the peace movement, we find three basic tendencies in organizational form. First, toward the "Right" wing of the movement are the traditionally bureaucratic and hierarchical associations in which centrally formulated policy is executed through a series of organizational levels. This was the tendency especially among the transcenders, a feature discussed in chapter 10 by William Brigham concerning Beyond War. The suggestion in that case, also, is that the transcender beliefs of Beyond War seemed to fit a relatively hierarchical model of organization.

Second, the tendency in the middle clusters of the movement (the educators, intellectuals, and politicians) was toward democratic organization (the classic preference of American voluntary associations). Hierarchy as a principle was accepted, but the upper-level occupants were selected and controlled through elections and other voting practices. In chapter 9 Dee Wernette profiles one such local-level organization that operated in this democratic manner. Wernette frames his report in terms of the macrostructural question of effects—namely, an assessment of features associated with success. Linking his focus on success to a concern with organizational form, we would suggest that the very organizational looseness of the nuclear weapons freeze group studied contributed to the buffeted organizational life he describes. Lacking a strongly formulated longer-term program to which participants adhered, and being democratic, the organization was captive to myriad emergent but short-term opportunities and proximate problems.

Third, the two peace movement segments furthermost to the "Left"—the protesters and the prophets—were more partial to equalitarian organization, to associations in which leaders were deemphasized and policies were, ideally, adopted by consensus. Treatments of these appear, in part, in Barbara Epstein's chapter 7 and Leah Rogne and Bradley Harper's chapter 13, the latter of which focuses on debate over civil disobedience as a tactic.

Given this internal differentiation of the Eighties peace movement, we are better able to understand why there is such a diverse nomenclature applied to it, even by the authors in this volume. In addition to the label "peace movement," we have seen these activities referred to as: the freeze campaign, the antinuclear war movement, the antinuclear weapons movement, the disarmament movement, the antiwar movement, the arms control movement, the nuclear disarmament campaign, the arms reduction movement, the antiintervention movement, the antiimperialist movement, and the peace and justice movement. Clearly, some of these labels fit some of the segments better than the others and represent either the participants' or the analyst's attempts to identify or delimit the actors' goals. We have chosen to refer to the broader movement collectively as the peace movement, since this seems to capture the ultimate goal of all of the movement participants, regardless of their divergent change-theories, strategies, and tactics. In several of the chapters that follow, the authors refer to the groups they examine by some of these other names, indicating that their work focuses on a particular segment of the peace movement.

LOCAL

Movements are actually played out at the grass-roots or local level. At this level, the macrostructure of clusters is a microsocial field of interorganizational relations. Although loosely sorted by participants into clusters, a movement, taken as a whole, is nonetheless a sprawling ensemble of interdependent organizations that must carry on relationships with one other. Movement organizations jointly occupy a world in which money, space, volunteers, and times to stage events and mount campaigns are scarce. Although all of them may thoroughly agree on broad movement goals, differing emphases of different clusters produce divergent conceptions of exactly what to do at any specific time. And even such compatible differences give rise to competition over available money, people, and time (cf. Zald and McCarthy 1987: chap. 7).

Robert D. Benford and Louis Zurcher (chapter 8) trace these processes of instrumental and symbolic competition in Austin, Texas. They examine the conditions under which competition emerged among three local peace groups: a community-based freeze group, a university-based Mobilization for Survival chapter, and the citywide chapter of the Texas Mobilization for Survival. Whereas it might be expected that groups representing different clusters would compete for both material and symbolic resources—e.g., the freeze (political cluster) having different goals than Mobilization for Survival (protest cluster)—Benford and Zurcher found similar amounts of competition between groups within the same cluster (i.e., the two "Mobe" groups). They conclude that although the structural differences among the groups set the conditions for competition to emerge, social-psychological factors explain the forms the competition takes.

Part III:
Campaigns—Transcending, Educating, Politicking, Protesting

The heart of any movement, its raison d'etre, is campaigning to achieve desired social changes. The depiction of change-theories in chapter 6 is also a once-removed description of the six main forms of campaigning seen in the Eighties peace movement. That is, they focus on theory-in-use as an aspect of movements, but such theories are, of course, also actually acted on by organizations and individuals.

Viewed as campaigning microprocesses, we need to render each of these change-theories in an appropriate processual—gerund—form: transcending, educating, intellectualizing, politicking, protesting, and prophesying. Studies that analyze four of these—transcending, educating, politicking, and protesting—are reported in Part III. Previously discussed chapters contain descriptions (albeit indirectly in some instances) of the other two, as indicated in our cluster-coded list of chapters above (in the section on movement-wide structure).

William Brigham's description of Beyond War, chapter 10, suggests how a transcending strategy is oriented to the elucidation of consensual value themes that are presented in a conventionally showy fashion in order to appeal to audiences that might not otherwise have much interest in war-peace questions.

In chapter 11, Mary Neal details the educating campaign style of the most famous of the early Eighties educator groups, the Physicians for Social Responsibility. As part of the physicians' efforts to "balance passion and reason," she focuses on the rhetorical style of the person who was perhaps the most visible and effective of early Eighties educators, Helen Caldicott (although there was a later backlash against her style).

John McDougall's account, in chapter 12, of the anti-MX campaign reports on one of the most clearly successful political efforts of the Eighties, as we discussed in the section on effects, above.

Finally, in chapter 13, Leah Rogne and Bradley Harper examine the protesting campaign tactics of the Minneapolis-based Honeywell Project. The Project's reliance on civil disobedience as its primary activity (indeed, for many members, its raison d'etre), was criticized by other members as politically ineffective and an inefficient use of resources. This internal debate over the tactic of civil disobedience had an adverse impact on group solidarity and contributed to a factionalizing of the local organization.

Through their analysis, Rogne and Harper also provide an illustration of our contention at the beginning of this Introduction that movement actors are often so caught up in the process of "doing" social change that even when they attempt critically to analyze their own actions, their closeness to the issues and their ego involvement in a particular tactic may cripple their capacity to reflect.

Part IV: Participants—Mobilization, Self-conception, Participation

Like movements, participation in them is helpfully conceived as a set of stages or even as careers. The four studies of Part IV focus on successive stages in such participant careers.

MOBILIZATION

H. Edward Price, Jr., in chapter 14, examines an important dimension of the premovement, or preparticipation, stage. Acknowledging that many other factors were at work, social theories stressing the role of political generations in member mobilization seemed salient to Price. He collected data on this matter and found a remarkable age-specificity among participants involved in the politician change-theory cluster of the movement. People whose political consciousness was formed in a small set of years in the late sixties and early seventies turned up with very high frequency in the political cluster of the Eighties peace movement.

Studies such as Price's situate people in historical contexts in ways that help us understand the background of their movement participation. Complementing such a focus are studies that trace sequences of personal and intimate experiences as conceived and reported by activists themselves. This is the task James Hannon sets for himself in chapter 15, where he reports regularities in the "lived experiences" over time of people who became Eighties peace activists in, primarily, the protest and prophet clusters. The people interviewed by Hannon tended, on the whole, to be further Left politically than much of the peace movement and to have involved themselves in greater degrees of personal sacrifice and risk than did most participants. As such, we would expect the process of becoming a peace activist to be rather different from those in clusters further to the Right. (The degree to which there is movement of peace movement activists among the clusters is a dynamic yet to be explored. Cf. Marullo 1988).

SELF-CONCEPTION

The conception that participants have of themselves as actual members is one of two major aspects of the membership phase in movement participation careers. In chapter 16, Carmen Knudson-Ptacek explores the self-conceptions of the members of a transcender peace group in California. She finds that a sense of connection between the individual and the larger society to be the key element of the self-concept that distinguishes activists from their nonactive siblings, spouses, or friends. And even within this transcender group, she finds four qualitatively different types of moral connection between the individual and the whole.

PARTICIPATION

The second major aspect of participation is, of course, what members actually do in movements. Sam Marullo's detailed analysis, in chapter 17, reveals that movement involvement is not at all a homogeneous phenomenon. Based on his analysis of members of only one organization within only the politician cluster (a freeze group, specifically), Marullo distinguishes eight model types of participation. Similar analyses carried out within other clusters are likely to reveal a wide variety of yet other patterns.

Reading the Knudson-Ptacek and Marullo chapters together, a reasonable inference would be that at the local level, both the meaning and overt behavioral patterns of peaceseeking vary considerably—even within a single organization and even within a single cluster of the movement. How these individual models of participation become the distinctive clusters described by Lofland et al. in chapter 6 is a topic yet to be examined.

Social Science and the Peace Movement

We conclude with several brief observations on each of the two main topics discussed in this volume: social science and the peace movement.

SOCIAL SCIENCE

When a movement "breaks forth" in a contemporary society, social scientists in some numbers are drawn to it both as participants and as analysts. The occurrence of this pattern in the peace movement in the Eighties was only a recent episode in a longer history. Among other post-World War II movements in the United States in which social scientists have played both roles are those concerned with civil rights, the Vietnam war, student rights, feminism, the new religious movements, antinuclear power, and gay/lesbian rights. In fact, it is our impression that more social scientists were involved (both absolutely and proportionately) in the movements just mentioned than in the Eighties peace movement.

Such a regularity of involvement needs to be a topic of social analysis. There is a movement analysis trade, subject to the problems and hazards of all trades. Among them are the difficulties of studying something too soon and too close. Thus, although a large amount of social scientific work was done on the civil rights movement in the midst of its unfolding from the late Fifties to the middle Sixties, the most perceptive studies of it may well have been performed only in the middle and late Eighties. This point also applies to the other movements mentioned. The present volume will likely suffer the same fate; the most knowing analyses are yet to come and will be dated 2020 or so.

It is important to note the dual role of social scientists in the peace movement (as well as in other movements). Virtually without exception, the analysts one reads here have also been activists, sometimes simultaneously, sometimes sequentially. Indeed, several of these authors have been and are major activist leaders. Furthermore, new insights on the movement will undoubtedly be provided by yet other leaders once they are removed from their activism.

Research workers have leaned to qualitative rather than quantitative methods of data collection and analysis. Only four of the sixteen studies here are based on questionnaires or other numerical sources, and the larger universe of all such studies is in like proportion (that is, we have not excluded quantitative work). Given that the bulk of mainstream social science is moving in exactly the opposite direction, this is an anomaly. It may have to do with the emergent character of movements making field and qualitative methods more feasible. But, in addition, there may be a selective affinity between the philosophical values dominant in the peace movement, with which social scientists tend to be sympathetic, and the epistemology of qualitative studies.

Both the studies herein and the larger universe of which they are a part have tended to the microsocial rather than to the macrosocial, an imbalance that may have to do with the same kinds of factors just mentioned with regard to a penchant for qualitative work. In addition, as we have noted, the macro issues of the movement's impact on society and features of its national structure are difficult topics to analyze, especially for lone and largely unfunded researchers. We simply have to hope that more macro-level work will emerge. (In the next section, we speculate on what such hoped-for research may find.)

We, as editors, need to acknowledge that several important aspects of the Eighties peace movement experience are, as yet, dealt with by social scientists only in passing or not at all. Among such matters we have to include are: the early crystallization initiative and referendum success of the freeze idea; the political debate over the Freeze Resolution in Congress (cf. Waller 1987); the peace movement's electoral activities, especially in 1984; the organization behind and the impact of large, nationally coordinated demonstrations, such as the June 12, 1982, rally and the national lobby days; the merger of SANE and the Nuclear Weapons Freeze Campaign in 1987; the dissolution of several important peace movement organizations and the decline of Washington arms control lobbying organizations at decade's end; the late Eighties rise of the idea of common security among peace movement intellectuals and its adoption in other clusters; the nationwide campaigns of civil resistance (and the rise of that conception as against civil disobedience); and the confluence of peace and environmental issues in the late Eighties.

THE PEACE MOVEMENT

What can we say in more general terms about the effects of U.S. peace activism in the Eighties?

As a first matter, we can point to the movement itself as an effect. When we contrast the peace movement of 1980 with that of 1990, we see many highly significant changes. Although all of them are not documented in these chapters, we know from additional sources that between 1980 and 1990 the movement went from

—Counting peace groups in the few thousands to counting them in the many thousands;

—Numbering members in the tens of thousands to numbering them in the hundreds of thousands;

—Measuring peace spending in the hundreds of thousands of dollars to measuring it in the millions;

—A participant social base that was very narrow and relatively radical to one that incorporated an expanded array of occupational categories and other groups (including the addition of many liberals);

—A miniscule-sized transcender cluster to flourishing programs of consensual peace themes, peace travel, and peace events;

—Minimum inclusion of war-peace topics in formal education to widespread incorporation;

—Virtually no organized peace intellectual activity to networks of peace research institutes and circles;

—Only a few national and local officials concerned with peace topics to nationwide networks so concerned, including establishment of a new government agency, the U.S. Institute of Peace;

—A very small national lobbying force and electoral program to vigorous lobbying and electoral efforts;

—Virtually no protest of the war system to a panoply of on-going protest activities; and

—Only the most modest of moral witness and prophetic dissent to a number of regional networks so dedicated.

Taken together, these and other changes represent a significant transformation of the movement itself. In 1990 we are witnessing not simply a larger peace movement than we saw in 1980, but a different one, involving a scale and breadth of effort that amounts to a new peace presence, or peace establishment. That presence, that establishment, is a truly major achievement.

But what of the movement's impact on U.S. society and international relations? Clearly the arms race has continued, military intervention has not stopped, and the policy process remains elite-controlled. Nonetheless, we would argue—at least tentatively—that there has been an impact. Although a number of nonmovement factors certainly contributed to the changes listed below, we believe the movement also played a role. We hypothesize, then, that the peace movement of the Eighties contributed to

—Changing public opinion of the Soviet Union from hostile—based on extreme fear—to neutral or even positive—based on a more cautious, live-and-let-live attitude;

—Increasing knowledge and awareness of the United States' important but limited role in an interdependent global order;

—Heightening public outrage over defense contracting fraud, abuse, and mismanagement, leading to more oversight and regulation;

—Creating scientific, cultural, and educational exchange programs with the Soviet Union;

—Slowing or reducing nuclear force modernization and defense spending increases that otherwise would have occurred;

—Preventing a new generation of weapons from proceeding through the research and development stage without careful scrutiny;

—Forcing a reticent president to enter into arms control negotiations; and

—Influencing Congress to play a more active role in shaping foreign policy, hindering or blocking some of the administration's more aggressive initiatives.

As we have indicated, claims such as these, because of the complexity of the factors involved and, in some instances, their historical uniqueness, are extremely difficult to confirm or refute. Nevertheless, with the passage of time, future researchers should have additional clarity regarding both the direction and reversibility of these processes and the myriad factors influencing them. The analyses contained in this volume are only the beginning of this enterprise.

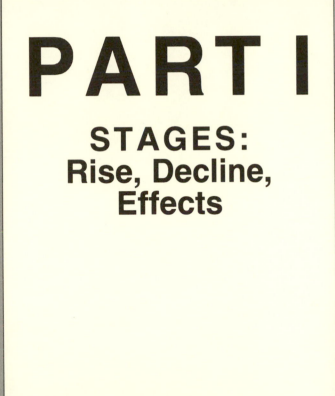

PART I

STAGES:
Rise, Decline, Effects

CHAPTER 2

The Early Eighties Peak of the Peace Movement

ELISE BOULDING

To clarify the use of the term peace movement in the United States, I suggest that we consider it to be made up of various sectors. One sector is that of the historic peace churches, who have traditionally taught a doctrine of personal as well as social pacifism (i.e., disarmament for the state as well as the individual) that is intended to apply to all situations. Another sector consists of those peace organizations in the United States dating back to the days of World War I which have consistently promoted disarmament policies. They contain a broad spectrum of attitudes toward personal and social pacifism. They include church members from many denominations and humanists of many political views, who may reserve their position on personal pacifism but who support disarmament as a political doctrine on the grounds that political problems require political, not military solutions.

A third sector consists of the antiwar movement born in the Vietnam era, which includes the antidraft movement. The antiwar movement represented a tremendous revulsion of feeling against war as an instrument of the haves against the have-nots, and added to the ranks of longtime peaceworkers many middle-class moderate-to-liberal citizens, both young and middle-aged, who had strong political and social objections to what were perceived as wars of colonialism and neo-colonialism. *Just Wars* fought to oppose undeniable evil were seen as a phenomenon of the past. This sector had been quiescent during the 1970s but was once again aroused during the 1980s by the threat of nuclear war and by the threat of U.S. military action in Central America.

The fourth sector, mobilized for the first time in the antinuclear movement of the Eighties, was much more diverse than the other sectors and harder to characterize. What the new antinuclear groups had in common was an opposition to the use of nuclear weapons in war, but not necessarily an opposition to the use of conventional weapons. War itself was accepted by many antinuclearists as a necessary evil. It was this fourth sector, the antinuclearists, that gave the peace movement of the 1980s its distinctive character. It included professionals from the communities of medicine, business, law, science, education, art, labor, and veterans. It also included conservative politicians and fundamentalist, politically conservative churches. It is this new sector of the peace movement of the Eighties that serves as the focus of this paper.

Historical Context of the American Peace Movement

Although this paper focuses on the U.S. peace movement of the past decade, it is important to recognize the continuity of this movement with the great public response to the Hague Peace Conferences at the turn of the century. The resulting movement can be traced through this century in the great multiplication of bibliographies about peace making, peace keeping, and peace education, a tangible record of continuing involvement of citizens as well as professionals and governments in the issues of peace and war. The monumental bibliography of bibliographies on war and peace by Carroll and Fink (1983) makes that continuity of involvement accessible and visible.

At the symbolic level, the threat of nuclear war stirred deep feelings about the possibility of human extinction and the adequacy of political and economic arrangements in the modern world. The movement, therefore, has macrohistorical significance; it questions the very paradigms on which modernism and "development" are based. At an intuitive level, balance of power concepts are struggling with interdependence concepts, and ecological thinking pushes against the hidden agendas of dominance that underlie so much of our power politics and economic exploitation of the natural and social environments.

Symbols of a new order recognized in every country of the world were created by the peace movement internationally—the Campaign for Nuclear Disarmament's peace symbol, the broken gun, the dove, the flower, and the green earth. The acknowledgment of these symbols is the best testimony to the change in world view the peace movement has nurtured. Whatever the outcome of the most recent peak of activities of the peace movement, the international system cannot return to its nineteenth-century ways.

The U.S. peace movement can be seen as a series of peaks and troughs in a century-long trend line as larger publics are first aroused to the dangers of war and lulled back into acceptance of its necessity. The baseline movement consists of the historic peace churches and longtime peace organizations. There was a peak in peace movement activity just prior to World War I, when a core of social reformers and lifelong peace workers helped launch a broad antiwar coalition that fought military preparedness and military budgets (Chatfield 1971). Preparedness was portrayed as a dinosaur—the symbol around which antiwar rallies were held. Groups sponsoring the rallies included labor, farmers, social workers, churches, the women's peace party, and a significant group of congressional leaders. The American Union Against Militarism broke apart when Wilson declared war. Antiwar fervor turned into prowar fervor for all but the core of committed peace workers.

There was another peak in peace movement activity just prior to World War II. The Emergency Peace Campaign was a massive two-year public effort—1936 to 1937—launched again by a core of committed peace workers and again with the support of labor, farmers, women, a variety of civic groups, the churches, and an even more significant group of congressional leaders than in the anti-World War I movement. The two opposing interests of isolation and world responsibility joined forces against involvement in this particular war. There were peace committees in two thousand cities and towns, organizations on five hundred college campuses, and nearly seven hundred nationally prominent men and women (not the old familiar peace workers) who donated their time traveling across the country to speak against military involvement in Europe (Chatfield 1971). Huge sums of money were donated to these educational efforts by well-to-do citizens.

As war clouds gathered in 1938 supporters fell away, and by 1940 the Keep American Out of War Congress was the only national peace movement activity left. When the United States entered the war after Pearl Harbor, it had already been effectively involved in supporting the allies for two years.

In the Vietnam era of the late 1960s and early 1970s, the Mobilization for Survival created another antiwar peak. This time, unlike the pre-World War I and II peaks, the movement did in fact contribute significantly to ending a war. Success in attaining its political objectives was responsible for ending that particular peak, as failure had been in the two previous movement peaks. During the long decades in between peaks, the core of committed peace organizations, adding slowly to their numbers over time, continued their work.

The peak and trough phenomenon should not be taken as a signal of futility, but rather as an indicator of the Sisyphean character of working for disarmament and peace. Because the social order is always changing, Sisyphus' stone never rolls back to the original starting point, but to a different plateau on the long hill. It is important to know the terrain of that hill, and where future plateaus might be. It is also important to be aware of the peace movement's committed core— those directly behind the stone. It would be foolish for analysts of the peace movement of the Eighties not to acknowledge its roots, not to be aware that many of those who were working in it had been active on behalf of peace issues for forty years or more, and shared their knowledge with younger generations. It is from these historical roots that the peace movement peak of the 1980s sprung. However, it assumed a new form in response to the social context and mobilized new constituencies. It is this new form of the movement to which we now turn our attention.

The Organizational Base

The recent peak of the peace movement, like other U.S. social movements, demonstrated a tradition of local organizing that has been a characteristic feature of this country since its inception. At the base were several historical layers of organization, including associations founded during or after World War I, when world responsibility was the theme; the peace organizations founded after World War II, to counter the ugly rumbles of the Cold War; and those founded during the era of revulsion against the Vietnam War.

Added to these were the organizations formed in the Eighties in response to the threat of nuclear war. Table 2.1 lists the national peace organizations active in 1983 with established headquarters which had 18 or more local branches, giving their time of founding.[1] We can see that the organization with the largest number of branches (140) was the U.S. section of the Women's International League for Peace and Freedom. WILPF was founded in Europe in 1915. It has outlived several other women's peace organizations founded in more recent decades that did not take root locally as WILPF did. The three other World War I era organizations are the Fellowship of Reconciliation, with 83 branches, the American Friends Service Committee, with 47 local offices,[2] and the War Resisters' League, with 32 branches. The next four organizations in the table, SANE, Mobilization for Survival, Clergy and Laity Concerned, and World Peacemakers, were all formed either after World War II or during the Vietnam era, and are still very active. Three new national organizations, formed in response to the threat of nuclear war, also took root locally by 1983: the Freeze

Table 2.1. Number of Local Chapters of the Largest National Peace Organizations in 1983

Organization	Founding era	Number of local chapters
Women's Internat'l League for Peace and Freedom	WWI	140
Fellowship of Reconciliation		83
American Friends Service Committee		47
War Resisters League		32
SANE	WWII	26
Mobilization for Survival	Vietnam era	132
Clergy and Laity Concerned		52
World Peacemakers		26
Freeze Campaign	"New"	109
Jobs with Peace		80
Women's Action for Nuclear Disarmament		40

NOTE: Data from the files of the *American Peace Directory 1984* of the Institute for Defense and Disarmament Studies, and verified by phone calls in June 1983 to the organizations listed.

Campaign (109 branches), Jobs with Peace (80 branches), and Women's Action for Nuclear Disarmament (WAND) (40 branches). A nuclear freeze, to be followed by negotiated nuclear disarmament, was advocated by all of these groups. The newer groups tended to deal with more immediate issues like the threat to survival posed by current nuclear policies, the linkage of military production to unemployment, and the health effects of nuclear production. The older groups, however, tended to have a broader agenda for dealing with the long-term causes of war, and to link the peace issue to social and economic justice and human rights.

The role of religious organizations in working for peace is underestimated by Table 2.1. Four of the eleven national organizations listed are religious—the Fellowship of Reconciliation, the American Friends Service Committee, the Clergy and Laity Concerned, and World Peacemakers. However, there were also new peace initiatives with full-time program staff and legislative representatives in Washington, from half a dozen or more of the major denominations. For example, there was a large-scale Peace and Justice program of the Catholic church which reached into every local parish in the country to do educational work based on the pastoral letter on nuclear war by Catholic bishops (National Conference of Catholic Bishops 1983). Annual nationwide peace sabbaths in the local parishes of fifty other denominations by 1983 represented a rapidly expanding movement reaching people of all classes never reached before. After the Catholic Bishops' letter, several other national church bodies adopted similar pastoral documents, including the Episcopal church, the Presbyterian church, the Baptist church, the Methodist church, the United Church of Christ, and the Lutheran church. These are in addition to the continuing activities of the historic peace churches. As a result, there were many local communities in the United States that supported specific peace action as part of an ongoing church program, but were not organized in a way that would appear in the lists of peace organizations. The actions they undertook ranged from prayer to educational programs to peace marches, from writing letters to Congress to active lobbying in Washington, D.C. The fact that religious peace group activists repeatedly showed up in additional organizational formats outside of their own church organization, as we see in examining further data on the peace movement, suggests something of the dynamism of the religious sector of the peace movement.

Another important national group, which was not primarily organized by local branches but had members everywhere, was Citizen
Soldier, which carried on a long-term campaign to alert veterans, the
federal government, and the general public to the serious health consequences to veterans of their exposure to atomic testing in the fifties,
and of their exposure to the herbicide Agent Orange during the war in
Vietnam. Their work provided dramatic testimony to the dangers of
nuclear war.

The Professionals

One way to identify who were the most active initiators of peace
action in the United States is to look at the total roster of national
peace organizations in 1983. Table 2.2 summarizes data about 142
such organizations taken from the *American Peace Directory 1984*
files. Organizations have been grouped and rank ordered according to
type of initiator, with the organizational foci given for each group.
Next to peace groups with a general civic orientation and diverse
membership, we find that church activists, teachers, scholars, scientists, and women were the most frequent initiators. The great majority
of the groups focused either on a set of considerations related to disarmament, such as conflict resolution, nonviolence, and social justice, or
they focused very specifically on arms control and nuclear disarmament. If we add the groups concerned with global perspectives and
world order to the disarmament/conflict resolution group we get a total of 77 groups who approached disarmament within a broader framework of desirable alternative national policies. The more narrowly
focused arms control, freeze-specific, and area-specific groups (Middle
East, Central America) totaled 64 groups in all. Given the narrow,
strategic nature of the arms control issue as it had been presented to
the American public by several successive presidents, it is of interest
to note that a substantial majority of the organizations active in the
peace movement saw the issues in broader, rather than narrower,
terms.

The peace research movement, including groups such as the International Peace Research Association (IPRA), had a special relationship to the peace movement in the United States. Peace researchers
themselves do advocacy research on policy problems pointing to the
advantages of nonmilitary postures. A larger group of scholars and

Table 2.2. Initiating Interest Group and Thematic Focus for 142 National Peace Organizations

Initiating interest group	Number of organizations	Disarmament, conflict resolution, nonviolence, social justice	Foreign policy, globalism, UN	Arms control, nuclear disarmament	Freeze specific	Area specific
General civic	34	8	7	12	4	3
Religious	27	19	3	4	—	1
Professional & scientific (Total)	59	16	14	23	4	1
Teachers	16	6	5	5	—	—
International relations Scholars	14	4	6	3	—	—
Natural scientists	6	1	1	4	—	—
Lawyers	6	1	1	4	—	—
Students	4	0	—	2	2	—
Social scientists	5	2	1	1	1	—
Communications	3	1	—	2	—	—

Specialists						
Doctors	2	—	—	2	—	—
Artists	2	1	—	—	1	—
Business						
executives	1	—	—	—	—	—
Others (Total)	**22**	**9**	**1**	**9**	**2**	**1**
Coalition						
organizations	7	2	—	4	1	—
Women	8	3	—	4	1	—
Political						
activists	3	2	—	—	—	1
(radical)						
Children	2	1	—	1	—	—
Blacks	1	1	—	—	—	—
Youth						
volunteers	1	1	1	—	—	—
Total	**142**	**52**	**25**	**48**	**10**	**6**

NOTE: Based on data taken from the *American Peace Directory 1984* files.

scientists who do not identify themselves with the peace movement, such as the Federation of American Scientists, oppose the technological arms race. These include many of the scientists who worked on the first atom bomb at Los Alamos, as well as younger scientists who see the multiplying technical problems in succeeding generations of weapons systems and question their value for national security. *The Bulletin of Atomic Scientists* has long been the voice and the conscience of the physicists' community about the dangers of nuclear weaponry.

Natural and social scientists, doctors and lawyers, also became active in the past decades on war/peace issues. The Physicians for Social Responsibility had the most visibility in public education on the threat of nuclear war. Their pattern was followed by Educators for Social Responsibility, the Lawyers' Alliance for Nuclear Arms Control, the Nurses' Alliance for the Prevention of Nuclear War, and dozens of other professional and business groups that used the "social responsibility" concept as a basis for their involvement in community education on the threat of nuclear war. Scholars and scientists on college campuses had opportunities not open to other professionals. In the research area, many worked specifically on arms control issues. Others moved to interdisciplinary research and teaching in peace and conflict studies, coming in contact with more advocacy-oriented peace researchers. The United Campuses to Prevent Nuclear War (UCAM), and the Student/Teacher Organization to Prevent War (STOP War) were the largest such advocacy groups at the college and high school levels respectively. The new type of interdisciplinary teaching program coalesced into peace studies programs which have become an accepted part of the curriculum at a number of colleges and universities. Such programs originated in small denominational colleges before World War II, but they are now present in state and private secular universities as well.

The type and content of peace-related programs in 93 institutions of higher learning are listed in Table 2.3. The great difficulty that U.S. peace researchers had in finding support for scientific work shows up in the fact that only 16 of the 93 institutions supported both research and teaching. The lack of apprentice-type training for students in conflict resolution skills is notable, but a recent development that has changed this to some degree is discussed below. Looking at the program content in Table 2.3, we see that the majority of both secular and

Table 2.3. Ninety-three Educational Institutions with Research and Training Programs in Disarmament and Peace

	Type of Institution			
Mode of work	Institute or training agency	Secular college or university	Religious college or university	Totals
Research & training	2	16	—	18
Research only	—	1	—	1
Teaching only	1	54	17	72
Apprenticeship/ training	1	1	—	2
Totals	4	72	17	93
Focus of Program				
Conflict resolution, nonviolence disarmament, social justice	3	41	15	59
World order International relations with global emphasis	1	18	2	21
Arms control & national security	1	13	1	15
Total	5	72	18	95*

NOTE: Based on data taken from the *American Peace Directory 1984* files.
*Two programs were listed with more than one focus, and are thus double-counted.

religious institutions were dealing with the broader context of disarmament problems, including world order approaches, and only a minority confined themselves to the narrower issues of arms control and national security. This breadth of concern for developing the type of society that can handle disputes peacefully was both a strength and weakness of the U.S. peace movement. It was difficult to build strong political coalitions out of this diversity. At the same time, a core mission of the peace movement, and what gives it macrohistorical significance, was precisely the refusal to accept old ways of conducting international affairs.

Scholarship outside the traditional field of international relations was important in providing educational materials for peace studies programs. A significant amount of reading matter came from the writings of peace researchers in IPRA, and in the Consortium on Peace Research, Education and Development (COPRED). COPRED networks circulated teaching materials, and the Institute for World Order published peace and world order curriculum outlines for college use. The National Education Association developed a curriculum, "Choices," that focused on the issues of war and peace, and alternatives to violence, which was adopted by hundreds of school districts. Various social science associations formed sections on conflict and peace (as for example the American Sociological Association's Section on the Sociology of Peace and War), which also circulated materials useful for teaching. Peace research journals published in North and South America, Europe, Japan, and India all helped to shape a broader conception of the problem of disarmament than was available in conventional international relations publications. Materials more directly focused on arms control strategies were made available to campuses through such groups as the Federation of American Scientists, the Union of Concerned Scientists, the Arms Control and Disarmament Committee of the American Association for the Advancement of Science, and the interdisciplinary Social Scientists Against Nuclear War. The U.S. Section of the International Student Pugwash Movement also provided study materials. It should be emphasized, however, that only a very tiny segment of the student populations at any school was exposed to these programs.

Although academia was a source of expanding the understanding of the nature of war/peace issues, it also became the bastion of the balanced debate. The concept of the balanced debate on defense and national security policy was developed by university administrators in response to student demonstrations and demands for campus programs on the threat of nuclear war. The national student network (including more than 150 campuses that sponsored programs on the dangers of nuclear war) would show films made by the Physicians for Social Responsibility on the horrors of nuclear war, do simulations on the local consequences with packets of material provided by Ground Zero, and bring national figures to campus to discuss arms policy. Responsive to the "plausible" argument that scientific impartiality required a speaker favoring nuclear buildup for every speaker against it, the entire campus-based movement found itself largely debating the merits of one defense strategy versus another. There were relatively few occasions when alternative conceptions of national security and international conflict resolution were seriously examined (Remember that there were student committees on 500 college campuses in 1937, as opposed to 150 groups in the national student network of the Eighties.)

One important difference between previous peak mobilizations of the peace movement and the Eighties mobilization was in the involvement of professionals *as professionals*. The new opposition to war by doctors, lawyers, teachers, and other professional groups was rooted in their understanding of their professional responsibility, and had an institutional quality that earlier mobilizations lacked. As the movement receded, there remained a large new core of continuously involved professional activists that expanded the ranks of the old core of peaceworkers. Even on college campuses, while student activism disappeared, conflict and peace studies programs did not go away.

The Grassroots Groups

So far we have examined national peace groups and the contradictory developments on college campuses. Now it is time to turn to the more clearly identifiable grassroots part of the peace movement, the groups that formed locally and remained local in character. The names these groups gave themselves clearly reflected a sense of urgency, a need for action, and a sense of being a community-in-action. We know of their existence because of the determined network of the nuclear freeze movement, which uncovered and/or inspired many new local initiatives.

It was the nature of these grassroots groups to spring up in response to local perceptions of national and international problems. Some of these groups, therefore, came to nuclear arms control issues from an original opposition to conscription, to Central American issues, or from a concern for violations of human rights in various parts of the world (especially El Salvador and South Africa). In other words, they had other and perhaps wider agendas, but added nuclear arms control. Most of the grassroots locals, however, had agendas more narrowly focused on a nuclear freeze and arms control, based on their fear of a nuclear holocaust, with disarmament seen as a possible but distant goal. It was the dynamism of these new locals, a galvanized Nuclear Freeze Campaign's Clearinghouse in St. Louis, Missouri, plus the more sustained action over time of the older national organizations, that created the enormous political pressure for a nuclear freeze and arms-control negotiations.

Many grassroots networks were too new or too informal to be listed in the 1984 peace directory.[3] However, data on the distribution of about 400 locals (from a larger, uncountable set of locals) that were listed in the *American Peace Directory 1984* files indicated that the South and the Northwest had the fewest groups, but no area was unrepresented by locals. Three tiny underpopulated states in northern New England—New Hampshire, Vermont, and Maine—contained as many locals as the spacious population-booming Southwest. An east coast concentration from Boston to Washington, D.C., not surprisingly, had the most locals of any region. The Midwest, also not surprisingly, had more than three times as many locals as the South.

What kinds of people initiated these locals? The names that the local groups gave themselves did not always indicate the composition of the group, but I tabulated the categories of initiators that were revealed by group names. Thirty-two groups identified themselves as "people" or "citizens" in their names, eleven as "women," six as "interfaith," and six as "students." A few labeled themselves as "parents," "families," "children," and a few, artists, media, or business people. The majority of the groups took the name of the town or area in which they were located, such as "Upper Falls People for Peace." The message conveyed was that these were ordinary local citizens aroused by the threat of nuclear war.

What was impressive in these local peace movements was that individuals identified with a distinctive religious or ethical perspective were often willing to set aside their own ways of working in specific situations in order to assist a community peace group in finding its way on issues that were new to it. Longtime peaceworkers rarely insisted on working only with their own kind.

The other key words used in the locals' names revealed a sense of urgency combined with community and informality. I identified eight "high-action" words frequently used in names of locals: coalition (28), action (20), project (17), campaign (8), task force (6), mobilization (6), and initiative (4); ministry, crusade, team, impact, and alert were also used. Another set of words indicated a joining together in concern: alliance (58), committee (29), council (8), network (6); federation, forum, league, consortium, and collective were also used. Finally, the words center (45), group (17), and community (14) indicated a sense of belonging together among the group members. The names of these locals were on the whole distinctively different from the names of national peace organizations in the sense of both direction and informality.

The Role of Women in the Peace Movement

Recall from Table 2.1 that the venerable Women's International League for Peace and Freedom was the national organization with by far the largest number of local groups, and that Women's Action for Nuclear Disarmament was one of the largest new groups. Another new group in the 1980s, Peace Links, founded by Betty Bumpers, wife of Arkansas Senator Dale Bumpers, appealed to moderately conservative as well as more liberal women. Women appeared as initiators eight times for national peace organizations, eleven times for local women's groups, and uncounted times as organizers or contact persons for organizations containing both men and women. In local churches, mostly unreferenced here, they were frequently the organizers of the peace program.

It might be said that the peace movement of the Eighties owed much of its success to the vigorous leadership of a whole new cadre of extraordinarily competent and gifted women. Although there was an increased recognition of this, male names nevertheless tended to be featured in peace movement leadership. Some of the important women leaders were: Kay Camp initiated the STAR campaign (Stop the Arms Race) through the Women's International League for Peace and Freedom. STAR was both a predecessor and companion to the nuclear freeze campaign. Randy Forsberg, founder of the Institute for Defense and Disarmament Studies, was the originator of the nuclear freeze concept, and Pam Solo, a Sister of Loretto, was one of its leading strategists. Helen Caldicott was a prime mobilizer of the medical community in her role as president of the national PSR and later organized WAND. Representative Pat Schroeder was a strong voice in Congress for nuclear disarmament. Betty Goetz Lall, arms control specialist, was a U.S. representative to the UN disarmament working group. Anne Cahn, another arms control specialist, directed the Committee for National Security, which for several years brought together leaders of all the major women's organizations in the United States for seminars on nuclear war. Betty Bumpers created Peace Links for conservative women who wanted to identify themselves with arms control and to dialogue with women in the U.S.S.R. Betty Reardon was a major leader in the new peace education movement, organizing conferences and preparing and editing materials for teaching about alternatives to nuclear war. Pat Mische, founder of Global Education Associates, played a similar role among peace educators. Joanna Macy, creator of the Despair and Empowerment workshops, through her tireless holding of workshops across the country, helped move thousands of local citizens from the paralysis of despair about nuclear war to peace activism.

Women in the United States have consistently been recorded as being for reduced weapons expenditures, for disarmament policies, for a nuclear freeze, and against nuclear energy for as long as opinion polls have been taken. They have been ignored just as consistently. However, beginning with the 1980 election, a clear gender gap in voting was discerned which provided a strong and not-to-be ignored voice for a changed military policy. The increased presence and visibility of women in the paid labor force, in elected and appointed public office, and in civic and specifically peace organizations, imply added new force to a set of views about the need for disarmament held by women for a very long time. The feminist critique of militarism added a whole new dimension to policy debates, requiring men to reason on unfamiliar terrain.

Conclusions

The American peace movement has a long established tradition, dating back to the beginning of the century. During this ninety-year period, the movement has seen peaks and troughs in response to external events. The movement has gathered support and grown organizationally when war clouds began brewing, and, during the first half-century, disappeared quickly at the outset of World Wars I and II. During the Vietnam era, the movement resisted the unjust war in Southeast Asia and helped bring about its end. The 1980s peak of the movement focused its efforts on halting the nuclear arms race that threatens our very survival.

Each peak of the movement saw the creation of new organizations, some of which survived during the ensuing trough. Over the years, a core of experienced peace activists has remained actively engaged in peace work through these organizations. However, since each wave of peace movement activism has confronted different threats and has had to operate within a different context, the shape of the movement has differed from one peak to the next.

The early 1980s peak of the movement was built from the base of the historic peace churches, a small number of secular grassroots peace networks such as WILPF, Mobilization for Survival, and the War Resisters League, and a handful of D.C.-based lobbying organizations such as SANE and the Council for a Livable World. On top of this base, the major impetus for the eighties resurgence of the peace movement was the call for a nuclear freeze, which spawned an enormous growth in locally based freeze groups and its national office, the Nuclear Weapons Freeze Campaign. Most of the previously existing organizations endorsed the freeze, and all of the peace groups, local and national, experienced a tremendous amount of growth. Three other initiatives shaped the contours of the Eighties peace movement: those by the churches, professionals, and women. Most of the mainline Christian and Jewish religious bodies produced statements condemning the arms race and calling for a demilitarizing about-face, providing a much wider institutional base for the movement. Professionals in their work roles created organizations legitimating their concern over the continuation of the arms race. And finally, due to their increased control over resources, women's desires for and efforts in creating peace generated many new organizations, while feminist perspectives influenced the goals and operations of most others.

From the vantage-point of the early 1990s, we can once more see the "peak-trough" phenomemon that has occurred previously in American history. But, as I noted above, Sisyphus' stone has not rolled back to its original position. The Eighties peak of the movement assumed a quite distinct form from earlier mobilizations, being more grassroots based and more thoroughly embedded in other institutions. The movement now stands on a much higher plateau than ever before, actively engaged and poised for the next peak.

Acknowledgment

I wish to thank Melinda Fine of the Institute for Defense and Disarmament Studies and Laurel Schneider of Dartmouth College for their assistance with data for this chapter. An earlier version was presented for the Commission on Peace Movement and Peace Research, International Peace Research Tenth General Conference, Gyor, Hungary, 1983.

Notes

1.   I wish to thank Melinda Fine of the Institute for Defense and Disarmament Studies for sharing with me the data from *American Peace Directory 1984* (Fine and Steven 1984). The *Peace Directory* took several years in the making, with Melinda and other IDDS staff acting as compilers. The tables in this chapter are based on the original data, and I take full responsibility for all interpretations presented here.
2.   The American Friends Service Committee, as a service organization, is not really comparable to the other civic action organizations, but has always been closely associated with the U.S. peace movement.
3.   The most recent version of the Peace Directory 1988/89 (Institute for Defense and Disarmament Studies 1988) lists eight thousand local peace groups. The Topsfield Foundation, which produces the Grassroots Peace Directory, maintains data on eight thousand local peace groups in 1989. Certainly a substantial number of these organizations are no longer operational.

CHAPTER 3

A Threshold Analysis of the Antinuclear War Movement

EARL A. MOLANDER AND ROGER C. MOLANDER

This chapter offers an explanation for the rise and decline of the anti-nuclear war movement of the 1980s using a theoretical framework for the evolution of social movements developed by the authors (Molander and Molander, 1987). Inherent in the application of this threshold theory is the assertion that mismanagement by movement leaders at a number of critical developmental stages contributed significantly to the movement's failures and ultimate decline. In particular, this chapter argues that it was the movement's failure to understand the role of education in movement development, not political naïveté or a lack of a sufficient political base, that was the overriding cause of its failures and decline.

As a social movement, the antinuclear war movement had its origins in 1981 and peaked in the summer of 1982 with the disarmament rally in New York City. What followed afterward was a movement increasingly fractionated by competition for status and resources and deeply divided over goals, priorities, and strategy, including the appropriate balance of movement building versus political engagement. However, these divisions were largely papered over by the two-year campaign to promote the Nuclear Weapons Freeze initiative first in the Congress and then in the 1984 presidential election.

Through June 1982, the proposal for a bilateral nuclear freeze between the United States and the Soviet Union had played a key role in building awareness of the threat of nuclear war and stimulating movement development at the grassroots level. However, the deep division on movement goals that plagued organization of the June disarmament rally pushed the Freeze to center stage as an organizational and policy compromise. Here its simplicity appealed as much to movement adherents as to the media, which in early 1982 had been instrumental in the movement's growth. As a result, the Freeze became (1) the organizing framework for the movement (via the Nuclear Weapons Freeze Campaign Clearinghouse) and (2) the first major policy proposal for its move into the political arena. In so doing, movement leaders pushed the movement away from its decentralized grassroots social movement origins toward an increasingly centralized political lobbying effort.

The bilateral nuclear weapons freeze, which had been an excellent social movement building symbol, proved a poor policy proposal. It failed to capture significant support in the expert community, the Congress, the media, or the general public who could not be persuaded to ignore the nuances of unilateral disarmament its detractors frequently raised. Drawn on by opportunist members of Congress, movement leaders blinded themselves to a lesson they had learned early on—that despite the 70 percent support for the Freeze in public opinion polls, nuclear weapons and mutual deterrence were deeply ingrained in American political culture, and no whirlwind political lobby, even with a broad base of public support, would be able to turn the corner on the policy path of the past forty years.

In consciously choosing to leap into the political arena, rather than continue their movement-building efforts at the grassroots, movement leaders abandoned those areas where their awareness-building and educational efforts had been most effective—the political margins between the liberal community and mainstream America. Worse, they entered an arena where they had little experience, few strong allies, and no institutional legitimacy. When the Freeze initiative failed in the Congress and the 1984 presidential campaign, the disintegration of the freeze network and the antinuclear war movement that followed was simply the public revelation of a management and movement breakdown that originated in the summer of 1982.

A Threshold Theory for the Evolution of Social Movements

The threshold model employed in this chapter is a five-stage depiction of social movement evolution that highlights the importance of key intervening thresholds between stages. The stages and thresholds are summarized in Figure 3.1. The model is a variation on life-cycle conceptions of social movements as set forth by Blumer (1939), Turner and Killian (1987), and Tilly (1978). It is also an attempt to reconcile the debate between resource mobilization theory (which portrays movements as planned, structured, rational, consistent with prevailing norms, closely tied to existing institutional structures, and

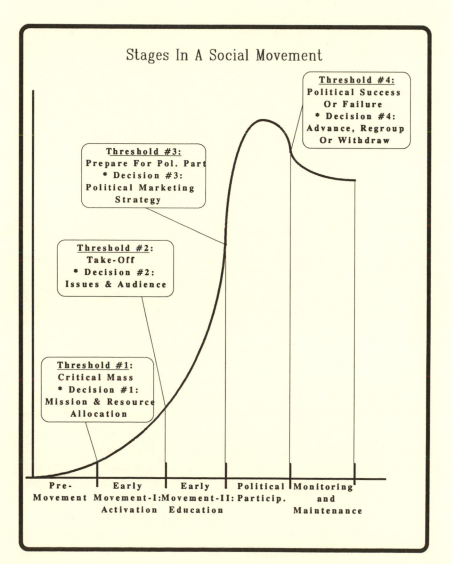

Stages In A Social Movement

Threshold #4:
Political Success
Or Failure
* Decision #4:
Advance, Regroup
Or Withdraw

Threshold #3:
Prepare For Pol. Part
* Decision #3:
Political Marketing
Strategy

Threshold #2:
Take-Off
* Decision #2:
Issues & Audience

Threshold #1:
Critical Mass
* Decision #1:
Mission & Resource
Allocation

Pre-	Early	Early	Political	Monitoring
Movement	Movement-I:	Movement-II:	Particip.	and
	Activation	Education		Maintenance

dependent on existing networks) and classical collective behavior theory (which conceives movements as spontaneous, unstructured, at odds with prevailing norms, outside existing institutionalized structures, and independent of preexisting networks) (Sorokin 1925, Zald and Ash 1966, McCarthy and Zald 1977, McAdam 1982, Walker 1983, Jenkins 1983, and Killian 1984).

Features of our threshold model that go beyond these earlier works in explaining social movement evolution are: (1) the nature of the discrete stages in multistage movement development, especially the education stage; (2) the importance of key thresholds between movement stages; (3) the need for sequential and deliberate passage through the intermediate stages of movement development; and (4) the importance of synchronization of movement progression with the evolution taking place within three institutions key to movement success—(a) the media, (b) the expert community, and (c) political leaders in the policy areas to which the movement is directed.

Stage 1.
Premovement: Strains in the System Equilibrium and the Prevailing Consensus on Nuclear War Prevention Policy

All social systems experience both internal and external strains that challenge the prevailing equilibrium. If the system is unresponsive, and the strains are sufficiently large to represent a major challenge to system equilibrium, spontaneous formation of the necessary elements for social movement evolution occurs.

The premovement conditions that ultimately led to the antinuclear war movement were broadly scattered in the external environment, and internally in the expert community and among policymakers. Externally, these strains included the economic impact of defense expenditures and the growing uncertainty about the threat of nuclear war in the domestic population, and the political uproar in Europe over planned deployment of intermediate range nuclear missiles there.

Internally, strains were apparent in the technological arena, where MIRV deployment was escalating the arms race with no end in sight, new first-strike weapons such as MX and Trident were being developed, and there was a seemingly inexhorable drift toward accidental war. Many of the specific strains in the policy system had arisen from the failure of SALT II to achieve Senate ratification. The consensus on

Mutual Assured Destruction (MAD) as the principal deterrent to nuclear war was coming unraveled, and the solutions under consideration, such as developing a limited nuclear war-fighting capability and civil defense, were not receiving broad-based support in the expert community, the political system, or the mass public.

Before entrepreneurs will undertake the commitment to build a social movement and individual SMOs, the movement channels through which the power of the movement can be expressed must appear to be open, i.e., there must be a sense of feasibility that movement goals can be achieved, whether that assessment is correct or not (Freeman 1983). In the case of the antinuclear war movement, this assessment moved a wide range of entrepreneurs to action, from Randy Kehler, a Vietnam War conscientious objector, who led the Nuclear Weapons Freeze Campaign, to Roger Molander, former National Security Council arms control expert, who started Ground Zero.

Finally, existing networks and institutions critical to success must be open to the movement in the sense that they are not occupied on other issues or policy agendas. The antinuclear war movement had the good fortune of emerging when the liberal peace and social justice political base in the United States was relatively free and unoccupied. It thus began with a significant political base in the liberal media, foundations, social justice groups, service organizations, and mainstream churches. The movement was able to use this political base and the growing number of activist elements within important professional categories—educators (Educators for Social Responsibility), scientists (Union of Concerned Scientists), lawyers (Lawyers Alliance for Nuclear Arms Control) being the principal groups—in taking the movement through its key early stages.

THRESHOLD 1:
THE MOVEMENT REACHES A CRITICAL MASS

Strains in the system are not enough to create a social movement. For emerging elements in a social movement to coalesce, it is necessary to have social movement entrepreneurs who can merge those elements in ways that create an actual product—a social movement.

For the antinuclear war movement, the strains in the social system reached a critical mass in early 1981 following the election of Ronald Reagan. His assumption of office saw the departure of a generally proarms control group of policy experts from the executive branch.

Within a few months, President Reagan set forth major initiatives to expand defense spending and declared his open hostility to and distrust of the Soviet Union, including the Soviet's perspective and record on arms control. As a result of these developments, a number of new social movement organizations (SMOs) were formed at the national level. With a quantum jump in the number of inquiries from the local level to these SMOs, especially the newly-formed national Nuclear Weapons Freeze Campaign, these organizations began to assess the receptivity of essential networks—specifically the Congress, national security experts, and the national media—to a grass-roots antinuclear war movement.

STAGE 2.
EARLY MOVEMENT-I: ACTIVATION

With the shell of a movement architecture in place, a movement begins to grow both quantitatively (the number of individuals, SMOs, and other institutions involved) and qualitatively (the breadth and legitimacy of the movement). This activation stage involves not only mobilization of potential movement adherents, but also funders, the media, politicians, and experts. As the movement progresses, it becomes important to synchronize movement development with the accompanying progression of understanding and commitment to movement goals in these other institutional realms.

Activating new movement adherents is a resource-dependent task. Few SMOs have the resources to be able to take large numbers of people from a state of apathy and ignorance about a movement to a state of activation and commitment. Virtually all need the assistance of the mass media. The activation process in the antinuclear war movement took a dramatic jump in early 1982 with the publication of Jonathan Schell's *Fate of the Earth*. In declaring that nuclear war was *the* "Fate of the Earth" issue, Schell, who had considerable legitimacy in the media from his early reporting of the problems with the Vietnam War, broke the dam on news coverage of the threat of nuclear war and the emerging antinuclear war movement.

For most of the first half of 1982, the antinuclear war movement was a major new story in the national media. Among the key movement events of the period was a week of nuclear war education activities organized by Ground Zero. Ground Zero Week involved more than one thousand communities nationwide, with extensive local and national media coverage. As a result, tens of thousands of new adherents were activated and brought into the movement.

Despite the breadth and media coverage of the Ground Zero Week event, many elected officials still were reluctant to endorse the new movement. Their reluctance was intensified by a huge disarmament rally two months later in New York City. Although half a million people turned out for this June rally, the strong disarmament, as opposed to arms control, themes were so at odds with current policy, not to mention the policy path of the Reagan Administration, that many people in the political center of political, media, and arms control institutions paused for a second look.

Threshold 2.
Take Off Legitimation of the Movement

Once a social movement is underway, there is a threshold at which movement leaders and adherents as well as media, politicians, experts in the policy community, and funders recognize the movement as a movement, and become aware that the movement's goals may indeed be achievable. Once this threshold has been cleared, the movement is for a time self-sustaining, made so by the herdlike character of all of these political actors (Freeman 1979).

Although it clearly had its detractors, the June disarmament rally following the success of Ground Zero Week proved the antinuclear war movement had clearly reached the take-off stage. It was addressed as a significant movement in the political arena and the media, and large numbers of mainstream social justice organizations were reorienting their agendas to include nuclear war and nuclear weapons issues. Simultaneously, the policy debate within the expert community on the nuclear arms race and the long-term viability of MAD was intensifying. Equally important, the funding base for the movement was rapidly expanding both in the foundation community and among large and small givers in the public at large.

Stage 3.
"Expanding the Circle" and Problems with Education

In the third stage of movement development, the movement continues its quantitative and qualitative expansion. In quantitative terms, movement entrepreneurs refer to this process as "expanding the circle," which implies attracting not only greater numbers of individual and institutional supporters, but also extending the outer reaches of the movement into the mainstream of society—political moderates and the institutions such as mainline churches, service clubs, community associations, schools and universities where new supporters tend to be found.

Qualitatively, energy and resources begin to focus on specific policy objectives that would require actions at some level of government. As a result, the importance of activation gives way to the increasing importance of education of movement adherents so that they can be effective and sustained advocates for movement objectives and tactics to potential movement adherents.

Synchronicity with Evolutionary Changes within the Expert Community. It is at this stage that parallel movements begin to emerge within the political system and the expert community. These movements focus even more specifically on those public policy measures that would be the appropriate first targets of the movement. As a result, there is considerable cross-fertilization of the grassroots movement with the complementary developments within the expert community and the political system. Simultaneously, parallel developments are taking place among countermovement forces.

Social movement entrepreneurs must be careful at this juncture to be certain that their movement is synchronized with parallel changes in the expert and policy communities. If these communities are not ready for the issues to be raised in the public policy context, the energy of the political participation phase of the social movement will be wasted because the experts, and politicians, being in most cases conservative, will favor the prevailing consensus.

Sequential Passage through Movement Stages. Activation followed by education (learning) and political participation is the sequence by which social movement adherents move toward their goals. Activation must precede the expenditure of resources on education, or educational materials and programs will have no audience. Education must precede political participation or (1) movement adherents will often misdirect their resources when they undertake political participation, (2) the pressures on public policymakers will not be sufficiently forceful to overcome the prevailing policy inertia, and (3) movement adherents will be unable to handle the inevitable defeats that will accompany any change process. All represent significant threats to the movement.

Problems for the Antinuclear War Movement. It was in this third stage of movement development that the antinuclear war movement began to have problems. These problems occurred despite the fact that, thanks to broad media coverage of the nuclear war issue and the active promotional efforts of local peace groups, by the fall of 1982 the movement was rapidly expanding its grass-roots membership into the political center of society.

The first major problems began to occur as antinuclear war SMOs sought to expedite the movement of citizens and loosely aligned middle-of-the-road social justice groups through the education stage toward political participation, most particularly on the freeze issue. At this point, some groups, including some elements within the flagship National Freeze Campaign, argued for a more protracted and thorough education phase. They identified three areas of support that movement adherents needed to sustain their efforts:

1. Intelligent and persuasive arguments for a broad variety of changes in policy that could be articulated to elected officials in one-way communication;

2. Responses to the countermovement arguments being made with increasing effectiveness by the Reagan Administration and traditional conservatives; and

3. Education to strengthen the commitment of movement adherents, or staying power, for what was anticipated to be a lengthy battle. It was clear to many movement leaders that the expert community was not likely to spontaneously and radically argue for alteration of the course of U.S. nuclear policy as it had been practiced in the United States for over two decades. Moreover, the state, in the form of the Reagan Administration and Republican majority in the Senate, was strongly committed to policies that ran counter to movement objectives.

Because of the passion of the freeze movement, the elegant simplicity of the Freeze proposal, and the general inclination of Americans to favor action over learning, those within the movement who argued for a longer education stage lost their battle, and the education stage was given only token attention as the movement pushed forward. As a result, at both the national and local levels, organizations and individuals with widely divergent "Nuclear IQ's" battled constantly on issues of strategy and tactics on the Freeze resolution as well as other issues at the same time as they tried to promote the Freeze initiative to the media, the experts, and the Congress. Exacerbating this problem was the fact that the antinuclear war SMOs were constantly competing for (1) funds and time from individuals, (2) institutional financial support, (3) media coverage, and (4) the designation of leadership of the movement.

THRESHOLD 3.
PREPARING FOR POLITICAL PARTICIPATION

Eager to engage the political process, the proposal for a bilateral nuclear weapons freeze became the movement's nearly singular focus. The national Nuclear Weapons Freeze Campaign and the other SMOs who were members of the freeze coalition were doing everything they could to prepare their members emotionally and organizationally for participation in the political process, but there was only a limited effort made to educate them to the possible counterarguments they would encounter from the media, members of Congress, congressional staffs, and freeze opponents. Even more importantly, little political groundwork was being done within the political system itself. Thus, the Freeze proposal was pressed on the Congress prematurely—before the members of Congress had a chance to work through the possible ramifications of such a proposal for national security, and how the Freeze proposal and its ramifications would be viewed by constituents back home in their districts. Senator Kennedy has been blamed by some for forcing the Freeze into Congress too fast (Solo 1988). However, it was ultimately the freeze campaign's leadership that decided to jump on the Kennedy-Markey bandwagon.

The experts were moving forward more rapidly, with many well-known arms control figures, including such former SALT negotiators and luminaries as Robert McNamara and McGeorge Bundy, giving cautious endorsement to the Freeze proposal. However, the administration remained strongly opposed to this single movement goal. Moreover, it became easy for the administration and countermovement critics to deflect a whole range of important antinuclear war movement issues by focusing their criticism of the movement on the criticism of the Freeze proposal.

STAGE 4.
POLITICAL PARTICIPATION

Social movements engage the public policy process as advocates for a particular policy position in the electoral, legislative, administrative, or judicial process. Engagement with the legislative process peaks with the introduction of a specific measure into the law-making body, followed by the lobbying effort for and against the proposed change.

Lobbying in the public policy process is dramatically different from social movement building, and social movements often have considerable difficulty making the transition (Molander and Parachini 1988). Locally, SMOs exhort their members to not only lobby their elected representatives, but also to lobby local elites and other public opinion leaders, and make declarations and create events to suggest there is a broad base of grassroots support for their position. However, unlike social movement building, much of the key lobbying work is done out of public view, and involves building a consensus within a majority of the body that a change in policy is appropriate. At the policymaking location—i.e., in Washington, D.C., movement leaders lobby public officials and their staffs privately. SMO leaders also exhort relevant experts sympathetic to their position to take those positions publicly.

If social movement leaders play their hand to the best advantage, pressures from grassroots constituents will reach elected officials simultaneously with pressures from on-site SMO lobbyists. Similarly, local media coverage of grassroots activities will occur simultaneously with coverage in the national media. Finally, experts and national opinion leaders will take public positions in support of movement goals. The objective is that together, these pressures will overwhelm legislators and lead to favorable action on the target legislation or other public policy form.

In 1983 and 1984, the antinuclear war movement mobilized at the national and local level to promote passage of a Freeze initiative in the Congress. The movement built a broad base of support in the public at large (public opinion polls supported the Freeze at levels as high as 2:1), among social justice, professional, and civic groups, in the media, and in the Congress. However, deprived of the necessary educational preparation that would have enabled them to be more effective in conflict with an administration and Congress that resisted their views, antinuclear war movement adherents and those elements they had captured of the media and the state (principally on the Democratic side in the Congress and the 1984 presidential campaign) proved unable to respond adequately on key policy questions raised by their detractors. Among informed interrogators in the media and Congress, these questions focused on verification of the Freeze and the impact of the Freeze on MAD.

Movement adherents were also poorly prepared to respond to the uncertainties and queries posed by ordinary citizens concerned about war and peace issues. In frustration with the complexities of technical issues, many movement advocates had no alternative but to focus all their energies on the highly-touted but simplistic Freeze resolution, or the highly visible but virtually impregnable fortress of the Reagan defense budget. They had no effective response to the lay person's question, "What about the Russians?" or their queries about verification and Soviet cheating on past treaties, even though substantive responses were available had they been properly schooled. Unable to achieve their grand goals or even their modest ones, unschooled in the Clausewitzian order of political battle, and uncertain as to how long and difficult the battle was sure to be, many movement adherents quit the battlefield to return to their homes and inactivity or to less technical and more accessible local social justice and environmental issues.

In the end, the movement was able to have only a limited impact on the major policy issues to which it gave primary attention: (1) the Freeze resolution that passed the House and failed in the Senate was a diluted version of what had been sought, and it was seen by the media and most political observers as a major loss for the movement; (2) Congress approved the MX, although in small numbers, and for silo, not mobile, deployment; (3) Congress continued to approve major annual increases in the defense budget through 1985; and (4) the president's SDI program took root and gained budgetary and popular support. Arms talks in Geneva were revived, and there was some indication that this was in response to grassroots pressures from the country's antinuclear war movement. However, no progress was made in limiting strategic weapons, and removal of intermediate nuclear weapons from Europe was claimed by President Reagan to be a response to his tough stance toward the Soviets.

THRESHOLD 4.
MOVEMENT COLLAPSE IN THE FACE
OF POLITICAL FAILURE

If defeated in this first trial by fire in the political process, internally a movement must immediately regroup, offering to movement adherents, funders, the media, and political supporters an explanation for the defeat in terms that protect the integrity of the movement, movement leaders, and the public policy positions they have championed. It must keep as many people and institutions on board as possible, avoid the acrimony that naturally comes as various SMOs blame each other for the defeat, and prepare to lay the groundwork for reestablishing movement momentum. If it fails in these efforts, the movement can go into "free fall" backward past Stage 3 or Stage 2 or 1.

When the modified version of the Freeze proposal passed the House of Representatives on May 10, 1983, the media declared the event a failure of the movement, depicting the resolution that passed as a watered-down version of what had originally been presented. When the freeze campaign protested vehemently, arguing that the passage represented a significant victory, it lost considerable credibility with the Congress and the media.

When the Senate failed to debate the Freeze proposal, the freeze campaign moved in two directions: (1) to prepare a new "quick freeze" measure for reintroduction into the Congress, and (2) to prepare "Freeze Voter '84," an effort to make the Freeze a 1984 campaign issue and to promote the reelection of those candidates who supported the Freeze.

When these efforts also were unsuccessful, the antinuclear war movement went into a tailspin. The movement rapidly fractionated, and many SMOs shrunk to a fraction of their former size in terms of budgets and numbers of active local members. To make matters even more difficult for the antinuclear movement, two competing national security issues emerged, and with them new movements that would draw adherents and funding away from the antinuclear war movement: (1) U.S.-Soviet relations and the the citizen diplomacy movement, which sought to build grass-roots contacts between the U.S. and Soviet people, and (2) Central America and the movement against Contra aid and other forms of U.S. military involvement in the region. As the freeze and other antinuclear war movement groups struggled to keep people focused on nuclear weapons-related issues, across the country local chapters of ESR, PSR, Ground Zero, and other peace and social justice groups turned their attention to one or both of these competing issues and movements.

Stage 5.
A Movement Becalmed in the Maintenance Stage

When the media declared that the freeze movement had failed, and the Reagan Administration's half-hearted approaches to arms control with the Soviet Union persisted, from 1985 onward the antinuclear war movement became becalmed. Many of the more policy-oriented SMOs, such as the Federation of American Scientists and Union of Concerned Scientists, turned their attention to the president's Strategic Defense Initiative (SDI)/"Star Wars" proposal.

Ground Zero closed its Washington, D.C., office and moved its operations, which by then consisted largely of suppying educational materials to schools, to Portland, Oregon. Educators for Social Responsibility and the freeze campaign saw many of their local organizations fold or shrink dramatically. A few local movement adherents turned their attention briefly to Star Wars and the Comprehensive Test Ban Treaty, but many moved on to other issues. Only the Center for Defense Information among the major organizations continued an active public education program, although that program had a limited outreach component.

Nuclear arms control was a nonissue in the 1986 elections, and in 1987 two of the largest organizations in the movement—the Nuclear Weapons Freeze Campaign and SANE—merged. Meanwhile, *Nuclear Times*, the most widely-circulated movement journal, despite its best cheerleading efforts, carried the tone of an exhausted movement. Although the skeleton of the movement remained in place, and despite the SANE/Freeze merger, by the end of 1987 it was far smaller and weaker than it had been at any time since 1981.

Conclusions

Reviewing the experience of the antinuclear war movement in the context of threshold theory, leads us to draw the following conclusions:

1. Failure to execute the "education" stage, a critical stage in this case because of the significant informational and technical component to nuclear policy, contributed to the movement's decline. The movement started with an educational commitment, but that commitment was subordinated to the rush to political action on the Freeze proposal.

2. The movement did recognize the need for sequential and deliberate passage through the agitation/activation, education, and political participation stages of movement development, and the role of timing as the movement "moves" between the various generic stages of evolution. But, as noted above, it did not stay long enough in the education stage.

3. The movement recognized and sought to execute a synchronicity of movement evolution with simultaneous evolutionary changes in the media, the expert community, and the state, and to establish its legitimacy with a segment of each. Although it achieved this goal to some degree in each of these institutional realms, it failed to effectively manage this synchronicity, and was unable to use those segments to expand their influence during the political stage of the movement's development.

4. The fact that national antinuclear war groups were (a) highly independent in the formulation of goals and strategies to achieve those goals, and (b) specialized along the activation-education-participation continuum, with few groups performing multistage activities, did not prevent their working cooperatively on the Freeze. However, it did mean that they would be competing extensively for funding, movement adherents, and the designation of movement leadership. SMO specialization led to the intramovement competition rather than intramovement cooperation.

5. In becoming the centralized, politicized "Freeze Campaign" in 1982, the antinuclear war movement abandoned the social movement-building activities at the margin between the liberal and mainstream communities in American society. This decision, made by the leaders

of the freeze coalition and its component SMOs, signaled the failure of the movement that would be publicly revealed with the dramatic movement contraction in 1984–1985. As a result, the antinuclear war movement is weaker today than it has been at any time since early 1981.

CHAPTER 4

Peace Movement Demobilization: The Fading of the Nuclear Freeze

DAVID S. MEYER

Protest movements like the nuclear freeze succeed when they present a credible challenge to politics as usual (Gamson 1975:72–88; Piven and Cloward 1979). By mounting such a challenge to state politics and policy, they force response, if not redress, from both government and the political mainstream, and alter the political landscape for subsequent political battles. The rapid emergence of the nuclear freeze campaign onto the national political stage in the first years of Ronald Reagan's presidency makes its equally rapid decline all the more curious. Although the movement's component organizations continued to grow after its apparent peak in 1982, by 1984 the movement found it increasingly difficult to agree upon goals and strategies or to command national attention. In the following years the movement coalition fragmented further; by 1986 the freeze campaign, pressured by serious financial and organizational troubles, negotiated a merger with SANE, an older arms-control interest group.

The 1984 presidential campaign proved critical for the freeze campaign; indeed, once underway the electoral effort seemed to overshadow virtually all other movement activities. Helen Caldicott, one of the movement's most powerful and prolific speakers, was particularly visible, urging her audiences to vote as if their lives depended upon the next election. "If Ronald Reagan is re-elected," she announced, "accidental nuclear war becomes a mathematical certainty"

(Coles 1985). Womens' Action for Nuclear Disarmament (WAND) produced a series of radio advertisements calling the 1984 presidential election, "the most important vote of the nuclear age," (Waller 1987:266) and many antinuclear groups were fully engaged in the campaign, contributing both volunteers and funds to sympathetic candidates (Taylor 1985).

For numerous reasons, the nuclear freeze movement was unable to translate its strength as shown in public opinion polls into votes for Walter Mondale. Not the least of these was that voting against Ronald Reagan seemed a timid prescription for action when one's life, and indeed the fate of the earth, was said to be in jeopardy. Among the other obstacles the movement faced were: the preponderance of other issues, particularly taxation; the nature of presidential campaigns in the United States, which emphasize personal and media appeal rather than issues; the disproportionate national funding of the two parties; and the Democratic challenger's weak campaign. Perhaps most significantly, the Ronald Reagan who ran for reelection was quite different from the one who was elected in 1980, and surely this was at least partly the result of the nuclear freeze movement. The president refused to allow the movement to define his positions on military and nuclear security issues. Midway through his first term he and his advisers abandoned much of the troublesome rhetoric about limited nuclear war and the Soviet Union that had fed the early mobilization of the freeze.

After the 1984 elections, Reagan's modest arms-control efforts bore some fruit, though the broad outlines of the United States national security policy, challenged by the nuclear freeze, remained essentially unchanged. In contrast, the organizations that made up the nuclear freeze movement endured serious self-evaluation and reconstruction. Coalition partners moved in several different directions, some advocated more radical approaches to disarmament and direct action as a political tactic; others turned to more modest arms-control measures and conventional politics. Some organizations shifted their attention to nonnuclear issues, such as the war in Central America. Still others vanished from the political landscape, much as the nuclear freeze did.

The transformation or demise of the nuclear freeze movement reflects a great deal about the American political system, the pressures it places on dissident movements, and the way in which it responds to dissent. This analysis examines three aspects of this problem: the internal pressures within the movement that contributed to the fragmentation of the nuclear freeze coalition; the portrayal and meanings given the nuclear freeze by the mass media and dissenting elites; and the way the Reagan Administration and national political leaders responded to the movement, by redefining its goals and refining their own presentation of nuclear issues.

The Fragmentation of Political Action

Social movements are characterized by a diversity of activity seen to be united in a challenge to the state or state policy. Participation entails an element of personal transformation as well as purposive attempts to change policy. There is a dynamic interaction between the movement and mainstream politics, but importantly, the movement remains on the edge of the mainstream. A successful protest movement must perform a delicate balancing act treading on the borders of political legitimacy. Movements that slip off the side of mainstream legitimacy become marginalized and politically insignificant. Those that reach some sort of accommodation with mainstream politics cease to challenge in the same way as a movement, being effectively co-opted. Movements generally undergo both marginalization and co-optation, as the coalition making up a movement fragments.

The nuclear freeze movement mobilized large numbers of people quickly and captured the public imagination largely because of the diversity it encompassed. Virtually any challenge to the Reagan Administration's nuclear and defense policies was widely, and incorrectly, seen as part of the freeze movement. Thus, former National Security Council member Roger Molander's nonpartisan Ground Zero project was consistently portrayed as a freeze group, though Molander was always candid about his opposition to the freeze proposal. Similarly, civil disobedience actions against weapons producers by religiously inspired activists were also seen as part of the freeze, though many of these activists castigated the freeze proposal as far too moderate (Solo 1988:85).

A movement employing multiple organizations, a range of activities, and a diversity of political perspectives enjoys certain benefits, as McAdam (1982) notes in his study of the civil rights movement. A broad and decentralized coalition allows a wide range of potential activists a variety of entry points to political activism. It creates waves of mobilization aimed at a variety of targets, and becomes far less predictable and less susceptible to repression or cooptation. The coalition supporting the nuclear freeze was more diverse and decentralized than that of the civil rights movement, with even less political cohesion. Although this made the movement especially vulnerable to pressures for dissolution from within, initially the net effect was that the freeze movement appeared far larger, more diverse yet united, and more powerful than it actually was.

Although Reagan's reelection marked the end of the "nuclear freeze" in political discourse, activists and political organizations continued activity, including virtually all the types of political action that characterized the movement in prior years: civil disobedience and direct action; symbolic demonstrations and educational events; and legislative lobbying and electoral campaigns. What had changed, however, was that this variety of activity was no longer united by a common face. Each action was widely perceived as discrete, divorced from other activities and from a larger social and political movement. Essentially, this happened in three different ways: marginalization, depoliticization, and cooptation.

Forced to the Margins

Partisans of direct action continued their efforts, engaging in dramatic attacks on weapons manufacturers or military installations, and calling for the abolition of nuclear weapons (Epstein Chapter 7). Rarely, however, were these calls connected to any conventional political activity or systematic program of political action. The costs of participation were generally very high; activists often received harsh jail sentences and heavy fines. In addition to these high costs, the intensity of participation required and the lack of apparent political efficacy severely limited the number of people who would engage in such activity. Those who did were politically marginalized.

There was more antinuclear civil disobedience immediately after Reagan's reelection than in the years immediately preceding. The White Train protests, directed against the transport of nuclear warheads, continued and grew along the train's route between Bangor, Washington, and Amarillo, Texas (*Washington Post*, February 23, 1985:A2), as did site protests directed against weapons producers (e.g., Schwartz 1984). Several groups of activists attempted to disrupt nuclear testing by invading the United States test site in Nevada, in an attempt to delay testing and gain publicity for a proposed test ban, though attempts to broaden this campaign by the American Peace Test (Clancy 1986; Solo 1988:174–176) were largely unsuccessful.

PROTEST WITHOUT POLITICS

Far more visible were activities designed for broader participation and extensive media coverage, which were intended to give people a sense of expression for their concerns without tying their actions to politics. Political analysis and specific demands were sacrificed with the intent of winning a broad spectrum of support. Although such activities often drew large numbers of participants, their political meaning was unclear, because they were divorced not only from any arms control or military reform proposal—such as the freeze—but also from either party, any candidate, or any political program. This depoliticization doomed several colorful events to political insignificance. The peace ribbon was one such project. A ten-mile-long banner produced in one-yard segments by activists across the country was unfurled in Washington; the only message to clearly emerge, however, was that many people did not want a nuclear war (*New York Times*, March 3, 1985:3; August 5, 1985:8; *Washington Post*, July 16, 1985:C7).

Even worse for antinuclear groups were similar events that failed to gain support or publicity. The clearest example was the Great Peace March, sponsored by a California-based group, PRO-Peace. The event was intended to continue over nine months in 1986, as more than five thousand people would march across the country from Los Angeles to Washington, D.C., under the slogan "Take 'em Down" (Cushnir 1986). PRO-Peace failed to win support from other disarmament groups, and two weeks after the march left Los Angeles in March 1986 its executive director acknowledged that the campaign had run out of money, dissolved PRO-Peace, and declared the event over. Five hundred marchers continued anyway, reaching Washington in November by raising subsistence support along the way. By failing to live up to its own grand designs, however, the Great Peace March seemed a hollow achievement, with unclear political intentions and minimal impact.

The trend toward apolitical or antipolitical expression of concern about nuclear issues was carried to an extreme by Beyond War, a California-based group that asked its members to "take responsibility for ending war and nuclear weaponry." As Brigham (Chapter 10) notes, Beyond War appealed primarily to middle-class and wealthy Californians, bearing closer resemblance to such self-help human development programs as est than to any of the freeze groups. Beyond War members sought to develop a "new mode of thinking" which would spread until people and nations stop fighting (Faludi 1987:23). The approach represented less a rejection of conventional politics than a repudiation of any kind of politics.

ENTERING THE POLITICAL MAINSTREAM

The kinds of activities outlined above had been components of the freeze movement at its height, but they were divorced from conventional political activity and politics in general, and thus robbed of potential impact and significance. In contrast, Washington-based lobbying groups and political action committees also continued their activity, most of them significantly stronger, larger, and better-funded than they had been prior to the emergence of the nuclear freeze movement (Clotfelter 1986). In order to support themselves and their activity, they became increasingly dependent upon their relationships with financial supporters and legislators. This entailed moderating their goals and approaches to improve prospects for financial support and legislative success. There was no doubt that this approach, conventional political action in pursuit of moderate goals, could generate some victories in Congress: aiding in the election of legislators who support arms control, working to achieve moderate reductions in funding for particular weapons systems, and lobbying for the ratification of future arms-control treaties. These goals, however, were substantially more modest than the comprehensive approach to nuclear weapons and foreign policy proposed by the nuclear freeze (Forsberg 1984). Abandoning the broader analysis and concerns that had animated the freeze, these groups were coopted.

Developing a legislative agenda modest enough to be achievable, yet ambitious enough to be significant was a difficult problem for most of the nuclear freeze coalition; indeed, the nuclear freeze initially had been intended as a solution to this problem. Lobbying and electoral groups needed to demonstrate both their political importance and their efficacy in order to maintain support. The national Nuclear Weapons Freeze Campaign (NWFC) redirected its own efforts to this congressionally oriented approach, shutting down its clearinghouse in St. Louis, and changing its central focus to lobbying for the negotiation of a bilateral ban on nuclear testing. Both symbolically and actually, this reflected a deemphasis on the grassroots activity and local organizations that had animated the nuclear freeze movement.

The test ban effort was a deliberate attempt to replicate the successes of the freeze with a more limited (and thus, achievable) platform. Organizers made a concerted (and fairly successful) attempt to gain the endorsements of prominent religious leaders and generate the requisite number of supportive op-ed pieces by notables (e.g., Carroll 1985). Closing the St. Louis clearinghouse and directing the organization's efforts primarily in Washington, D.C., reflected the national freeze's growing commitment to participation in conventional rather than movement politics. Replacing the nuclear freeze with a call for a test ban indicated a scaling back of goals.

This campaign, calling for the smallest part of the original nuclear freeze proposal that could be divorced from the whole, gained comparatively little support, either in Congress or among the general public. Difficulties with the public stemmed partly from a perception that the movement was retreating, and the failure to generate significant activity at the grassroots impaired the campaign's efficacy in Congress. Further, there was no consensus on goals within the freeze coalition, and several different proposals competed within Congress for support. Here diversity proved to be a serious weakness; the initial clarity of the freeze demands was gradually obscured (Solo 1988:174–175).

Clearly, there were other factors involved in the failure of the test ban campaign as well. Ronald Reagan, who had softened his political rhetoric about both nuclear weapons and the freeze movement, was less forthcoming about the test ban, arguing that testing was necessary to ensure effective deterrence as long as deterrence was necessary. The Soviet Union had already undertaken a unilateral test ban, and test ban opponents argued that this alone indicated that such a proposal was in Soviet interest and against that of the United States.

The shift to an emphasis on conventional political participation entailed a corresponding shift in mobilization strategies. Public support was less important than congressional endorsement; large demonstrations and media attention became less significant than financial support. Comprehensive analysis was secondary to legislative saleability, and political democracy took a backseat to political efficacy. In short, a large segment of the antinuclear movement eschewed extrainstitutional social mobilization in favor of competing within the established political institutions. For arms-control and disarmament organizations, this necessitated the cultivation of new resources, particularly funding sources, and correspondingly abandoning the tactics that had just recently given them legitimacy and enlivened the nuclear debate.

These factors all contributed to pushing the need for "credible" elite support to the fore. Such support would aid in gaining the political legitimacy that would help fund raising and enhance access to congressional leaders. The arms control elite, however, had never supported the nuclear freeze proposal as activists construed it: a first step toward ending the arms race and redefining the role of the United States in global politics. Instead, the arms-control elite saw the nuclear freeze as a vehicle to force the Reagan Administration to return to a traditional arms-control approach (Drew 1983). Cultivating such support was yet another pressure on freeze groups to moderate their goals and tactics.

The emphasis on congressional politics also entailed competition with better funded and more established lobbying groups and political action committees (PACs). Betsy Taylor (1985:5) notes that, despite tremendous improvements in peace movement fund raising, corporate PACs were able to outspend the Peace PACs by a significant margin. Lockheed contributed $420,000 to congressional candidates in 1984, topping the list of corporate PAC contributions. The top twelve corporate PACs included three other military contractors: Rockwell, Northrop, and General Dynamics. This funding imbalance is not limited to military contractors and disarmament activists. In 1984 the Republican National Committee, Congressional Committee, and Senatorial Committees outspent their Democratic counterparts by a ratio of nearly 4:1, $246 million to $66 million; conservative PACs spent $55,186,802 in contrast with $13,069,085 spent by liberal PACs (WAND 1986:41–44).

These figures, as lopsided as they are, overstate both the relative strength of liberal PACs and the potential for disarmament activists to achieve broad results through campaign contributions and lobbying. Conservative and Republican congressmen receive a much clearer message from their funders than do Democrats and liberals (Edsall 1984:86–90). Conservative interests provide approximately half of the campaign funds for Democratic candidates; as a result, the Democratic representative concerned about funding a reelection campaign receives an ambiguous message about political issues and is faced with pleasing a far more diverse constituency than a Republican counterpart. This leads to the tendency to seek a middle ground, which found the House of Representatives in 1983 supporting both a nuclear freeze and the revival of the much maligned MX missile (Drew 1983). By focusing their efforts on congressional politics, arms-control and disarmament groups chose to enter a political arena in which they were at a tremendous disadvantage.

The Organizational Imperative

The freeze coalition's membership organizations changed their styles and goals, fighting for their own survival as the movement faded. Many adopted organizational models that, although well-designed for organizational maintenance, were inimical to generating the kind of extrainstitutional mobilization that constituted a powerful aspect of protest. WAND, for example, in a slick report called *Turnabout*, announced a new priority for membership drives and volunteer efforts that would focus primarily on fundraising. Grassroots activism and decentralized democracy, the publication contends, represented old and archaic notions of political action; the disarmament movement should learn from the successes of conservative groups and emphasize professionalism and organizing through fund raising. "Too many progressive organizations are wedded to old-fashioned notions about citizen participation," WAND writes. "They continue to believe hundreds and thousands of volunteers can be persuaded to assume a broad range of organizing tasks." Voluntarism is less important than fund raising, *Turnabout* continues, adding that organizations with many donors are "far more powerful, enduring, and effective, than those built through traditional notions" (WAND 1986:38–44). The report urged the movement to adopt a more professional approach to politics, including expert survey research, marketing, and advertising—lest its message be overshadowed by those employing such tactics (1986:24).

WAND's analysis of the prospects for organizational survival was essentially correct. In times of growth for any movement, there is a concomitant proliferation of organizations (McAdam 1982; McCarthy and Zald 1977:1224–1225) that compete for the resources available to the movement as a whole. Certainly this was the case with the nuclear freeze movement. Although organizational proliferation and the endorsements of established groups enlivened the nuclear freeze movement and produced tremendous growth quickly (Miller 1982), it came at a price. The freeze came to be equated with the larger peace movement, getting credit for everything done by any group or individual in the name of arms control or disarmament (Solo 1988:88). The imperative of organizational survival, however, virtually forces social movement organizations to distinguish themselves not only from each other, but from the movement as a whole. Consequently, as a movement grows and draws more organizations into its wake, each organization is subjected to increasingly powerful pressures to specialize (McCarthy and Zald 1977:1234).

There is also the additional pressure to institutionalize, and to centralize and bureaucratize decision making (Freeman 1975:100; Michels 1962). This institutionalization is likely a prerequisite for organizational survival (Wilson 1973) and is associated with a movement's success (Gamson 1975:89-109). Although the nuclear freeze had initially been created as a coalition effort that emphasized decentralized governance, a campaign with "local self-determination and national coordination" (Solo 1988:62), the exigencies of participating in national politics virtually demanded a coherence and unity that this broad coalition could not provide. The NWFC quickly evolved into yet another distinct organizational entity, with its own staff, direction, funding needs, and struggle to survive. Power and responsibility gradually yet consistently shifted from the grassroots base that animated the movement to the staffs of the organizations included in the freeze coalition. By June of 1983 the primary decision-making responsibility for the freeze campaign had shifted from committees comprised of volunteers and members of other organizations to NWFC staff (Solo 1988:142).

This course of professionalization and bureaucratization of movement organizations is endemic to social movements in the United States (McCarthy and Zald 1973), and it is problematic. For the trend toward more secure institutionalization entails a redirection of goals toward more modest, and inherently more conservative, objectives. Wilson (1973:31) observes, "In the long run . . . all organizations seek some form of accommodation with their environment, because the costs of sustaining indefinitely a combat-oriented organization are generally too high to be borne by the members." For this reason, advocates of structural social change are often also critics of political organization (Lowi 1971:54; Piven and Cloward 1979). The leading edge of social mobilization almost invariably comes from outside the established organizations. The nuclear freeze idea, as a case in point, was the product of several activists and analysts working in concert, largely independent of the numerous established arms-control and disarmament organizations, many of which were slow in endorsing or working for the nuclear freeze (Meyer 1990:chap. 9). In 1985, desperately seeking survival, the NWFC began negotiations to merge with SANE, an older congressionally oriented arms control group (Rizzo and Harris 1987; Solo 1988:176).

THE PRICE OF ORGANIZATIONAL SURVIVAL

As the nuclear freeze movement faded, many organizations adapted to the new political environment by redefining their goals in more accessible and limited ways. WAND's *Turnabout* (1986:36) recognized a great "need for the movement to concentrate on politically relevant and potentially winnable items among those available on the progressive arms control agenda." Effective action, according to this view, would be contingent upon increased political sophistication, meaning a sort of legislative triage: abandoning the issues unlikely to win congressional support in favor of increased efforts for those with better chances. Naturally, congressional allies would play a key role in making these discriminations. These allies, WAND reports, advise deemphasizing emotional appeals based on fears of nuclear destruction, and concentrating instead on the congressional budget process.

For a social movement seeking comprehensive political change, there are several problems with this approach. First, a focus on incremental modifications in the budget, although responsive to congressional interests (Solo 1988:100), is unlikely to inspire broad public support or even interest. In taking this tack, arms-control and disarmament groups effectively abandon their greatest resource: broad, though perhaps shallow, public support and increased grass-roots political activism. Second, the intracacies of the long budget process require an ongoing lobbying presence, as the numerous committee and floor votes and compromises offer ample opportunity to undo any accomplishment. Though this serves the needs of organizational staff, it obsures their activity to the potential base of support. It is conceivable that antinuclear forces could win occasional legislative battles against stronger opponents, but the multiplication of significant votes diminishes the chances of making any changes in policy.

Third, by virtually ceding control of the arms-control and disarmament agenda to congressional leaders, disarmament advocates give up the ability to define themselves and their goals. Rather than injecting new issues and concerns into the political debate, as social movements can, they limit themselves to a competition in which they are weaker than their opponents, and over terms beyond their ability to define. By adopting an institutional focus, the antinuclear movement abdicated its special role in favor of playing a role in which established politicians and interest groups are more comfortable and far more powerful, effectively ceding its greatest political asset.

Fourth, the institutional approach necessitates an even greater dependence upon elite support, redefining not only tactics, but also political goals. For the most part, the differences elite arms-control supporters and legislators had with the Reagan Administration's nuclear and military policy were far more modest than those of the original nuclear freeze leaders. Significantly, these differences did not include the process by which defense policy was made, only the content of some policies. With the intent of maintaining good relationships with legislators and moderate and mainstream elite supporters, arms-control and disarmament groups readily narrowed their own agendas, winnowing out potentially controversial aspects of their programs. The notion of putting nuclear security issues on the democratic agenda—a powerful mobilizing idea—was downplayed. The institutionalized movement was also unable to respond effectively to new political issues; it could not, for example, incorporate growing public concern with escalating conflict in Central America or the Middle East, or increased public awareness of apartheid in South Africa. Citizens concerned with these issues, including many of those constituencies active in the nuclear freeze movement, had to look beyond their old alliances to express their concerns. The freeze movement ceded the political space for social movements to other issues and groups.

The Public Eye

Adopting a strategy based upon institutional activity also meant a much lower public profile, effectively ceding another advantage the movement had previously enjoyed. On this point, it is important to acknowledge that the greatest part of media coverage at the height of the nuclear freeze campaign had emphasized the movement's activities rather than its ideas. WAND attributed this to a "failed sales job to the media," advocating a more concerted effort to shape media coverage by convincing reporters that their proposals were good ones (WAND 1986:25). Although there is doubtless some truth in this, it is also true that mass media in the United States is more disposed and better equipped to cover events than ideas in any case.

The freeze proposal had never won the support of a significant segment of arms control experts, but had commanded attention because of its large-scale mobilization. Forfeiting this mobilization was giving up the only leverage the movement had in influencing expert debate on nuclear issues or in the more ambitious goal of creating a public debate. For this reason, there are inherent limits to strategies emphasizing organization building or public education directed exclusively toward mainstream politics (e.g., Molander and Molander, Chap.3). Emphasis on conventional means of political participation entailed the movement's sacrifice not only of its campaign to define its own political identity, but also the front pages. Less visible and colorful activity meant less media coverage (Hertsgaard 1985), and hastened demobilization.

Also costly in terms of media interest was the campaign's shift in focus from local to national activity. The nuclear freeze had percolated up to the national stage through hundreds of smaller newspapers and radio and television stations. Reporters and editors who normally covered local and regional issues were often eager to address national and international issues by providing coverage of local antinuclear activity (Leavitt 1983:32). This magnified the public face of the movement. For example, a two-week tour of European peace activists sponsored by the American Friends Services Committee (AFSC) and Clergy and Laity Concerned (CALC) generated more than one thousand press clippings in 1982, mostly in local and regional papers (Smith 1982). The local focus made the movement appear bigger and more widespread than it actually was. In national institutions and media, however, the movement received less attention because it competed with a broader variety of stories and issues.

There was also a sense in national media that the nuclear freeze movement story had been covered in 1982. "Reporting on social movements is faddish," explained *Time* magazine reporter Joelle Attinger. "The nuclear freeze was the story in 1982. Editors decided that Jesse Jackson was the liberal story last year" (Taylor 1985:9). Movements also must escalate in some way in order to continue to be newsworthy, as Todd Gitlin (1980:182) observed about the student movements of the 1960s. The June 12, 1982, demonstration, which drew one million people to New York City, was thus seen as the freeze movement's peak, one that would not be surpassed.

Although the more institutionally oriented wing of the movement chose activities that were essentially less visible, the mass media simply became less interested in the direct action of groups working on the margins. The first Plowshares action (featuring the Berrigan brothers) at a General Electric Plant in King of Prussia, Pennsylvania, had received extensive coverage throughout its long history in the courts, but subsequent Plowshares actions were generally ignored. In the few instances in which they received coverage, the stories usually reflected a human interest perspective rather than any sort of political angle (e.g., Grove 1986a,b; McGrory 1985; Plummer 1984). The fragmentation of movement action facilitated the separation on civil disobedience and direct action from politics.

The Changing Political Landscape

The nuclear freeze movement ceased to occupy a prominent place on the American political landscape, but that landscape had changed. This reality makes impossible a facile evaluation of the success or failure of the nuclear freeze movement. Organizations grew and were institutionalized, leaving a far more extensive network of potentially accessible resources than there were prior to the nuclear freeze movement. Nuclear and military issues received greater attention from politicians and the mass media. Nuclear education or peace studies programs were established in many colleges and high schools (e.g., Ringler 1984; Thomas 1987; Thomas and Klare 1989). All of this meant that expression of nuclear concern no longer required extrainstitutional social mobilization.

At the same time, antinuclear movements in western Europe ostensibly receded, partly as a result of elections, and partly as a result of the deployment of Pershing II and cruise missiles—both representing failures for peace movements. Heightened conflict in Central America, the Middle East, and South Africa came to occupy much activist concern, drawing antinuclear movement resources and supporters to other causes. The economic recession receded in the United States; significantly, the economic rebound came as freeze organizations were increasingly tying their own fates to business elites and upper-middle-class patrons, those drawing the most benefit from the Reagan-era recovery (Ferguson and Rogers 1986). Meanwhile, military spending stabilized, albeit at a level some 50 percent higher than the previous peacetime norm (Forsberg and Meyer 1985). Essentially, the strongest patrons of arms-control and disarmament groups had somewhat less volatile quarrels with the Reagan Administration and its policies.

Perhaps most significantly, the concerns that provoked the nuclear freeze movement were no longer so blatantly neglected. National politicians at both ends of the political spectrum repeatedly voiced their opposition to nuclear war, and reaffirmed their commitment to ensure that it did not take place. Reagan Administration officials tempered their own political rhetoric, abandoning talk of "limited nuclear wars" and nuclear "warning shots." In January 1984 Ronald Reagan announced his intention to resume arms-control negotiations with the Soviet Union, explicitly addressing the fear of nuclear holocaust that had fed the nuclear freeze movement.

The constellation of political realities that had made the nuclear freeze movement possible had shifted, as had the structure of political opportunity. Although the military and strategic nuclear policies directly addressed by the nuclear freeze proposal were essentially unchanged, almost everything else had, particularly the image projected by President Reagan. Waller (1987:300–301), claiming a victory for the freeze movement, notes that although the movement did not influence the Reagan Administration's policies, "it tempered Mr. Reagan's distaste for arms control. It chastened his rhetoric and changed his attitude . . . it forced his administration if not to achieve concrete results, at last to continue the quest for arms control." The somewhat softer Reagan stance made the president a more elusive target for arms-control and disarmament advocates.

Reagan also used his Strategic Defense Initiative to assuage the nuclear fears that animated the freeze movement (Krauthammer 1985; McGrory 1985; Tyrell 1985). SDI, soon termed "Star Wars," allowed the president to alter the terms of the nuclear debate. Calling nuclear deterrence immoral, Reagan urged the development of a system that he claimed would make these instruments of destruction obsolete and allow large reductions in offensive nuclear weapons. It is doubtful that many strong freeze advocates were convinced by these arguments, but in refuting them they were often forced to alter their own, criticizing Star Wars because it would threaten the system of mutual deterrence (e.g., Ball 1985; Kassebaum 1985; Tirman 1983). Effectively, SDI put the movement in the position of defending the status quo it had decried as terrifying and immoral, while the president promised to move beyond this reality to a safer and more peaceful future.

Although the Strategic Defense Initiative was a controversial program from the moment the president proposed it in March 1983, it quickly became a firmly established element in the United States' defense budget. Skillful political management of the initial research awards created an institutionalized bureaucratic and corporate constituency for the programs (Kaplan 1987). Subsequent debates on Star Wars are likely to turn on incremental levels of funding, rather than the desirability of spaced-based missile defenses. The secure institutionalization of Star Wars programs within the Pentagon and the defense industry is likely one of the legacies of both the Reagan presidency and, in a circuitous way, the nuclear freeze movement. The other apparent victory for the movement is, as Waller points out, the Reagan Administration's resurrection of the arms-control process.

The president has refused to credit the nuclear freeze movement with influencing his approach to arms control or military policy, repeatedly claiming that reopened arms-control negotiations with the Soviet Union resulted from, and vindicated, his administration's military build-up, and that he had never taken the threat of nuclear war lightly. These arguments are not surprising; politicians are gerrally and understandably loathe to credit protest movements with influencing their decisions on important matters of policy. Given the historical record, however, of a president who vocally opposed every previous arms-control agreement, it is reasonable to consider the revised

Reagan rhetoric and approach to arms control at least partly the result of a strong and visible opposition movement.

Conclusion

The demobilization of the nuclear freeze movement informs analysis of it prior mobilization. Although activity at the height of the movement's strength was characterized by diversity, in the movement's decline the same kinds of activity appeared diffuse. The movement had provided a bridge between political action within established institutions and on the margins of political legitimacy, expanding the opportunities available to advocates of either approach. This bridge vanished when the nuclear freeze faltered as a viable political concern, resulting in larger rifts within the movement constituency than in mainstream political space. The liberal arms-control institutionally oriented wing grew more moderate and less mobilizing. The extrainstitutional wing, freed from association with mainstream politics, adopted a rhetoric and style of action ultimately distancing it from the political relevance. Meanwhile, antinuclear concern was increasingly expressed in apolitical and demobilizing forms.

The nuclear freeze movement grew beyond the efforts of a few relatively small antinuclear and pacifist organizations because the Reagan Administration gave it the opportunity and the space to do so. Marginal changes in military policy constituted part of this opportunity, but more significantly, the Reagan Administration excluded moderate and liberal elite forces from the policymaking process. Though advocates of minimum deterrence, for example, had enjoyed little influence in previous administrations, their presence was always visible. The potential for antinuclear social mobilization was enhanced because other strategies for success were foreclosed.

The effective purging of previously mainstream figures from the circles of policymaking greatly expanded the potential coalition of opposition to the Reagan nuclear policies. The nuclear freeze proposal, by avoiding language tied too closely to any other organization or political position, proved to be a good vehicle for uniting this broad coalition. Conceived as both an arms-control strategy and as the standard of a social movement, the freeze proposal was both easily intelligible and comprehensive in its implications. It also was well-suited to a mobilization strategy that emphasized decentralized control and populist community participation. This decentralized approach allowed the nuclear freeze movement to encompass a broad variety of political activities, expand rapidly, and to avoid confrontation with heavy opposition. The freeze quickly came to unite a social movement.

By the middle of 1982, the nuclear freeze movement emerged as a force in national politics. The cumulative impact of many local actions and a few national and regional events, aided by the well-publicized support of numerous elite figures, brought the movement to the attention of national media and politicians. This gave the movement both an element of legitimacy and an infusion of political resources, allowing it to continue rapid expansion. The proposal ostensibly uniting this movement was defined in increasingly vague terms, however, to avoid straining the growing coalition. Many activists embraced a "least common denominator" strategy to build the largest and broadest coalition possible. Although this facilitated rapid growth and mainstream legitimacy, it also allowed supporters to redefine the meaning of the proposal and the movement, essentially moderating its goals. What had begun as an attempt to find a first step toward ending the arms race came to be seen as an expression of opposition to nuclear war and support for the arms-control process. Politicians seeking a vehicle for mobilizing support, raising funds, and opposing the Reagan Administration, effectively coopted the movement.

Movement leaders participated in this process because they appeared to be making political gains. Moderation in analysis and tactics generated concrete political benefits, most significantly, access to mainstream political institutions. The nuclear freeze proposal was debated in Congress, endorsed by numerous politicians, and ultimately passed by the House of Representatives. Nuclear freeze activists were given currency by national media, met with politicians, and attempted to establish themselves as a permanent force in national politics. These gains seemed to justify the political compromises the movement made, and many nuclear freeze leaders were unwilling to risk jeopardizing their newly achieved access.

The rapid movement of the nuclear freeze, from the margins of political legitimacy to the halls of Congress in less than two years, also created certain problems for the movement. The nuclear freeze was subjected to the rigors of legislative compromise very early in its life. Policymakers genuinely seemed to be responsive. As a result, movement leaders were not as wary as they might have been if they had been forced to spend a longer period of time in the political netherworld. In U.S. politics the open door to political institutions effectively preempts the development of more powerful dissident movements.

Access, however, does not equal influence. Although political institutions proved to be permeable for the nuclear freeze movement, they continued to represent an impenetrable barrier between citizen pressure and public policy. Though both opponents and self-described freeze supporters in positions of influence were quick to adopt the rhetoric that had been used to animate the nuclear freeze movement, very few were willing to incorporate any of the political analysis that had initially spawned the proposal and the movement. Thus, while almost all politicians eagerly expressed their opposition to nuclear war, virtually none were willing to take stronger positions directed toward nuclear disarmament or democratic control of foreign policymaking.

The nuclear freeze movement demonstrates both the extent and the limits of popular influence on U.S. military and strategic policy. In one view, the movement can be seen as the triumph of a pluralist society, effectively forcing an extremely popular president to return to long-established bipartisan policies he had not only consistently eschewed, but had vigorously criticized. The movement vanished when it was no longer necessary. From this perspective, the nuclear freeze movement was a demonstration of a responsive democratic polity and the limits on executive power. It is also possible, however, to see instead the movement's failure. The nuclear freeze proposal demanded a change not only in Reagan's policies, but in those of the United States since the dawn of the nuclear age. What it "won" was an apparent return to pre-Reagan policies, with a notable addition of the Strategic Defense Initiative. This is a victory of sorts, but far more modest than the movement's goals. The shell of the movement remains, however, in the form of stronger political organizations potentially ready to provide greater support for subsequent peace movement efforts.

CHAPTER 5

Effects on Scholarship and Higher Education: The Case of Sociology

Michael R. Nusbaumer

The study of social movements in general and the American peace movement in particular have often focused upon the amount and nature of social change brought about by the efforts of the particular social movement under scrutiny (Freeman 1983; Kurtz 1988; Wittner 1984). Most of this research, however, has concentrated on either particular politically made policy decisions or more general changes occurring within the target group/population. Analyses of the social change wrought by the American peace movement have concentrated upon changes in governmental weapons and warfare policies (Kurtz 1988). Although these lines of inquiry are certainly important, changes brought about in the larger society that may be attributable to the movement's efforts frequently are neglected (Freeman 1983:193). Thus, in an effort to explore this often neglected topic, the current inquiry explores the impact the American peace movement has had on a specific aspect of higher education: the discipline of sociology.

The Peace Movement
and the Discipline of Sociology

Social movements are loosely organized networks of various organizations immersed in a larger society (Gerlach and Hine 1970; McCarthy and Zald 1973). Social movements researchers identify in the larger society the beneficiary constituency in whose interests the movement claims to be acting, the target group toward whom the movement's efforts are directed in the hope of inducing certain actions, the opposition groups that are composed of those trying to influence the target group in directions opposite to the movement, and the publics. There are three major, identifiable subtypes of publics: cooptable publics, which share some common interests with the movement and under certain conditions may become supporters; bystander publics, which share few interests with either the movement or the movement's opposition and normally will not become involved in the issue; and potential oppositional publics, which share some interests with the opposition and under certain conditions may become active opponents of the movement (Turner and Killian 1987:149–152; Geschwender 1983:236). Any attempt to assess a social movement's effects on the larger society must recognize that a movement's activities are likely to impact differing publics differently and therefore must clearly identify the type of public under scrutiny.

As witnessed by various works in the current volume and elsewhere, the American peace movement of the Eighties comprised a large number of national, regional, state, and local groups. These groups displayed wide-ranging membership from diverse backgrounds and occupations, including intellectuals, educators, officials, politicians, the professions, and students (Lofland, Colwell, and Johnson, Chapter 6,). These groups also offered a wide array of ideological bases for peace movement participation which were rooted in economic, political, moral, religious, and technological analyses (Benford 1988; Kurtz 1988). As a result, any attempt to assess the peace movement's impact upon any particular public needs to specify what aspects or components of the movement have contributed to specific changes. Because of the diversity of the peace movement of the Eighties, any attempt to delineate all of the ways it differs from its predecessors would be a major undertaking, so current attention is given to three major differences and their impact upon change within the discipline of sociology.

First, in the peace movement of the Eighties, attention was clearly focused upon the prevention of nuclear war as the main area of concern (Benford 1988; Kramer and Marullo 1985). Not that conventional warfare was perceived as unimportant, only that the possibility of nuclear war was defined as society's "ultimate social problem" (Eitzen 1986:146).

Second, this recent era experienced a high degree of involvement from groups of professionals. Although a few professionally based groups were formed in and survived from previous eras, such groups grew in size and proliferated throughout a range of professions including medicine, law, education, social work, and architecture (Benford 1988; Boulding, Chapter 2). It is also important to note that Physicians for Social Responsibility (PSR) appears to have provided the organizational model for these groups (Rizzo 1983).

The third factor considered here is the "medicalization" of nuclear disarmament claims. The recent peace movement placed an obviously large and growing emphasis on the health consequences of nuclear war and its aftermath (Nusbaumer and DiIorio 1985). In a society that is generally witnessing growing concerns for improved health- and medically based analyses of a number of social problems, movements driven by a similar ideology should find increasingly cooptable publics (Fox 1977; Conrad and Schneider 1980; Zola 1972).

In this light, the current inquiry attempts to assess both the extent and the nature of changes that have occurred in one particular cooptable public—sociology—as a result of recent peace movement activities and efforts.

Sociology's Historical
Study of War and Peace

The relationship between the study of war and peace and the discipline of sociology is best reflected in activities related to research and teaching in sociology, as these are the two main activities of academic sociologists that are directly related to the discipline's subject matter. It also should be noted that this discussion and analysis is limited to American sociology and the impact of the American peace movement. Finally, it must be stated as succinctly as possible that the inquiry is concerned only with the coverage of peace and war. There is a long and rich history of sociological research and teaching that deals with the military as a complex organization, and the treatment and experiences of warriors within it. These topics are distinct from the topic of war and peace and therefore outside the scope of the current inquiry.

Sociological research, or at least that which is relatively widely disseminated and presumably read, appears in the form of books and scholarly journal articles. One of the first major book-lengths works in American sociology to deal with the topic of war was written by Pitirim Sorokin in the late 1930s and dealt with the relationship between cycles of cultural patterns and the frequency of war and revolutions (Sorokin 1937). This was followed some years later by the classic works of C. Wright Mills titled *The Causes of World War III* (1958), a book by Amitai Etizioni entitled *The Hard Way to Peace* (1962), and the work of Charles Osgood which culminated in publication of *An Alternative to War or Surrender* (1962). These were not the only books written by sociologists on this topic, however. Boulding (1984), in an analysis of book reviews published between 1960–1971 in the *American Sociological Review*, the major official journal of the American Sociological Association, found twenty reviews of books written by sociologists on the topic of war and peace.

Sociological journals have published a small number of articles dealing with war, peace, and closely related subjects since the late 1940s and 1950s, but in no systematic fashion. For example, Boulding (1984), in an analysis of articles published in the *American Sociological Review* from 1960–1977, found only four articles directly related to these topics and another five indirectly relevant. It was not until 1963 that any sociological journal devoted an entire issue to the topic of war. This particular issue of the journal *Social Problems*, edited by Peter Rose and Jerome Laulicht and entitled "The Threat of War: Policy and Public Opinion," contained twelve articles dealing with a topic the editors considered "the number one social problem in the world today" (Rose and Laulicht 1963:4). In an analysis of this journal's coverage of the topic of war from 1953–1975, however, Henslin and Roesti (1976) found that only 24 (3 percent) of the 844 articles dealt with "international tensions" and another 13 (1.5 percent) dealt with issues related to the military, yet 12 of these articles were from the 1963 special issue.

Coverage of the topics of war and peace through the teaching of sociology is most likely to occur in widely offered introductory level social problems courses or in advanced courses dealing more specifically with the topics of war and peace. To the extent that textbook content reflects topical coverage within particular courses, Robert Lauer's (1976) analysis of social problems textbook's coverage of war and peace is insightful. In looking at thirty-four social problems texts published between 1935 and 1975, he found that these topics were covered in only ten texts and this topic ranked last in frequency of some fourteen topics examined.

From this brief analysis of the discipline of sociology and its interest in and coverage of the topics of war and peace, it becomes evident that although generally not involving mainstream activity, a small segment of the discipline has been aware of and concerned with these issues. This history additionally suggests that although the discipline has not been a participant in the American peace movement, it was in a position to be considered a potentially cooptable public for the most recent resurgence of the movement.

Changes in the Discipline of Sociology, 1976–1987

The time frame selected for analysis of the impact of the American peace movement on sociology is 1976 through 1987. This allows for the establishment of a baseline of activity in the mid to late 1970s, when the movement was relatively inactive, through most of the 1980s when the movement experienced dramatic growth and expansion.

The impact of the peace movement on research activity is explored through examination of the coverage of war and peace in leading sociological journals and ASA annual meeting programs. The publication of books in the area should be reflected in the number of books dealing with these two topics that are reviewed in *Contemporary Sociology,* the ASA journal of book reviews since 1972. Journal coverage should be generally reflected in articles published in the *American Sociological Review* and *Social Problems*. Annual meeting programs for the ASA are examined as an indicator of research activity because many papers presented there become published articles a few years later, and opportunities for paper presentations (usually three to five papers are presented per session) are much greater than publication opportunities, which are limited by available journal space.

As shown in Table 5.1, the publication of reviews that cover books dealing with war and peace by *Contemporary Sociology* do seem to be increasing, especially from 1985–1987. When we recognize that it normally takes at least two years to write and publish a book and then at least another year before a review of it is published, this increase does appear to coincide generally with increasing peace movement activities. This apparent relationship notwithstanding, an examination

Table 5.1. Coverage of the Topics of War and Peace in Selected
Sociological Journals and Meetings 1976–1987

Year	Contemporary Sociology*	American Sociological Review†	Social Problems†	ASA annual meetings‡
1976	2	0	0	2
1977	2	0	1	3
1978	1	0	0	3
1979	0	0	0	2
1980	1	0	0	2
1981	1	0	0	4
1982	0	0	0	2
1983	1	0	0	2
1984	1	0	0	3
1985	2	1	0	4
1986	3	0	0	2
1987	6	0	0	4

*These figures represent the number of book reviews which deal with at least one book covering these topics.

†These figures represent the number of articles covering these topics.

‡These figures represent the number of sessions held which covered these topics. Each session usually contains 3 to 5 papers organized around the session title.

of the titles of the eleven books reviewed between 1985–1987 reveals that only one of these deals specifically with nuclear war, whereas three deal with past wars. Most of these books (six) focus on the relationship between international conflict and political structures and ideologies, suggesting that they were just as likely written by political scientists as by sociologists.

Coverage of war and peace in the *American Sociological Review* and *Social Problems,* as shown in Table 5.1, clearly indicates that there is very little attention given to these topics in this research dissemination medium. This does not mean there is no research being conducted and published in sociological journals since *The Sociological Quarterly* contained a special feature of four articles in a 1985 issue, under the heading "The Sociology of Nuclear Threat." Such attention to this topic in sociological research journals does, however, appear to be an anomaly.

In Table 5.1, the distribution of sessions at the annual ASA meetings that deal directly with the issues of war and peace generally show a small increase in sociological research activity in these areas from

1984–1987. More importantly, a content analysis of the titles of these sessions indicates that of the thirteen sessions held between 1984–1987, five dealt directly with issues surrounding nuclear war and four with the need for the profession of sociology to become more involved with the topics of war and peace. Additionally, three sessions dealt with the peace movement specifically. Of the twenty sessions held between 1976–1983 that dealt with topics of war and peace, only one dealt with nuclear war and none with the issue of the discipline's involvement in the topics of peace and war. Five sessions dealt generally with the topic of peace, but only one session in 1983 focused on the peace movement itself.

What this survey of sociological research activity dealing with war and peace suggests is that, to date, the discipline of sociology has not given much attention to them and therefore the recent resurgence of the peace movement has had little impact upon sociological research activities as a whole. Not only is there a definite paucity of research published in the journals, but when we recognize that *Contemporary Sociology* typically reviewed over six hundred books per year in recent years and annual ASA meetings averaged well over two hundred sessions per year for the time period under study, recent increases in attention remain minimal at best. Clearly, inquiries on these and closely related topics represent only marginal areas of sociological research of interest to just a comparative handful of research sociologists.

Still, this does not mean the peace movement has not had some impact upon research activity in the discipline. Recent ASA sessions do seem to indicate peace movement strategies and thrusts are being reflected in this marker of research activity. Why has this increase and change in activity not been more reflected in the printed, more widely distributed outlets for research? Possibly it is simply a problem of lag time, or of greater restrictions on available space, and possibly it is because those in control of these research outlets are not yet ready to recognize the importance and validity of this type of research. As Lang (1983:2) has queried, "One cannot help but wonder why the sociological analysis of war, . . . which occupied such an important place in the theorizing of pioneer sociologists should over the years have been so readily ceded to other disciplines." There have, in fact, been attempts to explain this lack of interest by the discipline because of such problems as the difficulty in maintaining scientific objectivity, the complexity of the subject matter, and turf wars and politics (Archibald

1963; Boulding 1984; Hannon and Marullo 1988), yet it is obvious that similar disciplines like political science, history, and anthropology have overcome such research barriers. Finally, despite the general lack of research activity on these topics, the number of calls for sociological participation in research on war and peace are increasing (Boulding 1984; d'Antonio 1983; Grimshaw 1983; Kramer and Marullo 1985; Kriesberg 1984; Lang 1983; and McCrea and Kelley 1983).

In looking at the impact of the American peace movement on teaching activities within the discipline of sociology, I have chosen to examine the contents of social problems textbooks. Textbooks seem an excellent source of data in this regard for several reasons: they must be reflective of market demands as publishers typically survey teachers to make suggestions for topical inclusions to authors, there are a limited number of social problems that they can cover in the typical academic semester, and teachers likely cover most of the topics dealt with in the texts or they would probably use other texts. An analysis of texts designed for use in social problems courses is also appropriate, as most social problems courses are offered as introductory-level survey courses in which the discipline of sociology is introduced to a large number of nonsociology majors and, when compared to most other survey classes at this level, are the most likely place to find discussions of war and peace.

Content analysis was performed on fifty-three major social problem textbooks published between 1976–1987.[1] The identification of war and peace as a topic was considered present if any chapter or subsection thereof was listed in the table of contents of the text. Headings such as "military-industrial complex," "violence," and "terrorism" alone were not recognized as adequately fulfilling the definition.

In examining the findings, as presented in Table 5.2, an important shift can be detected. The percentage of texts covering war as a social problem from 1976–1982 was only 16.6 percent (five of thirty), whereas the percentage covering war from 1983 to 1987 was 60.9 percent (fourteen of twenty-three). To the degree that 1983 appears to be a transition year, as its distribution equals that of the total sample, the data from 1984 to 1987 is even more noteworthy with 70.6 percent (twelve of seventeen) of the texts covering the topic of war. When combined with the earlier findings of Lauer's analysis of social problems texts from 1935 to 1975, in which slightly over 29 percent covered the topic of war, these recent findings represent a dramatic increase.

Looking more closely at those texts published between 1983–1987

Table 5.2. War Identified as a Social Problem in Major Social Problems Textbooks, 1976–1987

Year	Yes	No	Total
1976	0	2	2
	(0%)	(100%)	
1977	0	2	2
	(0%)	(100%)	
1978	1	4	5
	(20%)	(80%)	
1979	1	1	2
	(50%)	(50%)	
1980	2	7	9
	(22%)	(78%)	
1981	0	5	5
	(0%)	(100%)	
1982	1	4	5
	(20%)	(80%)	
1983	2	4	6
	(33%)	(67%)	
1984	4	1	5
	(80%)	(20%)	
1985	1	1	2
	(50%)	(50%)	
1986	5	3	8
	(62.5%)	(37.5%)	
1987	2	0	2
	(100%)	(0%)	
Total	19	34	53
	(35.9%)	(64.2%)	

that cover the topic of war, Coleman and Cressey in 1980, 1984, and 1987; Lauer in 1978, 1980, and 1986; and Neubeck in 1979 and 1986, accounted for four of the books published before 1983 and four published after. These data points simply represent updated versions of popular texts. Of the ten remaining texts published in this time period, six represented new texts in the field, and four represented new editions of previous texts that included the topic of war for the first time.

Further analysis of the content of these texts strongly suggests the authors were influenced by the current peace movement. Not only did all of these texts discuss the health-related consequences of warfare, but twelve of them included specific discussions of nuclear war, ranging from two to twelve pages in length.

What is suggested by these findings is that recent social problems texts, and presumably teachers of social problems, have actively and purposely "discovered" war as an important social problem deserving coverage at the introductory levels of the sociological curriculum (Nusbaumer, Kelley, and DiIorio 1989).

These data dealing with social problems textbook coverage do remain somewhat suspect measures of sociologists' increasing attention to the teaching of issues related to war and peace, however, because text coverage does not necessarily mean the topic is being covered in the classroom, and the coverage of these topics along with fifteen or sixteen other topics typically covered in introductory-level classes hardly signifies drastic changes in curriculum and teaching practices. Further evidence is therefore needed to confirm this apparent shift in teaching practice. In order to do this, an analysis of change in the participation of sociology departments in peace studies programs was conducted. Utilizing the 1984 and 1988 *American Peace Directory's* listings of "peace-oriented educational programs" that were available in conventional four-year colleges and universities as our samples, these programs were explored for evidence of participation by sociology departments at the respective schools.[2] The existence of such program participation is particularly noteworthy because it not only signifies a specific, conscious effort to extend relevant teaching efforts outside the sociology program, but typically indicates the offering of at least one upper division sociology course that is devoted entirely to peace, war, or a closely related topic.

The 1984 sample of thirty-seven programs indicated that fourteen (37.8 percent) exhibited some level of participation by sociology departments. By 1988 the sample had grown to seventy-five programs, of which thirty-eight (50.1 percent) exhibited sociology department participation. This four-year change not only indicated the growth of peace programs within higher education generally, but clearly indicates an increasing involvement by sociology in the creation and/or operation of these programs. This trend is further supported by the fact that six programs in the 1984 sample that did not indicate participation by sociology departments did indicate such participation in the 1988 sample. This evidence suggests that sociology is indeed actively expanding its teaching activity related to war and peace and sees itself as having an important role to play in broader study of these topics.

Acknowledging that of those professionals who create and disseminate the knowledge contained within the discipline of sociology only a small number actively engage in research activities when compared with teaching activities, the increased teaching attention given to war and peace represents both a crucial shift in orientation and a major accomplishment for the American peace movement and its adherents in the profession of sociology.

Conclusion

The current inquiry into the ability of the American peace movement to have an impact upon a particular potentially cooptable public has rendered some interesting results. Although caution must be taken in assigning responsibility for change to a single factor in any naturalistic research setting, the evidence presented here seems to indicate that the peace movement affected change within the discipline of sociology. In addition, the manner or level in which the movement's efforts influenced the discipline of sociology within academic settings also provides crucial insights into this relationship.

Upon establishing the potential cooptability of the discipline of sociology through an historical review of its coverage and concern with the topics of war and peace, the current analysis clearly indicates the recent peace movement efforts have influenced the discipline and have in certain ways successfully coopted sociology. Most noteworthy in this cooptation, however, is that it has not been a process that has occurred equally between the discipline's two main academic activities of teaching and research. The present evidence suggests that those comparative few, more prestigious creators of the knowledge in the discipline have either overlooked or refused to create and publish sociological research in the areas of war and peace. At a minimum, the research activity that has been published on these topics appears to have been influenced little by the peace movement. A rather large number of calls for more research coupled with recent increases in research activity, especially in terms of peace, at recent annual ASA meetings does point to an increase of research activity in these areas. This increased research activity, in turn, suggests that increasing pressures might be brought to bear upon major sociological journals to publish more work in the areas of war and peace. It also indicates that the peace movement is having an impact upon sociological research, but such research seems to be having difficulty achieving dissemination through mainstream sociological outlets.

The place where the peace movement has had the greatest impact upon the discipline is unquestionably the activity of teaching. It is within the arena of teaching that not only the largest number of academically based professional sociologists have the opportunity to actively define the content and orientation of the discipline, but it is also the source of sociological knowledge that most likely is disseminated to the largest audiences. The analysis also indicates that the recent discovery of war as a social problem warranting coverage in relevant sociology courses and the broader inclusion of courses deaing with war, peace, and related topics in the sociology curriculum through increased participation in peace studies programs has come about because of decisions on the part of sociologists to purposefully play a professionally active role in the discussion and educational presentation of these topics.

What this analysis suggests is that the peace movement has influenced the discipline of sociology in two respects. First, the peace movement's differential influence upon the discipline seems to suggest a distinct separation of research and teaching activities within the discipline. Indeed, one must wonder about the disciplinary sources of information utilized in sociology courses that deal with war and peace. This separation of teaching and research may be softening somewhat, however, as *Teaching Sociology*, a journal that publishes research on the teaching of sociology, contained no articles dealing with peace and war from 1976 to 1987, but published one in 1988 (Hannon and Marullo) and one in 1989 (Nusbaumer, Kelley, and DiIoria). Such disjunctures within an academic discipline, however, do pose a variety of theoretical and practical problems that could potentially harm its academic credibility. This issue clearly warrants additional attention, but may in itself be a divisive line of inquiry for the discipline.

Second, the recent peace movement, especially the professionally based groups, have adopted education as their major strategy (Boulding, Chapter 2). Therefore, it is probably not coincidence that the greatest amount of influence the movement has had on the discipline appears to be in the area of education. This connection suggests that those professionals who are engaged in primarily teaching rather than research activities may be most open to influence through professionally and scientifically based educational efforts. Social movements that utilize educational strategies containing information from reputable, professional sources may be most persuasive with other professionals engaged in educational activities, and thus create a multiplicative educational effect. Here again, further inquiry into the relationship between a movement's strategy and ideology and the activity of a potentially cooptable public is warranted but beyond the scope of this chapter.

In summary, the success or failure of any social movement is highly dependent upon its ability to mobilize potentially cooptable publics. The present exploration into the peace movement's ability to coopt the academic discipline of sociology begins to shed light upon some of the factors crucial to attaining such mobilization. This research does make one point particularly obvious: The success or failure of the peace movement must not be judged only on the short-term impact upon political decisions of target groups. The societal impact of the peace movement is much wider and ultimately must be judged from a longer-term perspective. The recent peace movement has had a greater impact upon the discipline than previous peace movement efforts. If this impact does not fade, the peace movement will likely gain a valuable ally.

Notes

1. A full description of the sample selection process and listing of texts contained in the sample for 1976–1986 is presented in Nusbaumer, Kelley, and DiIorio (1989). This methodology was extended into 1987, and two additional texts were included in the current sample: Coleman and Cressey (1987), and Farley (1987).
2. Note that both the editors and title for the 1988 edition changed as follows: Conetta, Carl. *Peace Resource Book: 1988–1989.* Both samples were based only upon those schools that offered a specialized program and curriculum related to peace studies and maintained a variety of wide-ranging degree programs across a typical college curriculum. Also, when no information could be obtained either from the peace directories or the specific college bulletins as to specific departmental participation, these programs were dropped from the sample. In the 1984 sample a total of 32 program listings were dropped out of a total of 69 and in 1988, 36 programs were dropped from a total sample of 111.

PART II

STRUCTURES:
Movement-wide, Cluster, Local

CHAPTER 6

Change-Theories and Movement Structure

JOHN LOFLAND, MARY ANNA COLWELL, AND
VICTORIA JOHNSON

As ends-means calculating entities directed to changing social arrangements, social movements are in the business of propounding theories of social change.

Much of such theorizing found in movements is, to be sure, hurried, pragmatic, uninformed, and at times naïve and inarticulate. This is in contrast to the kinds of features we associate with and seek in "professional" social theory—careful historical or comparative grounding in relevant data, articulate propositions that are logically and elegantly interrelated, studious consideration of competing theories and their relative merits.

Nonetheless, such differences ought not distract our attention from the fact that social change theorizing and acting is the central and ongoing process of every social movement. Social movement practitioners are practical theorists who devise hypotheses, act on them, assess their actions, confirm or revise the theory, and act again.

In analyzing social movements as applied or practical theories of social change, the first cognitive step we want to take—as analysts —is to focus on the entire range of behavior we discover in a movement. By this we mean that we need to look at what exactly movement people are doing, as distinct from what they may conceive themselves as doing and what they may claim they are doing. The latter two matters are obviously relevant but hardly definitive. What is definitive, instead, are our direct observations of the physical activities of a movement, combined with movement claims.

Activist-codified Theories of
Social Change

We do not want to be limited by movement-articulated conceptions, but it behooves us to begin by taking account of such views and by acknowledging that a more-or-less standard set of means-end activities are in almost routine use in a great many social movements. Indeed, the numerous manuals on "how to do" movements published in recent decades contain a rather codified set of such categories. Thus, Lee Staples' *Roots to Power: A Manual for Grassroots Organizing* (1984:xxi–xxii) anthologizes "nuts and bolts" articles:

Guide to Public Relations
Research for Organizing
The People's Lobby
Actions From Start to Finish
Lawsuits for Leverage

Staples' selections are informed by the community organizing tradition of movements, but equivalent conceptions are found in other traditions and they provide the actor-activist-grounded theorist a starting point for understanding working theories of social change.[1]

Change-Theories of
the American Peace Movement

Taking account of these activist-codified theories as we have encountered them in peace movement social change manuals of the Eighties and otherwise attending to movement activity,[2] we have found a set of practical change-theories that are in some respects the same as those commonly set forth in movement how-to manuals and which reflect ordinary movement practice. The set of such theories-in-use we observed, however, were rather broader than those provided in the how-to manuals and we want here to set forth our understanding of them.

As best as we can discern, six competing and often contradictory, yet in some ways complementary, theories were encoded in the movement. These theories centered on cognitively transcending, on educating, on intellectualizing, on politicking, on protesting, or on prophesying. The middle four are close to those codified in movement how-to manuals (such as Staples 1984), but the two on each end are not commonly discussed.

TRANSCENDER THEORY:
RAPID SHIFTS OF CONSCIOUSNESS

The transcender theory of social change in the peace movement conceived of domestic and international conflict as some manner of misunderstanding. According to the theory, an honest reexamination would reveal the basis for the misunderstanding and the needed change would then come about quickly. Or if there were, in fact, true disagreements, these were insignificant relative to a vast range of matters upon which everyone did agree. Therefore, rapid and significant change would occur once the proper realization by individuals at all levels of society took place. This most conservative of the peace movement theories strode the "high road" of being above ordinary ways of thinking about war and peace, and "above politics."

Situated in the context of historic traditions of social change theory, transcenders were idealists in two senses of the term, and this combination of characteristics sets them off from the rest of the peace movement.

First, they were idealists in the sense of the realism versus idealism used to characterize opposing approaches to the "realities" of international relations. Realism is a hard-headed "taking things as they are" between nations, a planet composed of states that act amorally and in a self-interested fashion in a field of chaotic and anarchic inter-nation relations. Idealism, in contrast, holds that moral values can and should be brought into international relations—a view that realists see as naïve folly or worse.

Second, they were idealists in the sense of the couplet, "materialism versus idealism." Materialism stresses the role of people's objective circumstances in causing interest in or resistance to social change, whereas idealism stresses the causative role of what people believe in facilitating or inhibiting social change. Stated in extreme but clear form by Brian Fay (1987:24), idealism as a theory of social change consists of three claims: "First, that it is people's ideas . . . which solely cause social behavior; second, that in order for people to alleviate their dissatisfaction, all they have to do is to change their ideas about who they are and what they are doing; and third, that people are willing to listen to rational analyses of their lives and to act on these analyses." As Fay documents, all three of these claims are quite contentious and decidedly out of fashion in the "higher intellectual circles" of at least the Western world. But, they were fashionably "in-use" among the affluent classes who participated in the transcender segment of the American peace movement of the Eighties.

Moreover, in the view of transcenders, the rational case for the irrationality and obsolescence of war was so obvious and overwhelming that mass change of consciousness could be expected to take place quite quickly. One organized expression of transcender theory—that of Beyond War—had even adopted Everett Rogers' (1983) theory of diffusion of innovations into its formal scheme of social change, propounding that at a certain percentage of adoption in a human population an idea was "unstoppable." No systemic or collateral changes in social, political, or economic structures seemed necessary. Such a theory was understandably attractive in emotional as well as philosophical terms to the upper middle class and wealthy who tended to be its adherents.

Theories of social change vary in the degree to which they feature rapid and dramatic "triggers of change" as distinct from small, incremental, and evenly paced steps to change. Transcender theory was very much toward the trigger end of this continuum and was partial to characterizing events as "epochal." The character of such triggers was, however, relatively benign, involving, for example, glitzy, high-tech events such as satellite-televised space bridges and publications of books such as Beyond War's tellingly titled *Breakthrough* (Gromyko and Hellman 1988).[3]

Educator Theory:
Communicating Facts and Reasoning

Construed narrowly, the term "educator" refers to people who are employees of educational institutions, that is, of schools. Although some people in the peace movement were educators in this narrow sense, we use the term in a broader fashion to include all people who (1) collected and (2) disseminated information on war-peace subjects and who did so (3) in a continuing and reasonably systematic fashion in order (4) to provide instruction. Understood as a theory of change and action, to educate was continually to process, update, manage, and systematize a flow of information for purposes of communication to broad and public audiences.

These features of their activities distinguished educators from the transcenders on the one side and the intellectuals on the other. Like educators, transcenders disseminated information in a systematic fashion for instructional purposes. Unlike educators, they managed no incoming flow of data. Instead, having generated their input, transcenders simply shut down. Efforts to collect information ceased because appropriate courses of action had already been decided upon. Additionally, transcender communications reflected exclusively their theory of change. In contrast, the content of information disseminated by educators related to numerous theories of change and activities within the peace movement.

Educators and intellectuals largely shared a theory of social change. The latter, however, claimed not only to receive and disseminate information, but also (1) assertively to collect, select, manipulate, and mold it and (2) to arrange it in terms of novel concepts, numbers, and arguments. That is, in their collecting, processing, and presenting of materials, educators tended to be passive whereas intellectuals tended to be active.

Of course, the line between educators and intellectuals was vague and subject to dispute. Some people worked both sides of the street and some who conceived themselves as important intellectuals were disparaged by others as mere educators (as in "he or she merely writes textbooks").

The more important core beliefs in the social change theory of peace educators were the same as those of educators in general; namely, a faith in the utility of facts and reason in searches for truth and the efficacy of facts in promoting appropriate actions. A quintessential educator slogan might be: "You shall know the truth and the truth shall make you free."

A large number of people reading these words are educators or, at the very least, extensively exposed to educators. It is therefore important to stress that the belief that facts and reason lead to desired social changes must be bracketed and treated as searchingly as we treat any other social movement belief. As a piece of ideology, it was not accepted as true throughout the whole peace movement. In the view of many movement theorists to the "Left" of educators, there was ample evidence that facts and reason had little or nothing to do with much of what people (particularly war system compromised people) thought to be true or with what they did. Or, if facts and reason were used (by, especially, high-ranking members of the war system) they were tortured and twisted beyond recognition. Along a different dimension, one classic peace movement button declared, "Knowing is not enough/Act for peace and justice" and a major (radical) educator PMO—Donnelly/Colt—used that slogan as a self-critical logo on its order forms. As analysts of social movements, then, we must not inadvertently accord some special cognitive status to educator theories of social change simply because of the unavoidably cozy relations all of us have had with them.

Intellectual Theory: New Facts and Reasoning

As indicated above, the core social change beliefs of intellectuals were similar if not identical to those of educators, but these beliefs were more strongly held. To go beyond systematizing and disseminating—the core activities of educators—to creating data and ideas committed one, by its logic, to the belief that facts and reasoning and specifically, new insights, would lead to desired social changes. As phrased by leading intellectuals of the Institute for Peace and International Security:

> Those who set the [political] agenda have significant, perhaps decisive power. . . . A powerful tool against war and the arms race, however, is unfettered imagination. The national security state cannot endure the release of political imagination, the invention of new language and new ways of thinking about and organizing the US global role. . . .

> Washington is the place where decisions are made. It is not, however, the place where all the power is or where the most effective campaigns are always fought and won. The real political battle is between those who innovate and introduce ideas intending to set the foreign and military policy agenda (Sasson, Solo, and Walker 1988:3, 2).

The change theory of the ordinary intellectual was not, of course, that new concepts and facts directly brought about the social changes sought. Rather, through dissemination to educators and through educational relations—particularly with politicians—they and others using the new concepts and facts generated by the intellectuals would create the appropriate change. To recycle and use anew the classic phrase employed by Katz and Lazarsfeld (1955) in studying the effects of media on political opinion, intellectual theory envisioned a two-step flow in which the intellectual was the fount of new inspiration, facts, and reasoning that provided the direction for educators and, especially, for action-involved politicians. Actually, this is at least a three-step flow, for the great public presumably is the target of all this.

Transcenders, educators, and intellectuals exhibited the idealism that beliefs were what really mattered, though, presumably, all three also looked to changes in domestic and international law as the ultimate outcome. Few stated this as an explicit objective (and some decried politics) but the logic of all their positions was that the public, once enlightened or educated, would act through their equally enlightened or educated legislators to bring about the desired end.[4]

Educators and intellectuals differed from transcenders in their views about the speed of change. The latter conceived of dramatic events producing rapid social change. In educator and intellectual theory, by contrast, the image was one of change achieved slowly and incrementally.

POLITICIAN THEORY: PARLIAMENTARIANISM

Liberal parliamentarianism was the change theory of the peace movement politician, a term we use broadly to refer to citizens who so oriented themselves as well as to office holders or activist members of political parties. Through public reasoning and dialogue in the legislative and electoral process, peace policies could be achieved by building majorities in a democratic process. Change required building credibility for feasible and realistic policies that could thereupon muster a preponderance of support.

Among populations of the Western, industrial nations this is, of course, the most familiar and famous of theories of social change. It is the official state ideology of perhaps the largest portion of current nation-states and *the* elite-sanctioned manner—now even in the Soviet Union—in which to set about changing things. It is, of course, simply a theory, one to be inspected as dispassionately as the other five before us. (Its less than "of course" status within the peace movement itself was communicated by such slogans as "Don't vote—it only encourages them," and "If voting mattered, they wouldn't allow it.")

The central concepts of this liberal parliamentarianism were feasibility, realism, and compromise. In order to "get" one had to "give." One settled for less than what one wanted in the tug and pull of competing interests. Further, one scaled one's desires to assessments of what was possible, meaning that one scaled down one's aspirations even at the start in order to achieve the possibility of a majority (cf. Solo 1988).

Like the theories of educators and intellectuals, peace politician theory tended to a slow, even tortured, image of how social change occurred. The Byzantine legislative battle was the centerpiece of its activities. There might be moments of exhilarating victory, but such successes were neither rapid, dramatic, nor glamorous achievements.

Protest Theory:
Forcing by Noncooperation and Disruption

The foremost tension within any social movement may be between those whose theories of social change lead them respectfully and conventionally to *present* movement issues and those whose social change theories lead them in one or another way to *force* movement issues. The four theories of seeking change just described were all respectable and conventional. They employed showmanship, education, intellectual analysis, parliamentary politics, lobbying, and electioneering. They all presented rather than forced. Such approaches presumed a faith in authorities to listen to reason and respond in satisfactory measure.

The essence of presenting was to allow opponents the option of ignoring you. They did not have to watch your television show, buy your newspaper, take your course, read your book, pay heed to your lobbying, vote for, or even vote on your candidate or issue. And, in fact, most opponents seemed most often overwhelmingly to ignore such peace movement "presentations."

This is a constant frustration for change-seekers. None of the four theories were very strong on telling their practitioners what to do after one had been ignored or turned away for the nth time. This weakness opened the way to the idea that perhaps showpersonship, education, reasoning, lobbying, and electioneering were not sufficient as strategies of achieving change. Opponents might have very powerful reasons for not wanting to be educated by or to reason with you. They might not want to know what you have to say. In fact, your proposed social change may threaten or undermine their interests and well being. Stated more generally, to educate and reason with people, you have to have their attention and openness. If they will not pay attention to or are opposed to your cause, you are simply out of luck.

How then might you get people's attention? Act in ways that interfere with the target's cognitive or physical routines, that upset either their expectations about ordinary behavior or their capacity to perform their own ordinary behavior. In either event, the object is to make the target believe that he or she has no choice but to attend. Once you have the target's attention, the more presentational kinds of social change theories and actions can be used. However, forcing tactics might still be needed because the target is likely to want to disattend as soon as possible and must continuously be discouraged from doing so. These were the central points of protest theories.[5]

Protest theory itself divided internally in terms of beliefs in the relative efficacy of noncooperation versus intervention. Noncooperation as a theory of how to achieve social change worked off a contrast with "lobbying, . . . petitions . . . [and] massive marches" in which these were portrayed as having little or no effect because none of them "hit them at the bottom line" (Cole, nd, fund solicitation letter for the boycott of General Electric). The bottom line consisted of money, and perhaps bodies, and therefore not providing one or both to corporations and/or the United States government was a key route to change. Corporations, in particular, were believed to be a target that the peace movement had missed by excessively focusing on Congress and the military. As profit-oriented entities, corporations were theorized to be more responsive than government bodies to economic pressure (Cole, nd). Other prominent forms of noncooperation with government and corporations included draft and tax refusal, boycotts, and alternative investments.

Noncooperation theory was espoused and practiced in a relatively minor fashion compared to intervention theory. The literature published by protester-intervention organizations very explicitly propounded that: "No signficant social change movement has ever succeeded in [the US] . . . without civil disobedience playing a significant role in its activities. The American revolution, the abolition of slavery, the labor movement, women's suffrage, and the civil rights movement all employed civil disobedience as an important and often central tactic" (American Peace Test 1988). The need, therefore, was for repeated and ever-larger and changing forms of mass intervention.

The trigger of change dimension of protest theory was clearly closer to the transcender image than to those of educators, intellectuals, and politicians. In both, change had to be rapid and dramatic, although protesters and transcenders clearly differed in the kind of trigger they envisioned. For transcenders it was a rather joyous transformation of consciousness—a so-called new way of thinking—whereas for protesters the trigger was a jolt, an intentionally created political crisis that gave politicians little option except to make the changes demanded by the protesters.[6]

Prophet Theory: Deep Moral Regeneration

Prophet theory of social change centered on the assertion that the war system, the state, the power elite (or other abstractions) were not the enemy. Instead, the evil (if that it be) was in ourselves—*all* our selves, members of the war system or not. Therefore, the goal was to "seek change from within, . . . to engage deeply the spirits of both sides of a conflict" (Douglass 1987:94). "Spiritually based non-violence," or "civil disobedience," was an act of striving to overcome the evil in ourselves that "lies in our cooperation" with nuclear war, for, "when we cease cooperating with evil at its source in ourselves, it ceases to exist" (1987:96). Further: "When we accept responsibility for nuclear war in the hidden dimensions of our own complicity, we experience the miracle of seeing [for example] the Nuclear Train stop and the arms race end. To paraphrase Harry Truman, the bomb stops here" (1987:96). Civil disobedience properly understood, then, was not "an act of defiance but an act of obedience to a deeper, interior will within us and within the world that is capable of transforming the world. . . . To live out the kingdom of God through such an action is to live in a loving relationship to our brothers and sisters in the police force, in courts, and in jails, recognizing God's presence in each of us. It is also to accept responsibility for an evil that is ours; as we are, so is the nuclear state" (1987:97).

In the view of Jim Douglass, a leading peace movement prophet, civil disobedience was, thus conceived and motivated, an act of prayer and love. It was "divine obedience." Indeed, Douglass observed, civil disobedience done in defiance rather than in prayer and love was "the right deed for the wrong reason. . . . Civil disobedience, like war, can be used to mask the emptiness of a false self" (1987:96). It followed that protest acts of the prophets were conducted with an air of religious solemnity, very much in contrast to the carnival/liberation/jubilation atmosphere often prevailing at protester actions (and the edge of anger expressed by the hard-left radical protesters sometimes present). We infer that prophets such as Jim Douglass were not supportive of such protest atmospheres, and in fact were infrequently seen at them.

Significant social change, then, required profound inner transformation, an overcoming of "the arms race within" (the title of a video documentary on Ground Zero, Poulsbo, and the Puget Sound Agape Community). The nuclear arms race and the war system were not merely errors in understanding—matters correctable by reason and education, or the tools of greedy and contending elites—although those factors might be involved. The causes went far deeper and signified something basically gone awry in the human spirit that required spiritual revolution. Prophets typically cast this "far deeper" matter as a radical form of Christianity, of which there were two main versions. Radical Catholicism was prevalent among prophets and particularly associated with the Plowshares network. In other networks, evangelical Protestant Christianity with a commitment to social justice was central, as espoused by, among others, the Sojourners Community. (Both are described by Barbara Epstein in Chapter 7, this volume.)

As articulated by Trident II Plowshares member Frank Panapoluos (1986), prophet theory, as a mode of action, had three levels. At the first and most basic level, adherents strove to build "life-sharing" communities among themselves. Premised on such communities, the second level required actually beginning disarmament by "beating swords into plowshares," i.e., engaging in disarming actions. On the third level, one was nonviolent, asserted that one had a responsibility to engage in disarming action, and accepted the consequences of those actions. In doing all of this, one hoped that: "People will see the truth of the action . . . and act on it in their personal lives. Our goal is a chain reaction of Plowshares actions around the country. Short of that we hope for people to alter their lives by engaging in *some* form of resistance" (Panapolous 1986:6, emphasis in the original).

Use of the term "chain reaction" suggests the degree to which prophet theory conceived change as occurring rapidly and dramatically. As a theory it would seem to lie toward the crisis end of the change continuum. Panapolos further observes: "To me, a million people taking the risk of *occupying* and *remaining* at nuclear weapons . . . sites would shut the system down, creating the moral crisis atmosphere necessary for disarmament to begin" (emphasis in the original). Prophet actions, such as those of Plowshares, then, looked toward such a day.

Change-Theories and Peace Movement Structure

Our main purpose here has been to draw out theories of social change as we find them in social movements (specifically the American peace movement of the Eighties) and to exposit them as pure types. We have, however, achieved such clarity at a price. The price is that we have decontextualized the theories. We have extracted them from the social locations in which we found them and taken them from the social organizations in which they were differentially embedded.

The contextual, structural, and social organizational facts are, however, that the pure theories found in the peace movement were not espoused randomly and conjoined willy-nilly with other social matters. Instead, the six had decidedly different conjunctions with a great many dimensions of social organization. Such linkages are drawn out in other chapters and we will therefore not detail them here except to provide a briefly stated set of overarching generalizations describing the major features of the peace movement.

Dominant Orientation

Peace movement organizations tended to adopt one or another of these theories as their dominant, even if not exclusive, orientation, and to specialize in one type of change action, even though they might also engage in other types of actions. For example, Grandmothers for

Peace and its moving spirit, Barbara Wiedner, were practitioners of protest theory, although both Wiedner and her organization did more than protest. The organization's statement of action in fact listed nine tasks: meditation and prayer for peace; speaking out for nuclear disarmament; participation in vigils; supporting other peace groups; educating themselves and others; voter registration; promoting peace studies in schools; making contacts with grandmothers in other countries; and, "when necessary, participating in nonviolent acts of resistance" (Grandmothers for Peace 1987). Only two of these nine (vigils and resistance) were protest. However, protest acts were viewed by her and her group and by advocates and enactors of other peace movement change-theories as the feature that provided Wiedner and Grandmothers for Peace a distinctive identity and *raison d'etre*. Much the same applied to most other persons and groups in the 1980s peace movement. We speak, therefore, of differentiating directions, distinctive competencies and dominant tendencies rather than totally exclusive features.

CLUSTERS

Peace movement organizations of the same or adjacent theory perceived a shared community of interest, selectively interacted with one another, and were partial to one another in undertaking joint activities. These selectively interacting communities of interest formed the six clusters (or segments) of the movement. Each presented a distinctive profile of activities; relationships with other movement segments, the war system and the public at large; characteristics of activists; forms of organization; modes of financing; features of membership; and cultural and emotional persona (cf. Gerlach and Hine 1970).

LIBERALS VERSUS RADICALS WITHIN CLUSTERS

Save perhaps for the transcender and prophet clusters, each of the other four divided internally in terms of how mainstream-liberal versus radical each was with regard to how much change was thought to be needed. There were substantively liberal versus radical educators, intellectuals, politicians, and protesters. Within clusters, liberals and radicals agreed on their theory of how to make change, but they disagreed on how much change was needed using that theory. Liberals envisioned more restricted social changes than radicals, who called for a wide-range of thoroughgoing social changes.

IDEOLOGICAL AFFINITIES
INTERLACED CLUSTERS

There were intersegment affinities and social commerce that interlaced the educators, intellectuals, politicians, and protesters along liberal versus radical lines. For example, liberal intellectuals such as Randall Forsberg had a following among liberal educators, politicians, and protesters, whereas radical intellectuals such as Noam Chomsky were followed more closely by radical educators, politicians, and protesters.[7]

AFFLUENCE AND CLUSTERS

Although it was only a main tendency, as we proceeded through the list of change-theories and their embedding clusters, the degree to which the leaders and members were socioeconomically privileged and culturally upscale declined. At the transcender extreme, leaders and members were quite affluent, and at the prophet extreme, leaders and members embraced a life of economic simplicity or even poverty.

The four middle segments were rather more complicated in that the economic level tended to divide between liberal and radical versions of educating, intellectualizing, politicking, and protesting, with the radical being the less affluent. Even so, compared among themselves, the educators and intellectuals tended on the whole to be more affluent than the politicians (with the exception of office holders) and the protesters. (A major reason for this was that the activities of the former two tended also to be ways they made their living, whereas the latter two were involved predominantly in volunteer and unpaid forms of citizen activism.)

CLUSTER SIZES

The great news about the peace movement of the Eighties was, of course, its surge in 1981–1983. Adopting a moderately restrictive conception of membership, we would estimate that the movement started the decade with about a quarter of a million members and perhaps 2,500 organizations. As it surged toward mid-decade it may have had as many has ten million participants involved in perhaps 6,000 organizations. In the later Eighties, membership declined, though the number of organizations continued to grow (even as some older ones closed their doors). By the decade's end, about a half a million people were involved in some 7,500 associations.

Viewed in terms of clusters, we estimate the relative strength of each as shown in Table 6.1. The politicians were by far the largest cluster in terms of participants, followed by the transcenders and educators. The intellectuals, protesters, and prophets, indeed, formed a kind of second tier, having only a tenth to a quarter of the membership of the larger clusters.

Degree Conflictful: Talkers versus Doers

Theories of social change can be ranked in terms of the degree to which they are conflictual—that is, the degree to which executing them brings one into a contentious relationship to the targets of change and produces a combative relationship with opponents. Indeed, we have so ranked the six theories of change presented above, ranging from transcending as least conflictful to prophesying as most conflictful.

The variable "degree conflictful" may be thought of as having at least two components. First, did the theory of change require only talk or did it mandate some regular form of action? In addition to uttering

Table 6.1. Estimated Number of Organizations and Participants in the Clusters of the American Peace Movement, Late 1980s

Cluster	Number of organizations	Number of participants
Transcenders	2,000	100,000
Educators	2,000	100,000
Intellectuals	200	10,000
Politicians	2,000	250,000
Protesters	1,000	50,000
Prophets	300	10,000
Total	7,500	520,000

words with movement content, by "talk" we mean writing and researching *and* activities attendant to these in a sustained way, most especially the activities of raising the funds that made concerted talking, writing, and researching possible. Talking in the narrow sense of uttering words with movement content includes the activities of public speaking, television and radio appearances, and the concatenation of these into tours.

Second, we can ask: "Talking (or doing) *to whom?*" Some important variations are: to people in one's cluster, the public at large in a general and disembodied fashion (as through articles, books, and television appearances), people in other movement clusters, and participants in the opponent world. Termed differently, what are typical objects of the talk (or action)? Who is targeted?

In these two terms of talking or doing to whom, the transcenders, educators, and intellectuals were the least conflictful. Their activities consisted mainly or totally of talk, and the talk was heavily directed to their own clusters or to the public at large. Such targeting may be thought of as indirect or unfocused generalized propaganda—as distinct from directed and direct social pressure.

The activities of doers entailed talking, of course, but went on to support the talk with persistent efforts to bring it directly to the attention of members of the opponent world. By "directly" we mean that, as a regular matter, the doer came into the immediate physical presence of members of the opponent world for the purpose of speaking about movement topics or against opponent policies, and perhaps also, for the purpose of performing acts that would communicate the seriousness of intent (e.g., acts of civil disobedience or resistance). Such targeting was focused and the three clusters that moved in this direction—politicians, protesters, and prophets—may be thought of as doers. They sought to make problems for opponents, to initiate situations that made it difficult if not impossible for opponents to ignore the movement.

CLUSTER RISK AND
SUBSTANTIVE RADICALNESS

There are yet other dimensions along which the six clusters can be ranked and we want, finally, to call attention to the degree of risk-taking each involved. Regardless of the degree of change they believed necessary, all talkers were engaged in relatively low levels of social risk-taking. In contrast, the doers subjected themselves to the possibility and reality of social disapproval, legal action, financial punishment, marginality and unemployment, and bodily harm.

Such risk-taking seemed to be associated, moreover, with beliefs that supported and facilitated it—beliefs that were more radical on the whole than those of the talkers. (Substantively, these beliefs were more "Left" in the sense of greater advocacy of equalitarian social arrangements and wide, democratic participation.)

The spectrum of ideological variation across the six clusters was really quite impressive because leaders and members differed on much more than sheer "Right-Left" talk in a narrowly political sense. The spectrum ran, instead, from a focus on technocratic arms-control perspectives, toward one end, to focus on the ultimate existential features of human life, at the other end.

Conclusion

We have addressed two basic matters about social movements in general and the American peace movement in particular. First, we have explicated the sense in which the ensembles of change-seeking organizations we call social movements espouse diverse theories of how desired social changes can be made to happen. Using materials provided by the American peace movement of the 1980s, we have isolated six such theories. Because we are speaking only of the peace movement, we do not claim these six are the only theories found in movements, although—impressionistically—we do think most of them occur quite commonly in other movements. Comparative analysis of other movements is obviously in order, however.

Second, we have suggested that such theories are embedded in clusters of like-theoried movement organizations. These clusters themselves have complex relations to one another. Among other relations, they are interlaced in certain ways and can be arrayed in terms of the degree they are conflictful and risk-taking.

Acknowledgments

We are extremely grateful to Lyn H. Lofland, Doug McAdam, Bill Moyer, and Carol Mueller for very helpful substantive and editorial suggestions on this chapter. An abbreviated version was presented at the Annual Meetings of the American Sociological Association, San Francisco, August 18, 1989.

Notes

1.   The works of Saul Alinksy (1946, cited in 1969 edition, 1972) are classic, of course, and there is an exceedingly rich and broad set of manuals in the tradition he pioneered.

2.   In the American peace movement of the Eighties such social change manuals included: American Peace Test 1988; Barash and Liption 1982; Conetta 1988; Coover et al., 1978; Freeze Voter Education Fund 1986; Hedemann 1981 (and later editions); Jergen 1985; Moyer 1977; Plesch 1982; Robinson 1982; Sweeney 1984; Taylor, Taylor, and Sojourners 1987; U.S. Out of Central America 1983; Wilcox 1980; Wollman 1985. For a more complete listing see Lofland, Johnson, and Kato, in press, an analytic bibliography of 625 books on peace movement organizations and activists that indexes social change manuals and that is coded in terms of the six clusters discussed in this chapter.

3.   One splashy transcender conference held in early 1988 was characterized by its organizers as an epochal event, under the banner of "A New Way of Thinking: Social Inventions for the Third Millennium." Transcender imagery of change is further conveyed in Ken Keyes, Jr., *The Hundredth Monkey* (1982), several hundred thousand copies of which circulated in transcender circles in the early and mid-eighties. For expanded discussion of transcender theory and practice see Lofland 1988; Mechling and Auletta 1986.

4.   It was likely, in addition, that laws governing the activities of tax-deductible nonprofit organizations (which prohibited more than an insubstantial amount of effort to influence legislation) were significant in causing this gap between what would appear to be the logic of educator and intellectual theories and what actually took place (McCarthy, Britt, and Wolfson in press). Conversely, the logic of politician theory presumed the importance of educating the public so it will undertake appropriate lobbying and electoral action.

We must recognize, moreover, that some intellectuals did engage in forging connections between ideas and politicians. For example, in the late Eighties, the Institute for Peace and International Security (whose intellectual theory is quoted above in the text), set about quite explicitly to carry ideas of "common security" into the political arena through grassroots political action: "Political power and short term success demand that the peace movement redefine the larger security agenda and engage in what right wing architect Irving Kristol calls the 'war of ideas.' In fighting to give legitimacy to our ideas, we push back the boundaries of what is now considered reasonable or politically possible" (Sasson, Solo, and Walker 1988:2–3, emphasis in the original).

5.   It is important to indicate that no theory advocating the positive relationship of violence to social change was found in-use among peace movement partici-

pants. This may, indeed, be a feature peculiar to the movement since the theory that violence-causes-positive-change is an extremely important in-use theory in a great many other social movements. Our exclusion of it in this report reflects the contours of our data rather than our assessment of its substantive or social significance. There is, however, the tricky question, "Who is in the movement?" A small number of people appearing at peace movement rallies did express sympathy with violence, and on rare occasions engaged in low level forms of it. Commonly, these people were members of Marxists sects. No Business as Usual (reputed to have links to the Revolutionary Communist Party) was one organized expression of this tendency and even represented themselves as a peace group of sorts. The vast bulk of the peace movement rejected or ignored this tiny minority and, in any event, such sectarians were not very active in the movement.

6.   A professionally articulated version of protest theory is presented by Piven and Cloward 1979. The social psychological side of being jolted into believing in the need for social jolts is nicely portrayed by Todd Gitlin in his account of his personal conversion from politician to protest theory in the presence of a Pentagon official who was defending U.S. government civil defense plans: "The world went obvious on me. *Men such as this were not going to be persuaded to be sensible.* They were grotesque, these clever and confident men, they were unbudgeable, their language was evasion, their rationality unreasonable, and therefore they were going to have to be dislodged. . . . I left the Pentagon a convinced outsider (Gitlin 1987:96–97, emphasis in the original).

7.   Despite some uneasiness, in order to save money and promote the movement, even radical and liberal peace movement organizations sometimes, however, formed coalitions for some purposes, such as producing newspapers, staging events, and renting office space (especially so in small cities where movement ranks were very thin). But when such joint ventures were among different clusters where the organizations were all either radical or liberal, cooperation was much easier. For example in one middle-sized West Coast city, a liberal politican group amicably sublet portions of its suite of offices to a liberal educator and liberal protest organization. Conversely, this same group was quite hesitant about joint actions with radical versions of organizations in those same two clusters.

CHAPTER 7

The Politics of Moral Witness: Religion and Nonviolent Direct Action

BARBARA EPSTEIN

Activist peace organizations in the Eighties, in the United States, tended to sort themselves out according to their tactics and structure. On the one hand, there were associations that relied primarily on the electoral process and lobbying Congress. These were for the most part conventionally structured organizations whose work was directed, and largely carried out, by paid staff members. On the other hand, there were the groups that relied on nonviolent direct action, employing civil disobedience as a dramatic, highly visible form of protest, and as a way of asserting a philosophy of nonviolence. This wing of the peace movement tried to avoid formal leadership structures, relied on consensus decision making, and was based on small, egalitarian affinity groups, sometimes as the components of large organizations, sometimes acting on their own.

The wing of the peace movement that emphasized civil disobedience was part of a larger network that was often called the nonviolent direct action movement. This node on the map of social activism was made up of activists in the women's, environmental, peace, and antiintervention movements who shared commitments to nonviolence and feminism, and who tended to be sympathetic to anarchism. Within the context of the movement, they wanted to create radically egalitarian communities that would prefigure the better society of the future. Many of the activists in the nonviolent direct action movement were drawn to various forms of spirituality, Christian and non-Christian.[1]

Radical Christians played a major role in the nonviolent direct action movement. Unlike the other groupings that the movement attracted, who tended to merge into the movement as a whole, the Christians maintained a quite distinct, semi-autonomous presence. There were, for instance, specifically feminist organizations within the larger direct action movement, but feminism was so widely shared that it was difficult to define the boundaries of the movement's feminist component. The religious, mainly Christian wing of the movement, however, was a clearly defined community with its own organizations. They based their politics on traditions that others in the movement were not expected to share, and practiced rituals in which others were not expected to participate, and which employed symbolism that others in the movement were not expected to understand. This did not necessarily mean that members of the direct action movement's religious community were uninterested in communication. The community was made up of practicing Christians, Catholics, and Protestants, and smaller numbers of religious Jews. Some of these people were members of regular congregations. For others, the primary, or only, religious affiliation was with alternative, often ecumenical, groups which identified with the peace movement rather than with any mainstream church or synagogue. In either case, members of the religious community were able to speak to enormous numbers of people whom the rest of the direct action movement had little ability to reach.

Perhaps because of its access to such large and powerful audiences, the religious community had a sense of its own actual and potential power that other sections of the direct action movement sometimes lacked. The organizations that the religious people created within the movement were more lasting than most others; the religious people themselves, once they became part of the movement, were likely to stick with it through thick and thin. Many of them were older than the people who made up the more counterculturally oriented sections of the movement; many of them had rearranged their lives so as to make movement activism a central part of it; they had found ways of reconciling activism with work and family pressures that they expected to last a lifetime.

Like the feminist community, the religious community espoused a politics of example rather than one oriented primarily toward strategic intervention or efficacy. But unlike the feminists, who came out of a mass movement and a tradition of thinking about politics in social terms, the Christians, who made up the core of the religious community, came out of a tradition that sees political or moral action as the expression of the responsibility of the individual to his or her own conscience. Feminism sees political action as a way of changing people's ideas or social institutions; there is a substantial current within Christian pacifism that sees political action primarily as a form of communication between the individual and God. The tradition of Christian pacifism has consisted largely of small groups of highly dedicated people engaging in acts of conscience, sometimes at great personal sacrifice, that have not been tailored to the needs of mass movements. But the religious groups that entered the mainstream of the direct action movement did so out of the conviction that a mass movement was required for the kind of social change that they wanted, a belief that such a movement can be built around a morally charged vision.

The religious community found common ground with the rest of the direct action movement in its commitment to a politics of example, but tended to define that politics quite differently than did others in the movement. For much of the feminist movement, exemplary politics was prefigurative politics: it meant living, insofar as possible, as one would in an envisioned future society. It meant self-realization through reconstructing the bonds among people, and between people and their natural environment. The power of such a politics came from the appeal of the vision that it projected, and from the hope that even in the present it might be possible to construct collectively a more whole and fulfilling life than mainstream society offers. Christian pacifism also involves prefigurative politics, but of a different kind: here the goal is not so much self-realization as it is self-abnegation, self-transformation through sacrifice. Sacrifice can also be a path to self-realization and to the creation of bonds with others, especially in a society in which materialism tends to drown out values and destroy genuine human connections. For this reason and also because of its deep roots in Christian tradition and its association with spirituality, self-sacrifice has had a genuine appeal. But it has led to a very different kind of politics than that implied by the feminist perspective.

To speak of a "politics of example" is to raise the question of effectiveness. Many in the more conventional wing of the peace movement argued that direct action had little impact on the political process: even the most massive blockade of an arms-producing laboratory or a testing site was not going to end the Cold War; at most it would stop work for the duration of the protest. Protesters who risked arrest or personal injury could be dismissed as eccentrics; even if they were admired for their willingness to act on their principles, relatively few were willing to follow their example; they controlled no votes in Congress.

This critique of the direct action movement engaged the movement only on the simplest level. It is true that the movement as a whole paid little attention to the question of strategy. Particular actions were planned with great care; but the larger question of how peace was to be achieved, what the path might be to the creation of a better society, was rarely discussed. Some, particularly among the radical Christians, rejected out of hand any discussion of the effectiveness of particular actions, arguing that one should take political action to express one's conscience and that the impact was in God's hands. Others were more interested in their effectiveness but were vulnerable to unrealistic expectations: in the charged atmosphere that accompanied blockades, inexperienced activists often more than half believed that the plant would be closed down, or that the blockade would persuade the workers at the plant to turn against the arms race and put down their work.

Critics of the movement who measured the effectiveness of political action by counting congressional votes and the activists who looked for immediate, tangible results both missed the point of direct action, which is that its impact is in fact not at all direct. Unlike the more conventional wing of the movement, which was most concerned with bringing about immediate changes in policy, the direct action movement wanted to change public attitudes, and it wanted to create a community within which activists could change their ways of thinking and of living, and which could serve as a magnet to others, a living demonstration of alternatives. Judged by these standards, the direct action movement was often quite successful. Civil disobedience actions often, I believe, focused public attention on the arms race or other issues, made real contributions to shifting public attitudes, and were often excellent terrains for creating community and living out alternative values.

Nonviolence and the Christian Peace Movement

The roots of the Christian direct action movement of the 1980s lie in the tradition of Christian pacifism, most immediately the legacy from the 1950s of such groups as the Committee for Non-Violent Action, which sponsored the attempt of the *Golden Rule,* with a crew of four Quakers, to sail into a nuclear testing zone in the Pacific in 1958, and the influence of the Quaker American Friends Service Committee. The practice of consensus, nonviolence, and the attempt to create communities that lived their principles were all attractive to many of the organizers of the antinuclear organizations that, in the mid-seventies, began to create a mass movement around nonviolent direct action. Many of those who were first drawn to the antinuclear movement were refugees from an antiwar movement that, by the early seventies, had largely burnt itself out with its own anger. Former antiwar activists, many with ties to the counterculture, who were disappointed in a movement that seemed to have lost touch with its own vision of a better society readily turned to the Quaker tradition for the articulation of a politics that could be the basis for community. They found allies in the two most radical American Friends Service Committee offices, in Cambridge and San Francisco. The early antinuclear groups, especially the Clamshell Alliance, were also assisted by the Movement for a New Society (MNS), a Philadelphia-based association that had its origins in A Quaker Action Group (AQAG), a group of radical Quakers formed in 1966. Members of AQAG had been centrally involved in the Southern civil rights movement; AQAG and, later, MNS took consensus decision making, nonviolence and direct action, as they had been practiced in the civil rights movement, as the building blocks of an envisioned nonviolent revolution. Convinced that antinuclear protest had the potential to develop into such a movement, MNS activists devoted themselves to building the antinuclear movement and to instructing its activists in consensus decision making and the techniques of nonviolent action.[2]

The Quakers thus had a formative influence within the nonviolent direct action movement. But although small numbers of Quakers played an important role in shaping it, in numerical terms Quakers never became an important component of the movement. And while the Quakers' commitment to nonviolence was based on religion, their influence in the movement was not experienced as particularly religious by the rest of the movement; their style has been much more secular than that of the various Christian groups that were to join the movement later, as it turned toward the issue of the arms race and then Central America.

Some of the religious groupings in the direct action movement originated in protest against the War in Vietnam. In May 1968 Daniel and Philip Berrigan, both Catholic priests, along with a group of Catholic peace activists, destroyed draft files in Catonsville, Maryland, with napalm that they had made according to directions that they found in the U.S. Special Forces Handbook. The sense of community among those who had participated in this action was strengthened over the course of several years in jail; they continued civil disobedience against the war upon being freed, and by the mid-seventies were making a transition to protest against nuclear weapons.

A number of those involved in these actions, including Philip Berrigan and his wife Elizabeth MacAllister, a former nun, established Jonah House, in Baltimore, where an occasionally shifting community of about ten adults, and, in the eighties, the two Berrigan/MacAllister children, have lived since. Berrigan and MacAllister, meanwhile, had announced their marriage and had been formally expelled from the Catholic Church. Jonah House has served as a basis for ongoing civil disobedience actions, as a model to other groups of Christian protesters attempting to establish "under the roof" communities, and as a focal point for the Christian pacifist movement as a whole, especially the groups in a number of East Coast cities that together made up the Atlantic Life Community. In addition to strengthening the bonds among protesters, communal living had the advantage of providing a relatively inexpensive way of life, and providing the children with care when their parents were in jail.

In 1980 the people from Jonah House, along with others, began a year-long campaign against the Pentagon. People came from around the country to take part in tours of the Pentagon led by Pentagon staff. During these tours, protesters would pour blood over models of weapons systems, kneel, pray, and would then be arrested. Some were able to leave the tour long enough to enter offices closed to the public and pour blood over files. The idea of holding "Isaiah actions," that is, of attempting to beat swords into ploughshares, came from this experience, and also from the experience of another Christian pacifist group, the Brandywine Peace Commmunity, which had held a witness against the Mark 12A missile. Several of the Brandywine people, along with several people from Jonah House, formed the nucleus of a group that would conduct the first of what would eventually be thirty-three "Ploughshares" and related actions. In September 1980 ten activists entered the King of Prussia nuclear weapons plant, severely damaged two missiles, and were subsequently given sentences ranging from eighteen months to ten years.[3]

Meanwhile, other Christian or Christian-based protest groups were forming elsewhere in the country. On the West Coast, Robert Aldrich, a nuclear engineer, resigned from his job in 1973, charging that the Trident missile that he had been working on was a first-strike weapon, and therefore in violation of international law. Aldrich persuaded Jim and Shelley Douglass, Catholics and former civil rights and antiwar activists, that the Trident base at Bangor, Washington, should be the focus of a campaign. In 1975 the Douglasses, along with thirteen others, came together to form the Pacific Life Community, which was committed to nonviolent opposition to the Trident and to the creation of a community in which self-transformation could take place. Most came from a Christian background, all had been repelled by the rhetoric and style of the antiwar movement in its last days, and were convinced that something different was needed. Looking to Gandhi, Martin Luther King, and the Catholic Worker movement for guidance, they organized a public education campaign against the Trident and conducted civil disobedience actions in which large numbers of people, at times in the thousands, would climb the fence and be arrested.[4]

Though the Douglasses and others hoped to draw large numbers of people to protest nuclear weapons, they also believed that action must originate in a core community in which self-education and self-transformation would be combined with politics. Seven members of the Pacific Life Community moved into a house together, and the community as a whole held regular meetings in which each examined his or her implication in the system of violence. For men, this often meant dealing with sexism and with insensitivity to feelings; for women, it could mean confronting problems of failure to take responsibility. After about three years, personality clashes within the group, along with the fact that some people decided to leave the area, led to a split. Those who remained decided to establish a permanent presence at the base. In 1978, now calling itself Ground Zero, the group moved to Poulsbo, Washington, and found a building adjacent to the base, from which actions at the base were subsequently conducted. Some of these drew large numbers of people from the Seattle/Vancouver area, some drew peace activists from further away. But Ground Zero itself remained a small group of religiously inspired activists who lived more or less at subsistence and who, although they did not share a house, shared resources, helped each other with child care and other responsibilities, and formed a tightly knit community.

Ground Zero then turned toward the creation of a broader community of nonviolent protest. In order to keep track of trains carrying weapons components, the Agape Community was created, a network of people across the country living within sight of railroad tracks; the contacts came from Sojourners, a Christian peace ministry based in the evangelical churches and other peace and social justice groups. Members of Agape monitored train movements and organized vigils. In 1982 Jim Douglass received a call from a reporter about a train heading toward the Bangor base carrying nuclear warheads; when he walked into the railroad yard outside the base, he found a train painted entirely white coming into the train yard, with heavily armed men in turrets on top of the cars. He noted the markings on the cars; later research confirmed that trains with markings such as these did carry nuclear warheads.

The Agape Community focused its efforts on spotting white trains. The first time a white train was located, traveling from the Pantex nuclear weapons assembly plant in Texas toward the Bangor base, vigils were organized in thirty-five towns and cities along the tracks; at two points people blocked the train's progress by sitting on the tracks. They were arrested. This required enormous courage, since no one could be sure that the trains would stop for those sitting in its way. Subsequently, thirteen more white trains were tracked, and protests organized along their paths.[5]

The Diversity
of Religious Direct Action

In addition to these larger networks, the religious community included many smaller groupings; those that were most involved in the direct action movement tended to call themselves affinity groups, others called themselves communities or, following the Latin American example, base communities. In the Bay Area, Spirit, organized by a group of seminary students, and Bardamaeus, also formed by young activists, were the foci of the most radical wing of the religious community. It was their members who tended to engage in the highest risk actions, such as entering offices to destroy files, and pouring blood. Mustard Seed, organized by members of the board of the Ecumenical Peace Institute, an umbrella organization for the Bay Area Christian peace movement, was composed of older people and was more cautious in its actions, for the most part simply participating in the civil disobedience actions of the religious community and the direct action movement generally.

Though the religious community was mostly based on ecumenical groups of Christians who came together outside the organized churches, there are some instances of congregations as such participating in the movement; San Francisco's Dolores Street Baptist Church, for instance, which was affiliated with the quite conservative Southern Baptist Convention, was represented by large numbers of its congregation in both of the major blockades of the Livermore Labs. In the Bay Area, where the religious community was strongest, starting in 1981 it held Good Friday services at the Livermore Labs every year. The first of these was organized by Spirit; after that the entire religious community became involved in planning and conducting them. As the service evolved, the distinction between Catholic and Protestant ritual largely dissolved. The traditional Stations of the Cross were presented in such a way that Christ's suffering became a metaphor for the sufferings of the world. The service always concluded with civil disobedience.

Though the activist religious community was overwhelmingly Christian, it also included increasing numbers of Jews, and, in a certain sense, the Pagans and witches had to be counted as part of this community as well. From the beginning there were many Jews in the direct action movement, but most of them were secularly oriented and did not participate in the movement as Jews. The large numbers of Jews who participated in the movements of the sixties were caught up in the same rebellion against their upbringing that shaped the movement as a whole; for most Jews, this meant dissociation from any Jewish identification. The revival of Judaism that swept this generation as a whole has touched many associated with the left, resulting in chavurot (religious study groups), kehilot (informal religious communities), and even a few radical synagogues with an orientation toward political activity. For many of these groups, the Sanctuary movement was the main point of entry into radical politics, because that movement was organized by congregations and has welcomed Jewish participation, and also because of the parallels between repression in Central America and in Hitler's Germany.

Faith, Politics, and History

The religious community brought to the direct action movement an ability to articulate the large questions of meaning that drew them into the movement and sustained their political activity. The connection between faith and political work that the religious people felt was described by Ken Butigan, a former member of Spirit, subsequently a staff worker for the Pledge of Resistance. Ken went with Spirit to Seattle to block the Trident; he was not a participant in the blockade, but provided support for those who were. For two weeks, the blockaders went out in boats each morning, not knowing whether that would be the day that the Trident would come in, and not entirely sure that they would return. The Trident might stop when it saw them, or it might plough right through their boats. Darla Rucker and Terry Messman-Rucker were both participants in the blockade; Darla, because of her disability, needed special assistance getting on and off the boat each day. Ken recalled,

> Each morning I would ago down to the water with Darla and Terry, I would carry Darla down to the Zodiac, one of the boats that Greenpeace had provided. Each time I did that I realized I might never see them again. There was the possibility they both might be killed. Then, after they floated out, there was the waiting, a contemplative vigil on the shore. That letting go, then receiving back again did more to create a sense of community than I've ever experienced before. By the time the sub actually came, I was reconciled to it. We are given our lives by the Spirit, for justice, for creating community; we offer our lives back. Sometimes our lives are taken, sometimes they're given back, a kind of continuous ballet with the universe, reciprocating, breathing in and out. Sometimes it takes a lot of courage, sometimes it takes putting up with boredom, or attention to details, so we can get the work done. That doesn't make it any less religious.[6]

The religious community brought to the movement an historical perspective that other sectors lacked. It is not that others in the movement were without a sense of tradition, but the Pagans, the witches, the anarchists, have adopted their beliefs rather than having grown up in them, and the traditions with which they began to identify lacked the solid continuity of organized religion. For both the Christians and the religious Jews who were increasingly being drawn into the movement, the holocaust, and to a lesser extent Hiroshima, were major points of reference, which they saw as having transformed the nature of both religion and social action, having set problems for humanity that required a new kind of response. Spiritually informed nonviolent direct action, members of the religious community argued, was a step toward such a response, because it addressed the problem of violence, it focused on individual responsibility for personal and social transformation, and it provided the basis for a prefigurative community that could sustain activism and serve as a model of a better society.

Jim Rice, a staff member of Sojourners, in Washington, D.C., told me that the Holocaust was the central image guiding his political work, that over the last few years he has read many books on it, that he was drawn over and over to the question of why it happened, and of the failure of German Christians to stop it. For him the Holocaust was a metaphor for the depravity of which human beings are capable. "It teaches an important lesson about the nuclear arms race. One of our defenses is, it can't happen; but it can, people have done that. The 'never again' image is important, and not just for Jews. I think a lot about that: what would I have done if I had been in Germany? Because of Hiroshima, because of the escalation of violence in World War Two, Hitler won. The good guys dropped the bomb."[7]

Radical Christianity and Marxism

Introduced to Marxism by liberation theology, the religious community has found it to be a powerful tool for understanding social conflict and for helping to outline a vision of a just society. Many Christian activists were attracted to Marxism because they saw it as compatible with biblical social criticism. Though the religious community has turned to Marxism for its focus on oppression and on class struggle, it understood those terms somewhat differently than they had been used by secular Marxists. Traditionally, Marxists have looked for groups that not only are oppressed but have as yet unrecognized access to power which will enable them to become agents of revolution. The working class is at the center of Marxist theory not only because of the claim that it would be in its interest to achieve socialism, but because the working class is so situated in capitalist society that, once self-conscious and mobilized, it would have the capacity to realize such a revolution.

The radical Christians in the direct action movement were much more interested in oppression than they were in whether a group was so situated to exert power. They were also relatively uninterested in the working class as such. The categories that the Christians were drawn to were, not surprisingly, fundamentally moral: they sought to organize those who were abused and powerless. The religious community, for instance, took up the issue of homelessness. Terry Rucker turned to full-time organizing of the homeless in Oakland, and he tried to develop ties between the people he is organizing and the religious community by efforts such as bringing busloads of them to the Good Friday services at the Livermore Labs. There was only a thin line between taking the side of the poor and taking on their burdens; within the religious community as a whole, there was a good deal of respect for those people who voluntarily gave up middle-class existence in order to live in poverty.

The willingness of many of the radical Christians to act on their consciences and suffer the consequences gave them a certain prominence in the movement, but it also made many of them particularly leery of attention to political strategy. Many argued that their responsibility was to offer witness; the results are in God's hands. This is an approach that led groups like that at Jonah House to ignore the question of building a mass movement and concentrate on actions that brought long jail sentences and were restricted to a small group of activists.

The Christian radicals who were more part of the mainstream of the direct action movement were much more concerned with building a mass movement on the streets than were the Jonah House people. Many of them also saw a need to find some balance between moral witness and political efficacy. Carolyn Scarr, of the Mustard Seed affinity group, who described herself theologically as a "Unitarian mystic," pointed out that actions that were designed only to offer witness could become ritualized. Police would be informed in advance that a group of Christians would, say, hold a service and then sit in the road in front of the Livermore Labs; the police knew that the action would involve a small group of well-behaved people, and they were likely to be cooperative and even friendly. Actions of moral witness could thus become just as safe as conventional political activity.

> It's easy to get pushed into a little place of permitted dissent carried out within the system, while the system rolls on unimpeded. Either way your actions are stymied. What you're left with is the uneasy middle ground of tension between the two, and uncertainty. And that's the only place where anything can get done, I think.[8]

Spirituality and Community

The ideal of community shaped daily life for the Christian activists to a greater extent than it did for most people in the direct action movement, with the exception of some of the Pagan anarchists. The members of Mustard Seed provided support for each other in a variety of ways: when members of the group were arrested, there was a bail kitty to call upon, and when in jail, others took care of the children and otherwise looked after the details of daily life. There was a sense of extended family among the members; children tended to regard the adults as aunts and uncles. The group met monthly for worship and political discussion; every summer there was a camping trip, and other events—such as wine tasting before a meeting at the house of a Sonoma County member—were likely to be organized spontaneously. Members of Mustard Seed tended to see it as a permanent fixture in their lives.

Many of the more radical Christian affinity groups were shorter lived, partly because members were younger and their lives were less settled, and partly because of the higher level of expectations, which not everyone could meet. While these groups lasted, however, the sense of community was even stronger. Spirit was formed out of about ten students at the Union Theological Seminary in Berkeley who came together through a Christian action at the Livermore Labs. When the affinity group was formed, they all lived within a two-block radius, close to the school. Darla and Terry Rucker were the only married couple in the group; they were also the only couple with children. Their house became the center for the group; meetings were held there, leaflets were produced there, anyone who temporarily needed a place to live was likely to stay there, and most days at least a few members of the group passed through the house on one errand or another. Darla Rucker remembers,

> There was always a group you knew you were going to act with, there was always support, always people to pick you up when you got out of jail. After one action, Pat got out before we expected her to. She called our house. Someone ran and got a cake, someone got champagne, we all got in a car, when she came out she was greeted by all of us. Every event that was important to one of us, we were all there; when my son was born every single person was in the room with me. We celebrated holidays together. People would sleep on our floor so they would be there on Christmas morning when the kids woke up. It was the most wonderful experience of my life.[9]

Spirit lasted for about three years. It broke up primarily because of its inability to absorb different levels of political commitment; some people saw political work as their central life commitment, others wanted to find room to pursue other goals. Darla, Terry, and Ken, who organized Spirit and were central to it while it lasted, have continued to be mainstays of the direct action movement and of the radical wing of the religious community. Darla pointed out that many of the radical religious groups consisted of a core that lasted more or less indefinitely and a periphery of others who came and went; this was true of Jonah House and of many of the Catholic Worker households around the country.

Communities such as Jonah House, which operated mostly on their own, avoided some of the pressures faced by groups like Spirit that tried to carve out a role for Christian radicalism within a mass movement, defining that role as one of higher commitment, of taking greater risks. One of Spirit's problems was that some of its members were not, in the long run, willing to take on that role. Differences within the group over each person's level of commitment came to the surface as many members of the group approached graduation and began to plan their future lives. But this was probably not the only factor in Spirit's demise. Another radical Christian group in the Bay Area, Bardemaeus, broke up over similar issues at about the same time, even though it was not made up of students. Both of these groups were formed as the movement as a whole was growing in the early eighties; both fell apart in the context of the decline of the movement as a whole several years later. In any cycle of the direct action movement, the early period of growth is the time when differences are easily tolerated, often, in the heady atmosphere of political enthusiasm, hardly noticed. When the movement becomes stronger and is forced to deal more seriously with issues of strategy, differences are likely to surface; as the movement declines, a general feeling of disappointment is likely to make these differences appear stark and seem insurmountable. These issues were particularly sharp for the religious activists because they held each other to such high standards. But even when affinity groups fell apart and the movement as a whole declined, many of the religious activists found ways of continuing their political work.

Radical Christianity
and the Politics of Moral Witness

The religious community was able to provide a more stable base for ongoing direct action than any other part of the movement because it drew inspiration from a powerful international movement, because its ties to churches and other religious organizations in the United States gave it resources that other sections of the movement lacked, and because it had access to a broad constituency. Most of the religious activists were members of churches; some of them were pastors or were very active in church affairs. The fact that their radicalism was rooted in religion tends to give it a certain legitimacy in the eyes of other religious people.

In addition to having access to a clearly defined and often receptive constituency, the religious activists had more access to institutional support than did other sections of the direct action movement. The religious community was particularly large in the Bay Area, partly because of the fact that there are many churches in the area that are sympathetic to the peace movement, and partly because of the presence of the Graduate Theological Union, which attracted students from all areas of the country on the basis of its orientation toward a radical form of Christianity. The Graduate Theological Union provided ongoing support for religious activism by sponsoring projects, seminars, lectures. The churches in the Bay Area, and in Northern California, both Protestant and Catholic, provided a base for social activism that often overlapped or merged with the direct action movement. Of the roughly two hundred churches nationwide that declared sanctuary in the Eighties, about a hundred were in Northern California, about twenty-five in the Bay Area. Because of the legitimacy that the churches provided for such activities, and the surrounding atmosphere of widespread public support, it would have been very difficult for the authorities to have arrested sanctuary workers as they did in the Southwest. An Alameda County sheriff, asked by the press what he intended to do about churches providing sanctuary, said that if he knew of a church engaged in such activities he would have to make an arrest, but that he knew of no such church.

The indirect support that the churches provided for the movement was most apparent in the Bay Area, but it was a factor on a nationwide level as well. Organizations such as Pax Christi, the Center of Concern, and the Christic Institute directly or indirectly nourished the radical strand within the Catholic Church; Clergy and Laity Concerned did the same for the Protestant churches. Although these groups had no organizational link with the direct action movement, they helped build an atmosphere of support that encouraged some church members to join the movement or to support it in other ways. The network of Christian activist organizations provided some members of the direct action religious community with jobs, which gave them access to national contacts and also often made it easier for them to organize their lives around political activity. In the sixties and early seventies, the influence of the Left was sustained in large part by a similar network of organizations. As the organized strength of the secular Left declined, the left wing of the churches in a sense took its place.

The religious community also strengthened the direct action movement by emphasizing a direct, immediate humanitarianism that tended not to be as prominent an element of nonreligious activism, and that broadened the movement's appeal. Witness for Peace delegations protected specific Nicaraguan villages by placing themselves between the Contras and their intended victims. Sanctuary workers risked their own freedom to protect Central American refugees from being returned to repression and possibly death. The efforts of nonreligious activists contributed to the same aims, but usually with more of a focus on broad political change, and less on the impact on the lives of particular people. This emphasis on giving help to those who need it attracted not only religious people but also others whose first interest was in making the world a better place in some concrete way. Will Lotter, who along with his wife Jane was a key Sanctuary worker in Davis, California, said that he was attracted to the movement because "it was one thing you could do that would actually make a difference in a refugee's life. This was something I could actually do to visibly say no to our government's policy. It has given me a real sense of satisfaction. We've met lots of refugees; it's been neat. You have some real substance to your activity."[10]

At a time of religious revival in the United States, and for that matter much of the world, the direct action movement's orientation toward spirituality was a major part of its appeal, and the ability of the religious community to link the movement to broader religious constituencies was crucial to the movement's vitality and growth. But the Christian perspective also reinforced some problems of the direct action movement that had other sources as well, and also brought new problems to the movement. Many people in the religious community regarded strategic thinking as incompatible with a spiritual approach to politics, which, they argued, meant acting on the basis of one's conscience, not calculating effects. In fact, the influence of the religious activists was enhanced by their obvious sincerity and their lack of interest in tailoring their actions and statements in accord with what the public might find comfortable. Small groups can afford to disregard strategy, and so can a mass movement, at least for a limited time, especially if it exists alongside other movements that are willing to devote more attention to it. If it were to become a larger component of protest generally, the direct action movement, including its religious community, would have to address the question of strategy more seriously.

There are also ways in which radical Christianity created problems for the development of a prefigurative and radically democratic movement. A politics that emphasizes self-sacrifice may command respect, but it is likely to have trouble attracting large numbers of participants. Liberation theology, which places the same emphasis on self-sacrifice as American radical Christianity, is the basis for massive popular movements. But in Latin America this politics takes place in a context of pervasive poverty and extensive political repression: it is more a matter of honoring the suffering that pervades most people's lives than of calling upon them to give things up. For Latin American priests and intellectuals, liberation theology implies foregoing a certain level of comfort and security, but it also brings incorporation into a powerful and inspiring mass movement, which has its own rewards. Radical Christians like to point out that poor people in the Third World understand the message of the Bible easily because it is about oppression and resistance in a society very much like the ones they live in. Biblical politics may require more reinterpretation to provide a basis for a mass movement in the United States. The pagan anarchists lacked the cultural legitimacy that the Christian activists could call upon, but it may be that their concept of prefigurative politics, which rejected the language of self-sacrifice and tried to create the basis for a whole and fulfilling life in the present, would be a better basis for a mass movement in the United States.

The most serious problem with the Christian perspective, for the direct action movement, was that its moral elitism led to some ambivalence about egalitarian democracy. Like the feminists, the radical Christians believed in leadership by example; but for the Christians, example was tinged with a heroism that was often incompatible with collective action. In believing that faith and willingness to take special risks gave them a special claim to morality, the radical Christians in particular implicitly set up moral hierarchies that were antithetical to the spirit of grassroots democracy that the movement tried to promote, and that coexisted uneasily with the consensus process. Debates in jail about whether to accept relatively lengthy sentences often took on overtones of moral superiority and inferiority. There were some differences on these issues within the religious community: the Catholics were likely to be more ready to take risky action, and also more willing to abandon democratic process. One Catholic priest, for instance, who has been to jail many times, and who was supported in his activity by only a minority of his church, declared his church to be a sanctuary for Central American refugees. He was condemned for not consulting the church first. He did not regret his action. "You don't vote on morality," he said. "Morality will lose every time."

Acknowledgments

This research was supported by faculty research funds granted by the University of California, Santa Cruz. I am also grateful to Jeffrey Escoffier for the substantial contribution that he made to this project through his close reading of drafts and his criticisms and suggestions.

Notes

1. Very little has been written on the nonviolent direct action movement of the seventies and eighties in the United States. There is a sparse literature on the antinuclear movement of this period, mostly emphasizing its electorally oriented side. The literature on the peace movement of the period is equally sparse. See Loeb 1987; Boyer 1984. On the historical roots of the peace movement of the seventies and eighties, including its nonviolent direct action wing, see Cooney and Michalowski 1977; Chatfield 1971; Wittner 1984. On the radical pacifism of the fifties, see Isserman 1987; Katz 1974.
2. The best source on the Movement for a New Society is their own newsletter, variously called *Dandelion Wine, Dandelion,* and *Wine,* and published by the Life Center, Philadelphia. MNS has recently been disbanded; the newsletter is no longer being published. My discussion of MNS and its role in the direct action movement is also drawn from several interviews with Fred Cook, in San Francisco, in the fall of 1984, and an interview with George Lakey, in Philadelphia, February 8, 1985.
3. Interviews with members of Jonah House, January 30, 1985.
4. The following account of the Pacific Life Community/Ground Zero is drawn from an interview with Jim and Shelley Douglass, June 17, 1987.
5. For an account of the White Train campaign, see Douglass, "Tracking the White Train," *Sojourners* 1984, and the accounts of local actions, in the same issue, by Don Mosley (Comer, Georgia), Mary Harren (Wichita, Kansas), Clare Hanrahan (Memphis, Tennessee), Mary Dell Miles (Birmingham, Alabama), and Archbishop Raymond Hunthausen and Bishop Methiesen (Amarillo, Texas).
6. Interview with Ken Butigan, March 18, 1987.
7. Interview with Jim Rice, April 30, 1987.
8. Interview with Carolyn Scarr, February 14, 1987.
9. Interview with Darla Rucker, February 3, 1987.
10. Interview with Will and Jane Lotter, March 23, 1987.

CHAPTER 8

Instrumental and Symbolic Competition among Peace Movement Organizations

ROBERT D. BENFORD AND LOUIS A. ZURCHER

In a multiorganizational field such as the peace movement, its component parts interact with one another (Turk and Lefcowitz 1962; Curtis
and Zurcher 1973). That interaction can take a variety of forms, including competition, conflict, and cooperation (Zald and McCarthy 1980).
In this chapter, we focus on the forms of competition that emerged
among social movement organizations (SMOs) making up a local peace
movement and on the conditions that were conducive to intergroup
competition. Competition refers to "the act of striving for some object
that is sought by others at the same time, a contention of two or more
persons for the same goal" (Mack 1969:330). The most visible forms of
competition are for instrumental resources such as money, constituents, and third-party supporters. SMOs also compete for symbolic
goods (McCarthy and Zald 1977; Zurcher and Snow 1981). Turf, status, and prestige are at stake in the competition for symbolic recognition (Gusfield 1963; Zurcher and Kirkpatrick 1976).

Most peace movement leaders eschew competition between participating SMOs. In fact, "progressive" ideology ostensibly encompasses
shared beliefs that regard competition as an inherently evil process
that deserves considerable blame for the existence of exploitation,
global human suffering, and the arms race. On the surface, there appears to be a norm of cooperation that is supposed to operate at both
the individual and organizational levels of the movement.

We will show that peace movement groups were unable to avoid
competition among themselves despite conscious attempts to create a

cooperative interorganizational environment in the pursuit of parallel goals for the well-being of society as a whole.

Setting and Method for Study

All nine major peace movement organizations operating in Austin, Texas, during 1982 and 1983 were examined. Three were studied directly by the participant observation of the first author, Robert Benford. The criteria for selecting the SMOs for intensive study were threefold. First, each SMO had to be observationally accessible. Second, only SMOs that devoted a substantial proportion of their resources toward antinuclear weapons work were considered for selection. Finally, each SMO had to have been observed in the preliminary stages of the study to have had direct interaction with other local peace movement organizations. Three SMOs met our selection criteria: Austin Nuclear Weapons Freeze Campaign (NWFC), University of Texas Mobilization for Survival (UM), and Texas Mobilization for Survival (TM).[1]

Robert Benford was accepted in each of those SMOs as a person concerned with the purposes of the organizations and as a researcher gathering data about their activities. There was no deception about his purposes. He was able openly to take notes, and recorded them fully within twenty-four hours after taking them. Formal intensive interviews were conducted with twenty-one key activists, and participants were interviewed informally. Pertinent documents (speeches, memos, newsletters, publicity statements) were analyzed for illustrative purposes.

Results and Discussion

Table 8.1 summarizes the goals, strategies, tactics, and structures of the three SMOs.[2] We will argue below that the structural differences between the three SMOs generally were less important than interactional phenomena in explaining the emergence of competition among the SMOs toward accomplishing the mutual goal of nuclear disarmament.

Table 8.1. Summary of Comparative Analysis of Three Austin Peace Movement Organizations

Structural dimension	*Movement organization*		
	NWFC	*UM*	*TM*
Goals			
Number	Single	Multiple	Multiple
Change advocated	Minor	Major	Major
Change orientation	Structural	Structural & people	Structural & people
Strategies			
Type	Bargaining & persuasive	Persuasive	Coercive & persuasive
Principle	Strategic	Expressive	Expressive
Tactics			
Scope	Narrow	Narrow	Broad
Style	Conservative	Moderate	Moderate to radical
Structures			
Type	Semi-centralized	Decentralized	Decentralized
Leadership roles	Primarily administrative	Mixed; no statesman	Mixed; no administrator
Number of members			
Active[a]	12-15	5-7	10-12
Passive[a]	75-100	15-20	50-75
Years operating[b]	2	6	7

[a]Active members: participate regularly in the activities of the SMO.
Passive members: participate only occasionally but are among those an SMO considers within its membership pool.
[b]Years operating as of 1983.

COMPETITION FOR INSTRUMENTAL RESOURCES

Oberschall (1973:102) defined social movement mobilization as "the process of forming crowds, groups, associations and organizations for the pursuit of collective goals." He suggested that in order to achieve its objectives a movement must accumulate, control, and strategically deploy resources. This suggestion contains the paradox faced by every leader of an incipient SMO. Resources are needed to achieve the desired goals, but their mobilization requires that those resources already be under movement control. The folk adage "it takes money to make money" in the social movement context can become "it takes resources to make resources."

In the earliest stages of an SMO's development, it must acquire a commitment of resources from its constituents in order to begin the accumulation of assets that can be used to achieve the organization's goals. An SMO needs cash for printing leaflets, banners, and brochures, as well as money for postage to conduct mail campaigns, to meet rent and telephone costs, and to provide capital that might be used in future fund-raising projects. Volunteers are necessary to maintain the organizational thrust, and if an SMO is to realize its goals, it typically will require external or third-party support (Jenkins and Perrow 1977), including the support of the media (Molotch 1979; Gitlin 1980), governmental officials, and technical advisors (Tilly 1978).

Whatever the types of resources that are required by an SMO, the availability of those resources is limited. Zald and McCarthy (1980:5) hypothesized that "under conditions of declining availability of marginal resources, direct competition and conflict between SMOs with similar goals can be expected to increase." This observation emphasizes the effects of the external environment (i.e., society's resource base) on the internal dynamics of a movement (i.e., competition and conflict). It did not fully enough consider the relationship between a movement's internal environment and interorganizational relations.

Unintentional SMO Competition. As a social movement grows larger, the resource base might not expand to meet the needs of the attracted groups. Consequently, even in the case of the peace movement, the leaders of which consistently discourage competition, the movement can find itself creating an environment characterized by pervasive competition.

To illustrate, in 1977 when TM was founded only two other local SMOs made up the Austin peace movement. By 1984 there were over thirty peace and justice groups, nine of which included nuclear disarmament among their goals. As a leader of TM noted, "We used to be the only group in town concerned about the arms race. Now we are competing against all these other groups for the disarmament dollar."

UM faced a similar situation. When it was established on the University of Texas campus in 1978, there were no other university groups focusing on nuclear issues. By the Fall of 1983, UM was directly competing with United Campuses to Prevent Nuclear War, University Peace and Justice Coalition and a university chapter of NWFC. They competed for money, constituents, and media attention.

The effect of these circumstances was an increase in competition. Assuming that the availability of resources remains constant as the number of peace movement organizations increases, the potential share of resources that any one SMO can control decreases. Hence, all else being equal, as the number of geographically proximate groups within a social movement increases, the intensity of the competition among them for instrumental resources is likely to increase.

In addition to competition for dollars, competition for community scheduling of key events emerges. One of the peace movement organizations in Austin attempted to eliminate potential overlaps by publishing a "peace calendar" as part of its monthly newsletter. Nevertheless, the Austin SMOs routinely conflicted with each other on plans for public events.

Given that many SMO activities are dependent upon a limited pool of participants who feel obliged to contribute time and labor, direct competition for their assistance among several ideologically similar SMOs is typical. Most movement events require an audience. The sponsoring SMOs plan and hope for media attention. The odds are that representatives of the media will report only one movement event if several occur on the same date.

Many SMO activities are dependent upon using ad hoc action teams. The potential members of these teams are drawn from the finite pool of adherents and constituents who are willing to contribute time and labor. When several movement activities are scheduled simultaneously or too tightly in sequence, competition for "visible" supporters and for audience obtains. As one TM organizer in charge of recruiting volunteers for a statewide antinuclear march reported dejectedly, "Everyone tells me they're too burned out from working on the freeze referendum." The diversity of commitment demands for member activity not only generated competition among SMOs but also between members' dedication to the peace movement and their other routine activities in daily life.

Intentional SMO Competition.   As indicated above, peace movement organizations generally view competition as an undesirable process. When competitive situations within the movement are attributed to a conscious effort on the part of an SMO or its leaders, tensions are pronounced. For example, a UM leader announced at a TM meeting that his organization had recently decided to hold "Nuclear Waste Awareness Week." The TM representative reminded him that the Union of Concerned Scientists and United Campuses to Prevent Nuclear War were sponsoring their annual "November 11th Convocation" during that week. She suggested that the UM leader check with those groups to ensure that their plans for Nuclear Waste Awareness Week would not conflict with the convocation. The UM leader repeatedly rejected the TM representative's subsequent pleas to reschedule the event to avoid an overlap. He asserted that that week was absolutely necessary for his group's activity because it was the anniversary of Karen Silkwood's death. "Besides, we [UM] already reached consensus on this," he declared.

Later in the month, TM participants decried the small audience turnout for the activity they had sponsored during "Austin Artists for Peace Week." A TM leader said, "Well, there is so much going on. . . ." His colleague responded that he was disgusted with the "lack of coordination" among the various peace movement groups in scheduling events. "It's almost like we are bent on self-destruction."

Zald and McCarthy (1980) observed that competition among SMOs within a social movement industry is not necessarily "zero-sum." That is, one SMOs gains do not have to come at the expense of another movement organization. They based their conclusions on literature (Bolton 1972; Curtis and Zurcher 1973) which shows that "few people affiliate very extensively, but that a small portion of people are rather widely affiliated" (Zald and McCarthy 1980:5-6). Thus, "since no organization commands the total loyalty of most of its constituents, this competition is not zero-sum and, consequently, should not be especially rancorous" (1980:6). Though we share their assumptions about that possibility, empirical evidence indicates that regardless of the objective conditions shaping an SMO relationship, it is the subjective evaluations that are most salient. An excerpt from Benford's field notes illustrates that point:

> I called (the Austin NWFC founder) to see if TM and a peace coalition could use a list containing the names and phone num-

bers of volunteers who worked on last fall's freeze referendum for purposes of recruiting volunteers for a march and for a concert in support of antinuclear activities. (The Austin NWFC founder) replied "I don't know whether or not I want to loan that out because I need it for getting volunteers also." I responded that if he loaned it to us, I would photocopy it and thus quickly return the original. He responded, "that's not the problem. If they commit to you all, we'll have trouble getting them to volunteer for us."

This leader seemed to perceive the availability of participants as a zero-sum situation. We suggest, therefore, that competition among SMOs that is perceived by the leaders as not being zero-sum will not be intense. Conversely, competition among SMOs that is perceived by the leaders of at least one SMO as being zero-sum will be intense and may lead to SMO conflicts.

COMPETITION FOR SYMBOLIC RESOURCES

Symbolic resources are abstract assets such as turf, status, and prestige. They are meaningful to and desired by social movement participants, but unlike money, facilities, and labor, do not have a precisely defined exchangeable value in the market place. Sometimes the distinction between "instrumental" and "symbolic" is a matter only of definition. More importantly, with respect to SMO competition, the two forms are interdependent. Successful competition for tangible resources is likely to result in greater symbolic rewards for an SMO, and vice versa.

Turf. Functional and geographical boundary distinctions among SMOs in a social movement are established by competition, by negotiation resulting in informal agreements and by unilateral decisions. Which group is to perform what tasks where is thereby determined (Zald and McCarthy 1980:11). Real or perceived violations of these arrangements are likely to lead to intense competition and, in extreme cases, can result in bitter conflict among SMOs.

Generally, leaders of the Austin peace groups honored the functional turf among them, particularly if an SMO was known to concentrate its efforts on a specific issue. For example, at a TM meeting, one leader announced that the national Mobilization for Survival was calling for civil disobedience actions as a part of a demonstration against U.S. intervention in Central America. Discussion turned to what kind of action could be organized in Austin to coincide with the planned nationwide protest. A TM organizer interjected, "I feel like if we are going to do anything we should approach other groups such as the Central American Committee, the Committee in Solidarity with the People of El Salvador and the Committee for Peace and Justice in Central America." The leader went on to suggest that it was inappropriate for TM to "take the lead" on a Central American action since there were several SMOs that focused on opposing military intervention in that region.

Geographical turf also tended to be respected among the Austin SMOs, although disagreements sometimes arose within a particular SMO regarding what constituted infringement. For example, those in attendance at a TM meeting were informed that the nuclear submarine USS *Corpus Christi* would be arriving in the Texas port of the same name. A TM leader announced that a protest was being planned by a Corpus Christi group and suggested that two or three carloads of people be recruited to travel to the coast and participate. All the members agreed that a protest would be exciting, and enthusiasm prevailed until one member noted that the planned activity was not a protest but a liturgy organized by a religious group. One activist suggested that TM should protest the vessel's arrival anyway. "Just because one group plans a religious ceremony doesn't mean we couldn't go down there and participate however we see fit." A TM leader objected to that notion, arguing, "We have to respect the fact that this event is being planned by another group." "We shouldn't muscle in," a member added. "We would be violating their territorial rights."

In the fall of 1983, the University Peace and Justice Coalition and a Freeze Campaign chapter were established on campus. Rumors circulated that more groups were in the process of being formed, including "Students for Peace" and "Engineers for Peace." United Campuses to Prevent Nuclear War, which remained at that time an elite organization made up solely of faculty members, appeared unconcerned by the proliferation of campus peace groups. UM members, in contrast, publicly argued that the proliferation was a violation of their jurisdictional claims. A UM leader complained, "There are too many groups on campus; it smacks of undermining our purpose." He continued:

Now [NWFC's founder] is starting a Freeze group on campus.
He didn't bother to tell us . . . but he always used University
Mobe [UM] whenever he wanted to gain access to campus. . . .
They [NWFC] just don't respect us enough. I don't know why
that is. We don't care about the credit. We just don't appreciate
people going around us. . . . The Freeze is going to have a paper
organization on campus anyway. They're not going to be stealing
any resources from us. They'll just use it for access to campus.
. . . The group will be a flash in the pan.

Clearly, symbolic turf issues were important to the UM leader.

Although instrumental resources can be at stake, symbolic competition occurs regarding functional and geographical turf. These boundary distinctions are often the result of informal agreements reached by the SMOs in a given social movement. Thus, we propose that perceived violations of informal boundary arrangements within a social movement are likely to increase competition among the involved groups and can lead to SMO conflicts.

Status.   According to Zald and McCarthy (1980:4), SMOs compete for "symbolic dominance: which SMO has the best program, tactics, and leaders for accomplishing goals? SMOs attempt to convince sympathizers to follow their lead." Although the peace movement can derive benefits from remaining acephalous and decentralized (Gerlach and Hine 1970) and although a cooperative norm usually operates to restrict competition, the groups nevertheless tend to vie for "symbolic hegemony." Some SMO leaders are satisfied to carve a functional or issue niche within the peace movement for their particular organization. Others, however, prefer to see their SMO as *the* vanguard group of the movement.

Competition for symbolic resources appeared to underlie the UM leader's intransigence regarding the rescheduling of Nuclear Waste Awareness Week. He refused to accept that TM, the sponsor of the event, was one of the dominant SMOs among the Austin peace movement groups. In a meeting with TM members, he appeared to gloat about the fact that TM was having financial difficulties, whereas UM had a surplus of cash at hand.

Zald and McCarthy (1980:6) suggested that "competition between inclusive organizations in an industry takes the form of slight product differentiation (offering marginally different goals) and, especially, tactical differentiation." Competition between UM and TM seemed to support that argument. In their pursuit of symbolic hegemony, given that their goals were essentially the same, both SMOs emphasized creativity and originality in designing where creative packaging often determines the success or failure of similar products. An event that was part of Nuclear Waste Awareness Week provides an illustration. UM sponsored a foot-race called "You Can't Run From Nuclear Waste Race." When a UM leader announced the race at a TM meeting, he explained, "The race will cover 3.2 miles, the same distance Karen Silkwood's car went the night she was murdered." TM members groaned at what they considered to be forced attempts at macabre symbolism.

Given these observations, we conclude that competition for symbolic dominance among SMOs having similar goals, ideologies, and strategies will tend to take the form of tactical differentiation.

In contrast, SMOs with disparate ideologies and strategies (though, by definition, similar goals) will, in the pursuit of symbolic dominance emphasize their differences in preferred approaches for social change. For example, in a feature story (Butts 1983) that compared a TM leader with the NWFC founder, each activist was careful to draw distinctions for the journalist that reflected disparities in the two SMOs' strategies and ideologies. The TM leader emphasized the importance of taking "issues to the streets," while the NWFC leader asserted that he preferred to work toward "positive votes on the freeze." An interview with the NWFC founder further demonstrated perceived differences in the rhetorical strategies of the two organizations:

> The goal of the nuclear freeze is just to get both sides to stop building more. . . . They have to stop before they can begin backing up. Also, another factor in that is that, at this point, after thirty years of being indoctrinated in how evil the Soviet Union is, the American public is not susceptible to hearing an argument saying "let's disarm; let's destroy all our nuclear weapons," because it's just such a leap from where the status quo people are. You know, there's a few people willing to hear it. The TM leaders think it's great, but it's a tiny fraction.

Competition for symbolic hegemony seemed to involve a process whereby a group would seek to enhance its own status within the movement, in part, by attempting to diminish the status of other movement organizations. One of NWFC's founders frequently accused the two Mobe organizations (TM and UM) of "preaching to the already converted" and "alienating more peace than they add" to the cause of nuclear disarmament. "The Mobes tend to make a spectacle of themselves, jumping up and down and shouting rather than just demonstrating or quietly vigiling," he added. "We're not like the KKK; we're not out to get just one or two new members." Although TM and UM leaders objected to such characterizations, they readily admitted that they were more inclined to devote themselves to activating adherents than to convincing skeptics or the undecided. "Besides," asserted a TM activist, "at some point you've got to stop talking about the problem and do something about it." In short, competition for symbolic dominance among SMOs that have disparate ideologies, strategies, and/or tactics may take the form of rhetorical exchanges that emphasize or exaggerate such differences.

Prestige. Competition among SMOs for prestige is closely related to competition for status. In the context of this analysis, prestige refers to claims of honor, distinction, or power that were generally recognized by the peace movement. The relative degree of prestige enjoyed by an SMO contributed, in turn, to that organization's status position within the movement.

The movement activists in the Austin setting were prestige-conscious. Claims of being "first" or being the "largest" were common. In spite of anticompetitive norms, postfactum public bravado was considered acceptable behavior so long as it tended to reflect favorably on the movement as a whole. The local freeze referendum, for example, was touted by an NWFC spokesperson as "the largest non-governmental election in the history of the world." TM representatives pointed out, in reference to the 1982 "March for Survival," that they had been central in organizing "the largest demonstration to be held in this state since the Vietnam era."

Other honors and distinctions commanded prestige only within the movement. For example, TM hosted an annual national Mobilization for Survival conference. The TM leaders were the sole local peace movement activists to be honored at the event. Their names appeared in the conference program as "coordinators." A TM activist was one of the two main speakers at the opening plenary session—a task referred to by other local peace leaders as a "plum." Moreover, TM decided where out-of-town guests would be housed, thus giving them greater opportunity to socialize with movement celebrities and leaders. As a consequence of this competition for symbolic movement dominance, UM/TM relations sank to an all-time low during the few weeks preceding and following the conference. UM leaders indicated they had been slighted and "upstaged."

Competition for symbolic rewards such as prestige can be quite subtle. A TM leader announced that he had taken the liberty of ordering a highly acclaimed antinuclear film without sharing the proposal with other peace groups. He commented, "I jumped on this as soon as the opportunity came up. I wanted us to be the first to bring it to Austin. We had to move quick on this to beat the Freeze."

Competition for prestige not only can be viewed as a means of achieving symbolic hegemony within the movement, but also can serve to establish or maintain an SMO's identity. To illustrate, a discussion took place at a TM meeting concerning the group's participation in Fall demonstrations that were being planned by a city-wide peace coalition. A TM activist recommended that TM organize civil disobedience as part of the demonstration. He explained the role he envisioned for TM, a role he hoped would enhance TM's prestige within the Austin peace movement: "We should be trying to move the peace community towards civil disobedience. . . . Another thing is that it would cut a niche for the Texas Mobe that sets it apart from the other groups. We need to call it soon . . . get our stamp on it right away. I don't care if other groups want to co-sponsor it with us after we announce it."

Conclusion

The Austin peace movement organizations competed for a variety of resources, both instrumental and symbolic. As emphasized in the preceding propositions we have offered for further research, SMO competition was affected by several circumstances that may now be summarized as follows:

External Factors
  Availability of Resources
  Geographical Proximity of SMOs
Internal Factors
  Overlapping Constituencies
  Number of SMOs
Turf Arrangements
  Functional
  Geographical
Resources Sought
  Instrumental
  Symbolic
Imputed Intentions of SMO Leaders
  Purposively Competitive
  Inadvertently Competitive
Perceptions of SMO Leaders
  Compliance with Shared Norms
  Violation of Shared Norms
  Normative Incongruities

The findings suggest that an important and frequently overlooked influence on competition interaction among SMOs is whether the resources pursued are instrumental or symbolic ones. All social movement organizations must acquire some concrete assets in order to achieve their goals. In a multiorganizational environment, however, tangible resources might not be sufficient. Acquisition of instrumental resources depends, in part, on the organization's symbolic status vis-à-vis other SMOs in the community. Symbolic competition may be just as necessary and prevalent as instrumental competition within a social movement. Competition flourished among Austin SMOs when the process was both intentional and for symbolic rewards. Thus, we suggest that competition among SMOs for symbolic resources within a social movement is likely to be more intense than competition for instrumental resources. When the objects being sought by more than one SMO are turf, status, and/or prestige in addition to competition for money, labor, and external support, intramovement rivalries will be more pronounced.

By definition, competition involves two or more individuals or groups simultaneously seeking the same object. In a sense, then, the existence of more than one SMO pursuing similar goals constitutes a competition relationship. The SMOs could, of course, elect to cooperate toward achieving their common goals. But as the preceding analysis suggests, movement organizations can be in competition with one another even when their goals are alike, as in the case of UM and TM. Consequently, knowledge of only the goals of SMOs within a social movement will not facilitate predicting whether competition will occur. Similarities and differences about the number and scope of the groups' goals can affect the form of competition. SMOs with goal disparities are likely to emphasize differences in the breadth and perceived achievability of their objectives when appealing for support from potential constituents, adherents, and third parties. Organizations with identical goals can be forced to distinguish themselves from one another by developing unique or distinguished tactics.

Specific strategies and tactics are both the objects and resultants of competition. The leadership of one group might juxtapose its strategy with that of other SMOs, as did both the NWFC founder and the TM leader. Each believed that his or her group's strategy was, in the context of the situation, inherently superior. Developing a marketable and effective strategy was, therefore, a competitive process.

Similarly, innovative and appealing tactics typically are in short supply. Although tactical borrowing from other SMOs and movements does occur, innovation is also valued. If a group develops unique and creative tactics, as in the Austin situation, it earns prestige and hence increases its symbolic status within the movement. Moreover, tactical differentiation can be a byproduct of the need for SMOs to attract the attention of potential adherents, the media, and the targets of change. As SMOs attempt to distinguish themselves from their competitors within a social movement, competition tends to shift from the purely instrumental realm to both instrumental and symbolic arenas.

The segmented and decentralized structure of the peace movement, as suggested by the Austin case, can give rise at a group level to competitive processes against which the structure was designed to protect. Movement leaders explicitly attempted to avoid constructing tall, bureaucratic pyramids in which power eventually becomes concentrated in the hands of a few persons. Instead, even in the case of NWFC, which was more hierarchical than UM or TM, there was a conscious effort toward "grassroots" organizing, locally based decision making and the creation of an egalitarian system. That emphasis contributed to the proliferation of peace movement organizations in the Austin area. Gerlach and Hine (1970:50) argued that segmentation within a movement is a result of competition. We do not question that assertion, but we argue that the causal arrows seem also to point in the opposite direction. Movement segmentation, as illustrated in the Austin case, serves to increase SMO competition. It might be concluded that a decentralized, segmented movement is conducive to competition among SMOs.

The conclusions presented in this paper are based upon participant observation, unstructured interviews, and document analysis among a few SMOs in a limited geographical area. Nonetheless, we intend the findings to stimulate further studies of the forms, antecedent factors, and effects of intramovement competition. Such studies should compare a representative variety of SMOs within or across social movements. They should also attend closely to the relative balance of instrumental and symbolic competition as those varieties emerge within the boundaries established by structural factors. Lastly, such studies should attempt, as Zurcher and Snow (1981), Fireman and Gamson (1979), and Jenkins (1983) have argued, to examine the interactional bases of social movement mobilization.

Notes

1. The other six major Austin movement organizations that failed one or more of our selection criteria were the American Friends Service Committee-Texas, Arkansas, Oklahoma; Pax Christi-Austin; Austin Physicians for Social Responsibility; Austin Professionals for Nuclear Arms Limitation; University of Texas-United Campuses to Prevent Nuclear War; and University Peace and Justice Coalition (a misnomer since it operated not as a coalition of groups but rather as an autonomous SMO). Though we did not directly study all of these SMOs by participant observation methods, we gathered data on each of these peace groups via interviews, informants, and documents. For more extensive descriptions of the selection procedures and methods employed see Benford (1984, 1987).
2. The elements of our classification are drawn from Barkan (1979), Blumer (1939), Curtis and Zurcher (1974), Gusfield (1957, 1966), McCarthy and Zald (1973, 1977), Turner (1970), Wilson (1973), Zald and Ash (1966), and Zurcher and Curtis (1973).

CHAPTER 9

The Freeze Movement on the Local Level

D. R. WERNETTE

This chapter assesses the strengths and weaknesses of the freeze movement by focusing on a single grassroots group. It uses the perspective and findings of William Gamson (1975) to do so.

The limitations of this study are related primarily to data gathering methods and to the characteristics of the group studied. Most of the data come from my participant-observations as one of the leaders of the local chapter, thus findings may reflect my biases. My observations have been supplemented by (1) informal, open-ended questions to a number of other members of the steering committee; (2) a review of the monthly newsletter and meeting notes, where available; and (3) observations of videotaped self-introductions by local leaders at a state training workshop.

The second limitation concerns generalizations from this group to the larger freeze or peace movement. Subfreeze, the pseudonym for the local freeze chapter under study, is located in an upper-middle-class suburb of a major Midwestern city. The vast majority of its members are drawn from the suburb and adjacent areas, and are well-educated, upper middle class, and older (average age is well over 40). Observations at state and national conferences suggest that these local freeze members are not greatly different from other freeze participants in their sociodemographic characteristics. The political climate in which this local chapter operated is, however, much more conservative than that of many other local chapters. As a result, the findings for this group may be atypical of those of the larger freeze movement. In any case, references to the freeze movement that follow refer to the local freeze movement organization under study.

The Approach of
The Strategy of Social Protest

Gamson (1975) studies social movements by focusing on movement organizations that act to accomplish movement goals. To qualify for study, an organization (or in Gamson's terminology, challenging group, hereafter "challenger") has to have two main characteristics. First, it has to attempt to mobilize an unmobilized constituency (i.e., create a willingness to act for the group and/or cause among its followers or would-be members). Second, it has to attempt to influence one or more antagonists (individuals or organizations) that are separate or outside the challenger's constituency. Subfreeze and the larger freeze movement qualify as challengers on both characteristics. Since the merger of the national Nuclear Freeze Campaign with SANE, the new coalition organization is the challenger on the national level. The effect of this merger on the local level has yet to be noticed.

A challenger's success is defined by Gamson along two dimensions: attainment of at least some of the challenger's goals, and "the acceptance of a challenging group by its antagonists as a valid spokesman for a legitimate set of interests" (1975:28). Acceptance is measured in terms of the challenger's consulting or negotiating with, being formally recognized by, or being included in one or more of its antagonist's groups. Attainment of the challenger's goals (which Gamson refers to as new advantages) is measured somewhat more subjectively: did (according to historians, the challenger in its statements, and/or its antagonists) at least half of the antagonists undertake one or more of the actions desired by the challenger in each area of its concern? If so, the challenger received new advantages. If not, it is coded as unsuccessful on this dimension.

By measuring success along two dimensions, Gamson makes two important contributions to the analysis of social movement success. First, both the challenger-antagonist relationship and the goal attainment dimensions are called into question. Second, two additional outcomes, intermediate to success and failure, are identified. These additional outcomes are: cooptation (no new advantages but minimal acceptance) and preemption (new advantages but no minimal acceptance). The value of receiving new advantages is obvious to anyone viewing challengers as goal-oriented organizations. The value of minimal acceptance may be less clear; it will frequently mean recognition of the ability of the challenger to legitimately attempt to influence future outcomes in its area(s) of concern. Given the significant fluctuations in levels of U.S. military spending, this dimension is highly significant for the freeze and the larger peace movement.

Using Gamson's Findings
to Assess Freeze Success

Why do some challengers succeed while others fail, and yet others have intermediate outcomes? Gamson examines four main sets of variables to explain the success and failures of U.S. challengers in the 1800–1945 time period: the challenger's goals, its techniques for mobilizing its constituency, the tactics or means it uses to influence its antagonist(s), and its internal organization.

GOALS AND CHALLENGER SUCCESS

Gamson finds that groups with the goal of displacing and/or destroying their antagonist(s) are much less likely to gain acceptance or new advantages than are challengers without this goal. Beyond this, the challenger's goals do not affect its chances of success.

The goal of Subfreeze and Freezevoter, the political action arm, is to end the superpower arms race through a mutual, verifiable freeze on the production, testing, and deployment of nuclear weapons and weapon delivery systems. Over its history, however, Subfreeze showed flexibility in its goals in two directions: willingness to accept partial steps toward a freeze, such as the defeat of the MX missile, passage of a comprehensive test ban treaty, and reductions in military spending; and expansion to other, related goals such as a halt to hostile U.S. actions toward Nicaragua. These changes in goal priorities did not occur without considerable internal debate. Strategic arms control nevertheless remains a top priority for the organization and its leadership, as reflected in comments by steering committee members.

Subfreeze's goal of freezing the nuclear arms race is somewhat ambiguous in terms of the destruction or displacement of its antagonist, the U.S. military and defense contractors. On the one hand, official freeze positions on both the local and state levels clearly reject the goal of unilateral nuclear disarmament. Recognizing the political dangers of appearing "too idealistic/pacifist," the freeze has consistently emphasized bilateral arms reductions, and has stopped short of demanding total disarmament. Thus, one can argue that the freeze goals do not entail destruction or displacement of the antagonist.

On the other hand, a successful freeze would clearly entail drastic reductions in government spending for nuclear weapons systems. The accompanying losses for defense contractors and their employees could border on destruction if accompanied by similar reductions in spending for conventional armaments. The freeze movement is thus clearly in a zero-sum situation with at least some of its political opponents.

Some within the freeze movement (proponents of a "military-industrial complex" analysis) view the freeze's goals as more radical: removal of traditional militaristic, war-fighting advocates from power. To the extent that such views see the government as identified with such a traditional defense and posture, the goal is clearly displacement of the antagonist. Thus, to the extent that displacement is counterproductive to goal attainment, Gamson's findings suggest that the freeze movement will fail to accomplish their goals or, in Gamson's terms, gain new advantages.

SIZE AND CHALLENGER SUCCESS

Gamson finds that larger groups (with peak membership greater than ten thousand) are more likely to gain acceptance, but are not more likely to gain new advantages, than are smaller challengers.

Subfreeze as an organization has grown in size from 35-40 at its beginning in 1982 to over 300 in subsequent years. Formal membership is defined in terms of payment of the ten dollar per year dues. It is clear that nationally, and indeed even within the Midwest region, the freeze movement has more than the 10,000 members that Gamson uses as a cutoff point between large and small organizations. On this basis one would predict that Subfreeze and the larger freeze movement would gain acceptance, but not necessarily new advantages.

MEANS OF MOBILIZATION
AND CHALLENGER SUCCESS

According to Gamson, virtually all challengers are confronted with the "free rider" problem: it is easiest and most profitable for an individual in the constituency to let others bear the costs of contributing to the common good, since benefits of the challenger's success are not directly tied to membership or level of contribution. One way of overcoming this free rider problem is through the use of selective incentives: benefits, such as subscriptions, cheap insurance, or protection from harm, which contributors receive and noncontributors do not. Challengers using selective incentives are much more likely to grow large in size and to gain new advantages and acceptance than are other challengers not using this means of mobilization.

Subfreeze does not use selective incentives, beyond receiving the monthly mailing, to induce individuals to join the group. Although the "hat" is passed for contributions at the monthly meetings, there is no real pressure on individuals to contribute if they are not so inclined. Members are mobilized to bring pressure on their congressional representatives by means of a telephone tree, by notices of upcoming votes in the monthly mailing, and by announcements at the monthly meetings. In addition, the group uses letters to the editors of local newspapers, announcements of future meetings placed in store windows, and public speakers as a means of gaining public exposure and new members.

The underlying set of Subfreeze's assumptions concerning mobilization of its constituency are as follows. Since everyone is equally threatened by nuclear war and the arms race, everyone should/will be interested in the topic once they are made aware of it. Furthermore, once people know about the threat, they will want to do something about it, i.e., pressure their legislators to enact the freeze. So, if we can only get people to our meetings, they will learn more about the issue and become mobilized automatically. Although somewhat oversimplified and never openly stated, this is the set of basic premises under which the group has been operating up to now. The leadership recognizes, however, that these assumptions are not leading to the desired mass mobilization of large numbers of individuals. The group lacks a clear alternative model of mobilization and recruitment, and so continues with its current methods and approach.

Applying Gamson's findings in this area to the freeze movement, we must conclude that Subfreeze's lack of use of selective incentives, which appears typical of the larger freeze and peace movement, hurts its chances of growth and success. Although the movement has grown in size, as noted above, its growth phase appears to be over, barring a resumption of cold war rhetoric.

Means of Influencing the
Antagonist and Challenger Success

Gamson finds that challengers who use either violence, or non-violent constraints such as strikes, boycotts, or other forms of pressure against their antagonists are likely to be more successful than their nonviolent or non-"pushy" counterparts. By the same token, challengers who are the targets of violent attack or arrest are much less likely to succeed than are other groups.

Subfreeze attempts to influence its antagonists—the U.S. senators and congressmen from its geographical area, and to a much lesser extent the president (Reagan in the period under study), who is viewed as a lost cause—by in-person lobbying, circulated petitions, and letters. Freezevoter influences the representatives by offering or withholding political support in elections. This is as close as the group comes to using constraints or pressure on antagonists. The group and its members do not use violence and have not been the targets of violent attack or arrest, with the exception of one member who traveled to the Nevada test site. In short, Subfreeze's chances of success are not helped by its means of influencing its antagonists or targets of influence.

Internal Organization—
Bureaucracy—and Challenger Success

Gamson finds that bureaucratic challengers, i.e., those with a written statement of the purposes and provisions of operations of the group, a formal list of members, and three or more levels of internal divisions, are more ready to act, and thus are more successful, than nonbureaucratic groups. Bureaucratic groups are especially successful in gaining acceptance, but are also more likely to gain new advantages.

Subfreeze has some elements of a bureaucratic organization: a written statement of purpose and a formal list of members. It also has a rudimentary degree of internal division of labor: subgroups responsible for outreach, resources (e.g., reading matter and speakers bureau), and lobbying/direct action have been created and are active to varying degrees. The group does not meet all of the criteria for bureaucracy, since no written provisions for operation of the group exist, and the levels of internal division are not very meaningful. Most of the work of the group is carried out by its chair, assisted by at most a dozen other activists. (Although no systematic study has been undertaken, informal observation suggests that a similar structure exists on the state freeze organization level.)

We can conclude that Subfreeze's chances of gaining acceptance and new advantages are not significantly aided by its low level of bureaucratic internal organization.

INTERNAL ORGANIZATION, CENTRALIZED POWER, AND CHALLENGER SUCCESS

Challengers with centralized power have a single center of power within the organization, in contrast to groups with some form of collective leadership or great autonomy on the local level. Gamson finds that centralized power is positively associated with success, especially with gaining new advantages. Centralized power is an advantage to a challenger in another respect: avoidance of factionalism. Challengers with centralized power are less likely to experience factionalism, or the creation of splinter groups within the larger organization, than are decentralized challengers. And decentralized groups with factions are much less likely to be successful, especially in gaining new advantages, than are either groups with centralized power or groups with no factions. It is also worth noting that bureaucratic organization and centralized power are both statistically independent, in terms of their frequency among challengers, and cumulative in their effects on challenger success. That is, challengers with both attributes are more likely to succeed than challengers with only one, and are much more likely to succeed than challengers with nonbureaucratic, decentralized organizational structures.

In analyzing the local freeze in these terms, we need to make a distinction between centralized power within the local organization, and centralized power within the freeze movement on the state or national level. Within the local organization, power is shared within the steering committee, although some steering committee members, including the chair, clearly have more influence than others. On the state level, power relationships and degree of centralization of power are less clear. The state office initiates approximately 60 percent of the state-local contacts; suggests actions for local groups to take; and provides information and literature for local group use. Strategy and programs are developed at annual meetings, and implemented by the paid state staff and local chapters to varying degrees. Being a voluntary organization, however, precludes "orders" being given. My assessment is that neither the state nor local organizations have centralized power, in the sense of individual leaders being confident that others will do what is asked of them without the need to be convinced of the wisdom of the action.

Neither Subfreeze nor the state organization has experienced factionalism, although differences of opinion and direction certainly exist within both. As Solo (1988) points out, major differences arose in the national freeze organization over issues such as the role of civil disobedience. Such differences did not, however, lead to organizational dissolution or fissure. On the local level this lack of factionalism may be due to the underlying norm of permissiveness within the organization: if an individual can claim that an activity or event is in some way related to the group's larger goal of peace, he or she is allowed to pursue it and recruit assistance from others in the group.

Although the local freeze organization under study is free of factionalism, a significant division within the group is found along the dimension of task/goal orientation versus socioemotional and value emphasis. This is most readily apparent at the group's meetings. Some members clearly need to express their feelings of concern (and, even after the Reagan era, frequently dismay) over international relations/arms-control developments, receive support and "we-feeling" from others who share those feelings, and relieve tensions through humor and expressions of hostility toward the antagonist. Closely affiliated with this is the desire to receive more information from public speakers at the group's meetings. Such information is, not surprisingly, largely supportive of the world view of the members and congruent with their values and concerns. These needs may be especially strong due to the largely "hostile" political environment in which the group operates and its members live; it is very easy to feel politically "deviant" supporting the freeze in such a politically conservative area. In any case, a very significant percentage of the group's meeting time is spent meeting these needs. To this extent the group borders on goal displacement, since the focus is more on maintaining personal values than on attaining group goals.

A second contingent within the group is primarily concerned with accomplishing tasks that will increase the group's chances of success.

For many of these individuals the group is clearly a means to the end of stopping and reversing the arms race. Time together is best spent in this view planning events that will win new supporters, gain media attention, and/or bring pressure to bear on the elected officials who can stop the arms race. The successful meeting in this contingent's eyes is characterized by a tight agenda with few digressions, many binding decisions taken following Roberts' Rules and majority votes, and a clear schedule of actions-to-be-taken and results-to-be-achieved by various individuals on or before the next meeting. The organization exists for this contingent because there is strength in numbers working together toward a common goal.

As noted, the internal divisions within the group have not led to formal factionalism. That lack of factionalism, according to Gamson's findings, should work to increase Subfreeze's relative chances of gaining new advantages.

Other Success-relevant Characteristics

From experience and informal discussions with other activists, it is my impression that Subfreeze, and perhaps the freeze or peace movement more generally, is primarily reactive rather than proactive in its orientation. On the local level there never seems to be enough time to adequately cover all of the items on steering committee meeting agendas, for example, which are primarily concerned with planning the next general meeting and related events. No short- or mid-term (not to mention long-term) strategy or sense of direction exists. Consequently, the group finds itself generally responding to national and international events, but never considering options of how to use possible future events for the group's purposes.

Assessing the Freeze Movement's Prospects for Success

What does the above mean for the (now SANE/) Freeze movement's chances of success? If Gamson's findings have predictive value, the signs are mixed, but appear weighted against the movement. Although its size and to a lesser extent goals are in its favor, it does not use selective incentives to mobilize its constituency, it uses few constraints to influence its antagonists, and it has neither centralized power nor a developed bureaucratic organization. The one characteristic clearly in its favor is its success in avoiding overt factionalism.

Despite this rather pessimistic assessment, one should note that the movement has experienced limited success, in terms of limiting the numbers of MX missiles to be constructed, some limited cuts in military spending, and in gaining acceptance as a legitimate political group deserving of attention. Also, the recent developments in arms control, such as the Intermediate Nuclear Forces (or INF) Treaty, START, and progress in the area of chemical weapons, clearly suggest that the superpower relations are moving in the general direction desired by the freeze movement. This may suggest that other factors beyond those used above are significant in explaining the success or failure of social movement organizations such as the freeze.

Using the Gamson findings as evaluation criteria, I conclude that the freeze movement's chances of success are not high, at least to the extent one can generalize from the study of one local group. Others (Solo 1988; Waller 1987) argue that the freeze as an issue and legislative initiative clearly failed. That may be the case, if one narrowly focuses on the original freeze proposal. On the local and state levels, however, attempts are still underway to close U.S. Department of Energy defense facilities, in order to curtail the nuclear weapons arms race. My interpretation is that such actions are close enough to the original intent of the freeze to justify classifying the current SANE/ Freeze organization as a continuation of the freeze. This is also consistent with Gamson's coding procedures for determining the endpoint of a challenge. In any case the findings presented above suggest that the current Sane/Freeze organization is likely to fail. If that proves true the timing of the failure will be of only academic interest.

Implications
for Social Movement Theory

Gamson draws two main conclusions from his study. One concerns the nature and purpose of challenging groups. Earlier views, such as Smelser's (1962), portrayed challengers and their members as acting from vague, emotional, transitory, oversimplified appeals or purposes. Collective behavior in this earlier view is different from routine political behavior in its greater reliance on myth, emotion, and magical thinking, and its lack of focus on how to operationalize and accomplish the group's goals in concrete political circumstances. According to Smelser, collective behavior, as evidenced in challengers, is primarily expressive in nature. Routine political behavior, in contrast, is more rational and instrumental: it is a means to accomplishing political ends. Gamson rejects this earlier view of social protest and challenger activities. He sees challenger participants as instrumental, but facing a different set of constraints and obstacles than do established interest groups.

The internal division in the group described above, in terms of two different kinds of members, parallels the different descriptions of challenger participants by Gamson and Smelser. In fact neither "ideal type" exists in the group, although a few individuals come close. This division is important and worthy of mention for a number of reasons, however. First, both "needs" or tendencies compete for time in a meeting, creating a certain amount of pressure on the individual running the meeting to arbitrate between the two. Second, this suggests that both theoretical approaches may have descriptive/analytical value in explaining the nature and dynamics of social movement organizations.

Gamson's second conclusion concerns the openness of the American political system to challenge and change. He concludes that, within the constraints identified in his study, the political system is indeed open to challenge and change. The case study of the local freeze group presented above suggests, however, that the odds of success are stacked against groups challenging the collective identity of the nation, as defined through opposition to other nations. Such limited successes as exist for peace groups appear at least as much related to the (at times illegal) actions of their domestic opponents, as to their own efforts. If true, this suggests that peace movements face significantly different constraints and opportunities from other movements. Identification of these constraints and opportunities is a key task facing movement activists and strategists.

Acknowledgments

The author gratefully acknowledges the valuable suggestions made by Sam Marullo and John Lofland to earlier versions of this paper, as well as the time and cooperation of the peace activists who dutifully answered his seemingly never-ending questions. This work was not supported by the U.S. Department of Energy or the U.S. government. The viewpoints expressed here are not necessarily those of Argonne National Laboratory or Lewis University.

PART III

CAMPAIGNS:
Transcending,
Educating,
Politicking,
Protesting

CHAPTER 10

Noncontentious Social Movements: "Just Say No to War"

WILLIAM BRIGHAM

Social movements vary in how ideology and organization combine and thereby determine strategy and movement career. A principal distinction is usually drawn between movements that are oriented toward structural or institutional change and those that intend to alter or transform the individual.[1] In the case of the former, the focus of social change is on the public arena, as in political revolution or reform movements, whereas the latter has more recently been exemplified by what is loosely referred to as the human potential movement.

The organizational structure employed will depend largely upon the goals that drive the movement and will include components selected from a set of oppositional elements: centralized-decentralized, bureaucratized-informal, exclusive-inclusive membership, professional-grass-roots "management," among others. Movement organizations that are institutional in focus tend to be centralized, bureaucratic, and have an inclusive membership, whereas personal change movements tend to be decentralized, informal, and have exclusive memberships (Gamson 1975; Freeman 1979; Jenkins 1983).

I want here to suggest that the sociocultural events of the 1960s, the focus on inner-directedness that characterized the predilections of many Americans in the 1970s, and the personal-not-governmental responsibility for social problems that characterized the advent of the Reagan era, provided a cultural springboard for a different pattern of social movement, one that confounds the patterns of ideology and organization just summarized and more commonly seen among movements. This movement type is noncontentious, not oriented toward conflict or structural change, and is of uncertain viability. The noncontentious social movement may have emerged from what Gusfield (1979:305) referred to as "the growing concern of populations with the transformation of self in human encounters, in religious experience and in the styles of work and leisure." Lofland (1988:174) has identified a corresponding type, the "consensus movement" and its "dominant emotional motif" of "joy . . . friendliness, optimism . . . and goodwill."

Since the late 1970s, at least three such social movements have come on the scene in the United States: Beyond War, The Hunger Project, and The Possible Society.[2] Although there are many similarities among these three organizations, Beyond War stands out as the "purist" illustration of this type of movement. Therefore, I will examine it in terms of commonly analyzed features of movements, and I will explore the sociocultural sources from which the noncontentious social movement emerged.[3]

Noncontentious Ideology

The ideology of a social movement organization will shape its strategy. The ordinary protest movement will, thus, aim its institutional or structural attacks according to the social change it seeks to accomplish or resist. But, in contrast, Beyond War strove to alter the way in which people think about war; it proposed, as did all noncontentious movements, "mass changes in perception or consciousness" (Lofland 1988:165). There was no real enemy, no upheaval necessary, no structural change called for—although any universal "new way of thinking" must result in such change. As Bromley and Shupe (1979) have pointed out, those movements that seek to transform individuals also see structural change growing out of this individual transformation. Thus, the strategy that emerged from Beyond War's beliefs was one of education, not action; one of personal transformation, albeit limited, that would lead to inevitable structural change.

Members of Beyond War were asked to make the decision[4] to adopt the "new mode of thinking" that was now necessary because of (1) the atomic bomb and (2) pictures of earth taken from space, the "two changes which [have] altered life irrevocably." These two changes had produced two "ideas" upon which the Beyond War philosophy was based:

First, "War is obsolete. . . . We cannot fight a limited nuclear war. . . ."

Second, "We are one. . . . We are one interconnected, interdependent life-system living on one planet" (Creative Initiative Foundation 1984).

I have identified five components of the new mode of thinking. First, rather than an exclusive sense of identification, the individuals had to see themselves as part of a "whole"; an identification inclusive of all humans. Second, there could be no projection of an enemy, no casting of blame. Third, the term "destroy" had to be replaced by "build" in the lexicon of the movement participant. Fourth, war was obsolete; nuclear weapons had irrevocably altered this method of conflict resolution. Fifth, the sanctity of life had to be recognized and realized (Creative Initiative Foundation 1984).

These tenets of the Beyond War ideology were presented in an educational format directed toward individual change. It was this ultimate goal—the transformation of the individual—that distinguished Beyond War from other "peace" or "antiwar" movements, and that distinguished other noncontentious social movements. The maxim that guided this educational process was that the individual must adopt the principle (that is, war is obsolete, we are one, move beyond war) as the first step toward everyone's accepting it in a codified, universal form.

Organization and Leadership

Somewhat different from other nonconentious social movements, Beyond War retained a lay leadership group, one that emerged from among those who were active in the predecessor organization, the Creative Initiative Foundation (CIF), and from its more recent (post-1982) members. Although the president of the Beyond War Foundation (Beyond War's board of directors) was paid, the rest of Beyond War's leaders were all volunteers and had no previous experience in such positions, but they were indeed professionals in ways that were crucial to the movement's strategy.

In order to reach 50 percent of their target populations with their message—a necessary precondition to 5 percent of the total target

population's fully accepting "the idea"—Beyond War developed sophisticated marketing campaigns not unlike those of the entrepre-
neurial firms from which so many of the organization's leaders had
come. Having originated in the technologically and, at the time, eco-
nomically rich area known as Silicon Valley in Northern California, the
Beyond War membership was equally rich in product development
and marketing skills. A typical CIF member in the 1960s and 1970s
was white, college-educated, professional, and twenty-five to forty
years of age. Many of these early members became involved in Beyond War, a project of CIF which, in 1982, subsumed the parent organization. By this time several of the young engineers who had joined
CIF ten or fifteen years before were successful entrepreneurs or man-
agers in the semiconductor industry.

The combination of their marketing know-how and, most importantly, their financial security contributed considerably to the growth
that Beyond War enjoyed in the ensuing several years. From a resource mobilization perspective, the leaders of the movement were
particularly valuable. Their professional marketplace skills and their
time—at no cost—allowed Beyond War to conceptualize, develop,
market, and sell a product that they labeled "A New Way of Thinking." The marketing sophistication of Beyond War was exemplified by
the glossy, slick quality of its printed materials and videotapes, the
test marketing of these materials, and the use of market segmentation
techniques (Mechling and Auletta 1986).

In the late Eighties, there were about ten thousand persons supporting Beyond War activities in forty states and six foreign countries.
In the words of the organization's spokespersons, these were not
"members" and this figure did not represent all of those who had attended orientation or information sessions (that number is not kept by
the organization). These several thousand were "workers" who had
"adopted the new way of thinking" and continued to be involved in
various Beyond War activities or, at minimum, to espouse their beliefs
informally to friends, coworkers, and neighbors. In addition there
were seventy-five full-time and ninety part-time volunteers at the Beyond War headquarters, and another 325 full-time volunteers around
the United States.[5]

The Beyond War organization operated with an annual budget of
about $3 million in 1987, about 60 percent of which came from indi-
vidual contributions that averaged just over $100; approximately 15

percent of revenues were generated by the sale of various materials, including videotapes, books, t-shirts, coffee mugs, and other items bearing the Beyond War logo. Beyond War published a newsletter that was distributed eleven times per year to twenty-five thousand households (Interview with Beyond War Information Desk and figures reported in Beyond War publications).

These characteristics of Beyond War—centralized, bureaucratic, and well-funded—differed from other personal change movements. That is, all printed materials were sent out from the headquarters, the structure and terminology of the orientations were highly standardized, and oral pronouncements of the official ideology were, on several occasions during my field observations, verbatim from printed materials. Additionally, in contrast to other personal change movements, Beyond War was striving for an inclusive membership. If indeed "we are one" and must all adopt that philosophy in order to move beyond war, then commonly used socioeconomic indicators of social movement membership must be reconsidered. The goal of inclusiveness had perhaps been marginally realized by Beyond War, especially as compared to its predecessor, CIF, which had a membership of exclusively upper-middle-class professionals with moderate to left-of-center political views. Occupational self-reporting by attendees at California Beyond War orientations revealed a broadening of this population to include at least some middle-class, skilled, trades workers and college-age students; members of Beyond War in the Midwest included farmers and small business owners/operators (Beyond War 1986).

Although the Beyond War membership might have been evolving in a socially heterogeneous manner, it was clear that the leadership and other full-time volunteers were upper-middle-class professionals whose lives could be disrupted by leaves of absence, and that the bulk of the membership was still drawn from that same socioeconomic group. As Mechling and Auletta (1986) have pointed out, there were a number of contradictions between Beyond War's key anthem ("We are one") and its membership and organization. First, notwithstanding the protestations of some adherents, Beyond War clearly had a hierarchical structure, as evidenced by a board of directors (who had responsibility for formulating policy, movement direction, budgets, etc.), a headquarters (from which standardized materials came), and regional and local leaders (who trained and oversaw orientation leaders). Second, the employment of consumer product market segmentation techniques suggested that, even in the eyes of the leadership, "we are *not* one." Third, there was a clear absence of any appreciable number of people of color in the organization, and women played largely behind-the-scenes roles. The values, structure, strategy, and leadership of Beyond War were not unlike the corporations that surrounded it in Silicon Valley, and from which its leaders had come.

Recruitment

The Beyond War recruitment strategy was based upon research employed in consumer product marketing. Proponents of this "innovation adoption" research claimed that "when 5% of a society adopts a new idea it is 'embedded' in its population. As the idea spreads and reaches 20% of the population, it becomes 'unstoppable'" (Creative Initiative Foundation 1984). In order to most effectively and expeditiously reach the 5 percent deemed crucial for "embedding" the new mode of thinking, Beyond War identified key states in which to begin their educational campaigns. The specific eleven key states selected were chosen because they were either new consumer product test markets, sites of key (1984) U.S. Senate races, areas that included populations "used to new ideas and [which exhibit] creative thinking," or they held early primary elections (Creative Initiative Foundation 1984).

The recruitment method was low-key and soft-sell. By employing rhetoric such as "we are obviously against all wars," the recruiter or orientation leader allowed the prospective member easily to agree with a noncontentious and self-serving philosophy. Therefore, it was unlikely that many would be opposed to such innocuous claims, and potential recruits would be easily gathered. This explains in some measure the success of noncontentious social movements in expanding their membership so quickly and easily: The new members do not risk harm to their social, occupational, or other status. By becoming involved in a movement that has, essentially, no opponents, there are few if any negative consequences. For example, although employees of a major defense contractor would most likely protest immediate disarmament as a solution to the nuclear threat, many of them might "adopt a new way of thinking" about war without jeopardizing their careers or diminishing their commitment to either enterprise.

The "embodied" (Lofland 1977) educational process of Beyond War was carried out primarily in three-hour orientations, usually held in a private residence and conducted by a trained orientation leader. A mixed-media presentation usually included a lecture, flip charts, handouts, videotapes, group exercises and discussions, and a question-and-answer session. The commitment asked for at the end of the orientation session (when donations were solicited in exchange for various movement materials) was (1) to adopt the new way of thinking, (2) to war the Beyond War lapel pin every day as symbolic support, and (3) to fill your chair at the next orientation.

In the eighties Beyond War representatives would not state how many persons had attended such orientation sessions, or similar Beyond War events. They did maintain that about ten thousand individuals were "working" on behalf of Beyond War. Either by taking this number as a measure of movement size, or by assuming that many more than ten thousand had been exposed to Beyond War's "embodied" communications, and even more to "disembodied" forms (newspaper or magazine advertisements, automobile window decals and bumper stickers, unsolicited literature), it was clear that a considerable number of people had been introduced to "the new way of thinking."

Quasi-religious Movements

The literature on religious proselytizing and conversion (Lofland 1977; Bromley and Shupe 1979), and on the "new religious consciousness" and "quasi-religions" of the 1960s and 1970s (Glock and Bellah 1976; Needleman 1970; Tipton 1982), provides several ideas that can help account for the apparent success of the noncontentious movements in attracting sizable numbers of attendees to their educational activities and, less clearly, significant numbers of ongoing members.

Lofland's (1977) two-fold approach to understanding the social psychological process of conversion to a cult—"predisposing conditions" and "situational contingencies"—is an initial, relevant conception. At the risk of negating their original meaning, I want to relocate these conditions at the cultural level. That is, a set of predisposing (cultural) conditions extant in the late 1970s and early 1980s were important precursors to the evolution of noncontentious social movements.

Changes in social institutions, in laws guiding social behavior, and in the values that lie at the core of social life, were numerous and far-reaching in the decades that preceded the advent of noncontentious movements. These changes included a questioning of traditional religious beliefs, and experimenting with Eastern religions and with "quasi-religious movements" (Glock and Bellah 1976). The human potential movement was one such quasi-religion that sought "to transcend the oppressiveness of culture by transforming [its initiates] as individuals" (Stone 1976:93). The human potential movement *qua* religion was thus attractive because of several features that fostered ease of access:

1. Low level of required commitment;
2. Low financial cost;
3. Participation did not require lifestyle alterations;
4. Low stigma (Stone 1976:112–113).

The tenets of Asian religions, which served as a principal basis for human potential movement philosophies, clashed with traditional Western values. Yet, these views resonated with a growing dissatisfaction with the oppositional nature of American political and economic life. The principles underlying the human potential movement and similar quasi-religious activities resulted in "criticism of existing society [which was] nonhostile, nonconfrontational, and often nonpolitical" (Bellah 1976:347–348). Also, a central belief of Asian religions is that of the "unity of all being. . . . *We are all one* and the conflict between us is therefore illusory" (1976:347; emphasis added). These perspectives, which were gaining widespread acceptance in the West, bear obvious resemblance to the ideology of the noncontentious movements that would evolve in later years.

The "predisposing conditions" of the late 1970s and early 1980s were formed from the search for, and reliance upon, noninstitutional, individualistic ways of resolving both personal and social problems. Because of the extent of quasi-religious and human potential-like activities in the 1960s and in the 1970s, at least in the geographical areas where noncontentious movements emerged, there were considerable numbers of "veteran seekers"—individuals who continually sought a new way of understanding life and self, who were "afflicted with a metaphysical lusting" (Lofland 1977:166).

Thus, coming into the 1980s, the human potential movement—now becoming more commonly known as New Age activities—shifted somewhat in focus, gained momentum, and grew in size. New Age spokespersons, such as Marilyn Ferguson (1980), suggested that a "historical synthesis" had taken place: social transformation was resulting from personal transformation; change was occurring from the inside out. By 1986 New Agers were big business, spending $100 million on the shining crystals that promised the healing of psychic and physical problems, and $300 million on audio- and videotapes that provided them with roadmaps to self-fullfillment (Blow 1988:26). These same people, these residents of the New Age "lifestyle enclaves" (Bellah et al. 1985:71–75), were most amenable to "participation" in movements that promised the amelioration of social (or global) problems simply by "visualizing" their resolution (Bordewich 1988:41).

Social Reaction

There was evidence of some antipathy between Beyond War and more typical antiwar, peace, and nuclear freeze movements. Although some proponents of these other organizations adopted the attitude that "we need all the friends we can get," many others believed that Beyond War was siphoning off potential recruits for activist groups, and that considerable money was being spent on efforts that had no tangible goals. Beyond War explicitly declined to align itself with other antinuclear organizations, eschewing coalitions with any groups that "projected an enemy" or in other ways decried the Beyond War philosophy. Yet other peace organizations were appreciative that Beyond War had so effectively reached large numbers of people with their message about the threat of nuclear war. But these same activists were equally critical of Beyond War's insistence that once their audiences were enlightened, they need not be encouraged to take action, merely to change the way they thought about war. Therefore, the greatest challenge to the noncontentious social movement might come from other organizations in the same general movement.

The reaction of major social institutions to the tactics of social movements shapes their careers. A challenge to dominant institutions and values is often countered with resources that easily overwhelm the movement. But the noncontentious movement presents no such clear challenge, no clear call for structural change. Beyond War was quite successful in adding to its ranks, either as workers or as honorary spokespersons, members of the very institutions (political, military, economic) that professed the "old way of thinking." It was this very success that suggested that the noncontentious social movement would not likely suffer defeat at the hands of institutional foes.

Indeed, one might look to these very institutions—particularly governmental entities in the era of Reaganism—for another explanation of how and why the noncontentious social movement evolved and prospered. The focus of how to resolve social problems shifted under the influence of right-wing conservatism and the strengthening of Christian fundamentalism. The individual, for either political or biblical reasons, did not look to the government for assistance, but rather to himself or to God's omnipresent spokesperson, the televangelist. In the 1960s and 1970s there was a perceived erosion of legitimacy in American institutions, and many people "looked within themselves"— via the human potential movement—for resolution of their own and society's problems. In the 1980s the legitimate role of governmental institutions clearly was not to comfort the afflicted. In his inaugural address, Ronald Reagan set the tone for the coming eight years: "Government is not the solution to our problem; government is the problem. . . . [For] if no one among us is capable of governing himself, then who among us has the capacity to govern someone else?" (quoted in Tipton 1982:258). Such an institutionalized self-help attitude, coincident with such governmentally supported activities as the "self-determination" and "self-esteem" commissions of then-California Governor Jerry Brown and Assemblyman John Vasconcellos, and the vacuous "Just Say No to Drugs" campaign of Nancy Reagan, underscored the belief that people can change themselves and society simultaneously by "trusting [their] natural decency" (1982:268). The noncontentious movement, in the case of Beyond War, proposed just such a self-help solution to the threat of nuclear war.

Movement Success

Because the focus of Beyond War was education, and because "membership" was a tenuous concept, measurement of movement success is problematic. Because many Beyond War participants might not have been involved beyond an initial orientation, measurement of continued adherence to the new mode of thinking would seem elusive. How exactly will the 5 percent or 20 percent be measured *and* kept "in the fold?" How can the impact on social institutions of the new way of thinking be determined? I posed these questions to members, orientation leaders, and official spokespersons, and the universal response was nebulous and evasive. They would not, or could not, state what would happen when or if 5 percent of the population accepted "the idea." They would not state exactly how "the idea" became "unstoppable" at that point. There was an apparent blind faith in the research often cited and in the rhetoric upon which the movement stands. Furthermore, because Beyond War did not maintain a tally of all those who had attended the various orientation and information sessions, it was not possible to determine when the 5 percent goal might have been reached. Although this may all seem problematic from an analytical perspective, it did not appear to trouble the "converts." Time and again, members of longstanding expressed their belief in and commitment to "the idea." It was apparently not troublesome to them that short-term and long-term goals had to be periodically altered, as was the Beyond War statement, which had been through more than sixty drafts. And it was this commitment to an uncertain outcome, to solutions coming from "an unseeable realm" (Lofland 1977:42) that characterized the noncontentious movement.

Conclusion

Beyond War would seem to illustrate an emergent social phenomenon that differed from classically identified forms of social movements. They were different in that they combined a focus on personal transformation, use of consumer product marketing tactics, a nonchallenging strategy, and an inclusive membership. They benefited from solid financial backing, and faced no considerable resource mobilization problems. A principal question to be addressed in further study is: How long can such movements enjoy increasing membership and other mobilization of resources without bringing about any measurable social change?

Acknowledgments

I am indebted to John Lofland for his continued support and direction. I have also benefited from discussions with Joseph Gusfield, J. Lee Meihls, and David H. Jacobs.

Notes

1. Such dichotomies have been presented by, among others, Blumer (1939) (general and specific movements), Smelser (1962) (norm-oriented and value-oriented), and Gusfield (1979) (public and private forms).
2. A much earlier instance of this type of movement was the Oxford Group Movement, an evangelistic, nonsectarian group founded by Frank Buchman in the 1920s (Eister 1950; Cantril 1941). The Hunger Project (HP) was launched by est (Erhard Seminars Training) founder Werner Erhard in 1977 (Keerdoja 1981). The Possible Society was begun by psychotherapist Jean Houston in the early 1980s as an organization that sought to teach individuals how to maximize their potential and thereby become "The Possible Human" (Houston 1982). A 1980s peace movement that roughly approximated the form and function of Beyond War was MEND (Mothers Embracing Nuclear Disarmament) (Mehan and Wills 1988).
3. I gathered data on Beyond War by means of interviews with team leaders, covert participation in orientation sessions, review of printed materials and videotapes prepared by the central organization, references in the popular press, and telephone interviews with spokespersons at Beyond War headquarters. In addition, while I was living in the Silicon Valley area in the late 1960s and early 1970s, several personal acquaintances of mine were participants in Beyond War's predecessor, the Creative Initiative Foundation (CIF). My knowledge of their later involvement in Beyond War, and of their professional careers in the semiconductor and defense industries, serve as the basis for some generalizations I make about the social standing and careers of CIF and Beyond War members.
4. In the Beyond War view, to make a decision is to take action; a conscious choice is not a passive act but a sign of commitment and of moving forward.
5. These latter full-time volunteers, most of whom had taken leaves of absence from their (professional) jobs and relocated temporarily from California, were paid $350 per week to cover some of their expenses. Financial support of volunteers represented only about one percent of the total budget; almost 70 percent of the total is used for educational programs and materials (Mechling and Auletta 1986:392; Beyond War 1987b).

CHAPTER 11

Rhetorical Styles of the Physicians for Social Responsibility

MARY NEAL

Sociologists have examined how social movements mobilize material resources such as labor and money. Movements must also mobilize the nonmaterial resources of ideas and symbols by defining a set of political arguments and then effectively communicating those arguments to key audiences in the political arena.

A central task in this communication is linking abstract political concepts with the personal concerns of audiences. Theorists have shown that these linkages are a key part of moving individuals to take action. David Bouchier, for example, suggests that individuals perceive the legitimacy of a political system in terms of their experience with that system. He argues that movements must therefore challenge the commonsense assumptions behind patterns of everyday life and demonstrate how these patterns are affected by broader political issues (Bouchier 1978).

Among recent U.S. social movements, for example, the women's movement stressed the politics inherent in personal acts. The environmental movement sought to "think globally and act locally." In the anti-Vietnam war movement, deaths of friends, brothers, or sons left no doubt as to the personal impact of the war.

For movements against nuclear weapons, health issues have been a central way in which this personal impact was made apparent. John Hersey's description of atomic bombing victims in his novel *Hiroshima* (1981) stimulated early discussion of nuclear arms, as did physician David Bradley's account of nuclear testing in the Pacific in

No Place to Hide (1983). In debates leading to the Limited Test Ban Treaty in the late 1950s and early 1960s, the health effects of radioactive fallout were a key issue in raising public consciousness (Sullivan 1982; Wittner 1984).

In the 1980s movement against nuclear weapons, Physicians for Social Responsibility (PSR) presented graphic portrayals of the medical effects of nuclear weapons. PSR activists organized major scientific symposia and formed a nationwide network of local chapters. They developed support within organized medicine and joined with other community groups to oppose civil defense planning for nuclear war. Their message was to alert the public to the fact that nuclear war could not be survived and must therefore be prevented, thus challenging the basic premises of strategic systems designed to fight and win a nuclear war.

These physicians conceptualized the problem of activating individuals in terms of "really knowing" the facts. Activists said that the medical facts of nuclear war were so clear that there could be no alternative conclusion; if people "really knew" these facts, they would have to agree with the need for prevention.

Part of this knowing came through the rational discourse of technical science. As psychiatrist John Mack stated, "The first step is to inform yourself, and then to inform others. Through accurate presentation of the facts, illusions are shattered and make-believe undermined" (1982:594).

Activists also recognized a second way of knowing, one that was emotional and experiential. Psychiatrist Robert Jay Lifton spoke of breaking through psychic numbing which kept the threat of nuclear weapons from emotional reality. In an address to a PSR annual convention, Jennifer Leaning (1983:3) stated:

> There is rational discourse, in which the intellect examines the world through abstract concepts; and there is acute awareness, directly transmitted through vivid language. We need to keep this second level alive in ourselves and in our audiences if we wish to imbue them with a true understanding of nuclear war, and if we want to move them to act.

To create this understanding, the physicians combined the reason of the technical authority of medicine with the passion of a discipline dedicated to the relief of human suffering. They generated extensive technical analyses of the effects of nuclear war and also developed ways to communicate that data which maximized its personal impact. PSR speakers presented not just abstract technical facts, but rather the specific and concrete facts of how a nuclear attack would affect the individuals in their audiences, their families, and their communities.

In this chapter I examine the physicians' speeches on the medical effects of nuclear war and explore how activists presented their arguments in ways that were both technically accurate and personally relevant. The discussion is drawn from a broader ethnographic study of the physicians' movement in the United States (Neal 1988).

First, I analyze the standard PSR speech that defined the effects of a nuclear attack on the city in which the presentation was taking place. Inside PSR, these speeches were known as the "bombing runs."

Two contrasting styles of balancing the passion and reason of the physicians' movement can be identified in these speeches. The most prominent style in PSR was a conservative, nonconfrontational approach designed to preserve technical and professional credibility. A second approach, exemplified by Helen Caldicott's work, stressed the urgent moral imperatives of preventing nuclear holocaust.

The Bombing Runs:
From Apocalypse to Action

The bombing run speeches placed the physicians' technical arguments in the context of moving an audience toward taking action to prevent nuclear war. The physicians were not simply attempting to frighten people, as their critics sometimes argued (e.g., San Francisco Chronicle, September 28, 1984). Activists sought to portray the personal reality of nuclear war in order to channel the resulting anxiety into specific actions the audience could take to prevent it.

PSR's position on the medical effects of nuclear war was originally defined in a series of articles in the 1962 *New England Journal of Medicine*, during debates leading to the Limited Test Ban Treaty (Physicians for Social Responsibility 1962). Two key articles described the effects of a nuclear attack on the Boston area and calculated medical care resources that would be available after the attack (Ervin et al. 1962; Sidel, Geiger, and Lown 1962). When PSR was reactivated in the late 1970s, these studies were updated and extended in further research (e.g., Adams and Cullen 1981; Cassel, McCally, and Abraham 1984; Chivian et al. 1982; Solomon and Marston 1986).

The bombing run style of presentation was introduced by Jack Geiger, one of the original authors of the *New England Journal* studies. Geiger adapted the Boston data for the PSR symposia series, setting the precedent of using the case of the city in which the presentation was taking place. Geiger's speech at the 1980 symposium in San Francisco was captured in the widely circulated film, *The Last Epidemic*, and published versions of his work became basic texts for the physicians (e.g., Geiger 1981a, 1981b, 1982).

As the movement developed, speakers' training workshops and handbooks formalized the presentations, refining and codifying style and content. Training sessions taught substantive content, developed basic speaking skills, and suggested specific techniques for communicating the facts of nuclear war (e.g., PSR/Greater Boston 1982; PSR/San Francisco Bay Area 1983).

The trainings stressed using audiovisual and printed materials to reinforce the content of the speech. The film *The Last Epidemic* was often shown with only a brief introduction and concluding remarks by the speaker. Other short films, slide presentations, and speakers' aides such as flip charts were used with longer speeches. Printed handouts were always available at the conclusion of the event.

The bombing runs began with an introduction designed to link the speaker's concerns with those of the audience. Activists referred to such topics as a recent political event, how PSR began, the problem of strategies designed to win a nuclear war, or a special interest of the audience.

The main body of the speech presented the medical effects data, essentially following the structure of the *New England Journal* articles. This framework was both technically accurate and effective in engaging the audience in considering the personal impact of the data.

The speaker first defined the conditions of the detonation in terms of such factors as the magnitude and distribution of the attack, the time of day, and the nature of the weather. Technically, the physicians stressed that studies of the effects of nuclear weapons were limited by uncertain assumptions about the nature of the attack and conditions that could affect the extent of the destruction. In terms of the dynamics of the speech, this detailed description prepared the audience for the effects data by describing the local setting in detail, encouraging the audience to visualize a concrete and familiar setting for a nuclear explosion.

The physical and medical effects of the attack were organized by a series of concentric circles moving out from ground zero, the point of the explosion. Each circle represented a zone of destruction for the purpose of estimating the magnitudes of radiation, blast, and heat and their effects on structures and people. This series of circles, like a bull's eye on a target, was a powerful visual device commonly used in posters and other formats.

Activists described the physical and medical effects of the attack in great detail. For example, in Geiger's (1982:141) description of the one-megaton explosion in Detroit,

> The first circle, with a radius of 1.5 miles from ground zero, encompassing an area of 7 square miles, is the region of nearly total destruction—and total lethality. Blast overpressures ranging from 200 pounds per square inch (psi) down to 20 psi would crush, collapse, or explode all buildings, including the most strongly constructed steel and reinforced-concrete structures. Winds of 600 miles per hour would hurl debris outward at lethal velocities. Temperatures in the fireball above ground zero would exceed 27 million degrees Fahrenheit, and in this area everything would be vaporized; elsewhere in the circle, the heat would melt glass and steel, and concrete would explode. Direct radiation would range from 11,000 rads near ground zero to 1100 at the circle's rim. All of the human beings in this circle would die almost immediately—vaporized, crushed, charred, or radiated. With no survivors, there would be no "medical problems."

This analysis was repeated for each of the six circles in the bombing run model.

The technical description was also reinforced by visual images of the power of nuclear explosives, such as slides of mushroom clouds or the effects of blast tests on buildings. Vivid images of the victims of Hiroshima and Nagasaki were often used: photographs of the total destruction of the towns, of patterns of clothing burned into skin and shadows etched into bridges, of haunting expressions in the eyes of victims.

These graphic images were combined with descriptions of familiar local places. Speakers defined the circles in regard to local landmarks or interspersed photographs of the local community with images of nuclear destruction.

The physicians then summarized the total casualties and calculated remaining medical care resources. For Detroit, Geiger estimated 939,000 deaths and 1,145,000 serious injuries. Health care workers and facilities would also be destroyed.

> Estimates of the ratios of surviving physicians to seriously injured victims vary from 1:350 to 1:1700. If we assume a ratio of 1:1000, and imagine that every surviving physician would find all of the wounded with no loss of time, spend only 15 minutes per patient on every aspect of diagnosis and treatment, and work 18 hours a day, it would still be 8 to 16 days before every surviving patient would be seen for the first time. Most of the victims, obviously, would die—many of them slowly and agonizingly—without any medical care, without even narcotics for the relief of their pain (1982:146).

Throughout their work, the physicians stressed the incredible scale of nuclear war, "beyond anything in all recorded human experience," (1982:146) phrasing abstract concepts in terms of personal experience. After seeing the devastating effects of the Hiroshima bombing, for example, audiences heard, "The total nuclear arsenals of the world are equal to one million Hiroshimas, or over three tons of TNT for every man, woman and child on earth." In regard to the Reagan Administration's proposal for a $1.6 trillion military build-up, audiences were told, "Each of the 61,019,000 families in the United States will pay an average of $30,996 in taxes for these weapons" (PSR/San Francisco Bay Area n.d.:12).

Concrete demonstrations of the scale of nuclear war also became popular. One such demonstration involved dropping BBs into a metal container. The few BBs representing the total firepower of World War II, including the Hiroshima and Nagasaki bombs made a small sound, which was then compared to the thunderous roar of the thousands of BBs carefully counted out to accurately represent current arsenals (Caspar 1983).

The physicians did not stop with the acute effects of nuclear explosions. Their work was based on a public health approach, a broad perspective that considers health and illness within its social and environmental contexts. Thus, after describing the immediate destruction, the physicians continued recounting public health problems, psychological effects, and long-term social and environmental devastation.

Here again the data generated vivid images of nuclear war. Animals blinded from ozone loss in the atmosphere, hordes of insects surviving from their superior resistance to radiation, and vast numbers of human corpses recalled visions of mutants and horrors long associated with nuclear imagery.

Finally, the physicians often included military and political issues in their speeches to place the medical data in context and further specify the problem of nuclear weapons. The probability of nuclear war was often addressed. As a speakers' manual stated, "Nuclear war is just a remote bad dream to most people. How it might happen (and indeed has nearly happened) is an important part of the presentation" (PSR/ San Francisco Bay Area 1983:20). Activists addressed such issues as accidents, escalation of limited nuclear war, first-strike weapons and strategies, terrorism, and horizontal and vertical proliferation of nuclear weapons.

The effect of this seemingly never-ending array of horrors was a repeated psychological battering for the audience. One would think the description could not be worse, and then hear even more devastating examples.

After creating this intense experience, the physicians always moved from stating the problem of nuclear weapons into "what you can do." Activists stressed the importance of ending with a positive and empowering summation, although they recognized that this could be difficult to accomplish after the presentation of such depressing material.

Activists typically discussed a broad approach to preventing nuclear war based on arms control as opposed to continued escalation of the arms race, and then described specific actions individuals in the audience could take. For example, "101 Ideas for Preventing the Last Epidemic," a popular resource developed by The Nuclear War Study Group at Harvard Medical School, listed such actions as writing to newspapers, calling congressional representatives, staging a run, and including world peace in prayer or meditation (PSR/Greater Boston 1982:123-126).

After the formal presentation, the speaker opened the floor for questions from the audience. At the end of the event, printed handouts reinforced the content of the presentation. Handouts provided information such as bibliographies and fact sheets; helped people become more active through "what to do" lists and legislators' contact information; and connected individuals with appropriate organizations through membership cards, brochures, and area organization lists (PSR/Greater Boston 1982:4).

The physicians also contributed to generating action through other movement organizations. PSR materials on the medical effects of nuclear war were often part of other groups' definitions of the dangers of the arms race. The Northern California Nuclear Weapons Freeze Campaign, for example, officially adopted the film *The Last Epidemic* as an organizing tool during the 1982 statewide nuclear weapons freeze initiative campaign (Californians for a Bilateral Nuclear Weapons Freeze 1982).

A Nonconfrontational Style: Maintaining Professional Credibility

In the bombing run speeches, the physicians' passion about the dangers of nuclear war was tempered by their strategy of using medical expertise to counter the technical expertise of the nuclear strategists, thus contesting the legitimacy of nuclear weapons (cf. Neal 1988). In this context, maintaining professional credibility was a key task. In the bombing runs, challenges to the speaker usually came in the question-and-answer period at the end of the presentation. How to handle these "tough questions" was a key part of speakers' training.

Activists developed techniques for establishing their expertise on the subject of nuclear weapons. The physicians stressed the importance of being technically accurate. A San Francisco Bay Area training workshop, for example, cautioned speakers against exaggeration and noted overstatements in the film *The Last Epidemic* that had been challenged in presentations. For example, the film stated that millions of people could be instantly blinded by focal retinal burns; in fact, such burns could happen only if individuals were looking straight at the explosion at night and the chance of being totally blinded was actually very small (PSR/San Francisco Bay Area 1983).

In regard to the military and political facts of nuclear war, the physicians were not so clearly technical experts. They cooperated with physicists and arms-control experts to develop expertise to counter established policy and then used public speaking techniques to draw on their colleagues' credibility. Quotes from authoritative sources were an important resource for speakers.

Another approach was to move from technical detail to general principles, or as the Bay Area handbook put it, "Remember the forest and don't get lost in the trees." The forest was defined as general issues such as "More weapons do not make us more secure" and "Verifiability does not have to be 100 percent to work effectively" (PSR/San Francisco Bay Area 1983).

In addition, organizers referred to common sense as a counter to technical arguments, using a variety of everyday analogies. For example, a popular story way, "The nuclear arms race is like two people standing in a pool of gasoline. One has eight matches and the other has ten. Adding more matches will not make anyone more secure" (PSR/San Francisco Bay Area n.d.:12)

Activists also pursued a nonconfrontational style of interacting with individuals, which they considered congruent with the image of the physician as scientific expert. Speakers were advised not to aggressively confront a questioner, but rather to find a way to acknowledge and build rapport with the person and then use that rapport to move him or her toward the speaker's position. This professional style was part of broader efforts to create a "respectable" approach to peace issues, as reflected in the American Friends Service Committee (AFSC) document, "Depolarizing Disarmament Work: Twelve Guidelines to Help Us Reach New People" (Mogey 1982).

The physicians targeted audiences in the middle ranges of opinion, not people who were already convinced for or against PSR's position. A normal curve was used as a model for the distribution of opinion, the trainers suggesting that the vast majority in the middle were the unconvinced. The Bay Area speakers' manual advised,

> Avoid becoming hostile or setting up adversarial relationships with the audience. Being too sympathetic with the "already convinced" or lacking sympathy with the "impossible to convince" may cause the loss of trust and credibility with those who "could be convinced" and it's this latter audience group we need to be especially concerned with (1983).

Specific techniques for fielding aggressive or negative comments were suggested, such as thanking the individual for his or her opinion or saying, "That's a very good point."

Finally, PSR's professional approach included a conservative attitude toward taking political positions. In the early part of the movement, the physicians maintained a tight focus on "nonpolitical" education about the single issue of nuclear war. The national PSR organization and local chapters had strict guidelines as to positions speakers could espouse. The Bay Area handbook advised speakers:

1. PSR's major goals are to inform the public about the facts re nuclear war and to encourage support for disarmament by *mutual* means.
2. PSR is not a political group; PSR is a medical group.
3. PSR is not for or against any political figure, Russian, American, or other. PSR does not condemn the Soviet Union, the United States, or any other country. Instead, PSR presents the facts of the matter from a medical point of view and does whatever possible to encourage all people to understand the dangers of nuclear weapons and nuclear war, dangers which do not limit themselves nationally or geographically.
4. If you express opinions in addition to those adopted by PSR, you must make clear to your audience that these opinions are your own and do not express PSR policy (1983:4).

Helen Caldicott:
The Moral Imperatives of Nuclear War

Helen Caldicott was one of the most visible spokespeople for the physicians' movement. She had been active in opposing nuclear testing in her native Australia and became involved in the reactivated PSR while a visiting faculty member at Harvard Medical School. For Caldicott, the planet was "at the crossroads of time" (Caldicott 1979). Urgent and immediate action was the only reasonable response to the nuclear threat. Her books, *Nuclear Madness* and the later *Missile Envy*, were widely distributed (Caldicott 1980; 1984), and her work was extensively covered in the press and in documentary films (e.g., Cevoli 1983; Rosenthal 1982; *Eight Minutes to Midnight* 1981; *If You Love this Planet* 1982).

Caldicott's presentations covered essentially the same content as the bombing runs, had essentially the same form of moving from stating the problem into action, and used many of the same techniques, such as vivid imagery and commonsense analogies. She also developed her own distinctive style and content, drawing from her experience as a pediatrician specializing in cystic fibrosis, a terminal childhood illness.

In contrast to the public health model developed by Jack Geiger and others, Caldicott used clinical imagery. She described the world with nuclear weapons as a terminally ill planet "infected with lethal macrobes (nuclear weapons) that are metastasizing rapidly, the way a cancer spreads in the body" (Caldicott 1986:1).

In contrast to the measured reason of the mainstream physicians' movement, Caldicott based her work on an intense moral critique of nuclear weapons. She stressed the need to educate people about nuclear issues, but for Caldicott, the essential issues were moral:

> This is a moral issue and it's very simple. . . . I call it mental masturbation to worry about all those scientific trivia. It's irrelevant. You don't even have to know what weapons Russia has, except that we'll be wiped out in twenty minutes and within 30 days after a nuclear exchange 90 percent of Americans will be dead. What more do you want to know? (1981b:2).

Instead of avoiding an emotional approach, Caldicott embraced and promoted it, asserting that emotional response was entirely appropriate to the issue. She proposed that the only way to end the arms race was to be "passionately involved with saving this planet" (1981a:9). Here again she used an analogy based on terminal illness: "If I had two parents who came into my office, and I told them that their child had leukemia and I showed them what the prognosis was and what might happen, and they showed no emotional response, I would get them to a psychiatrist straight away" (1981a:9).

Caldicott was direct and blunt, eschewing the need to be moderate and respectable. She defined an urgent and massive danger and stressed the immediate necessity to act before time ran out. An article about her work, for example, was entitled, "Nuclear War: This May Be Your Last Christmas" (1981c).

Caldicott was equally direct in her opinions about the nuclear establishment, " . . . It kills people. I'm here to look after people, to save people's lives, not to kill them" (1979:12). In regard to politicians, Caldicott talked about a "mad lust for power" and compared the superpower leaders to boys with arrested emotional development playing in a sandbox and arguing about who had the biggest bow and arrow.

Caldicott also discussed the role of women in stopping nuclear weapons. PSR psychiatrists stressed emotional aspects of the arms race, but rarely considered women's issues. Caldicott, on the other hand, spoke "as a mother, as a pediatrician, and as a woman," and in 1980 formed Women's Action for Nuclear Disarmament (WAND). She often used imagery of mothering and children. "To our government, 'nuclear war' may mean a struggle between superpowers. To women, 'nuclear war' means the threat of annihilation of all children. *Protecting children from that threat is the single most important act of parenting today*" (WAND, n.d.). Caldicott contrasted what she considered the rational orientation of men with the caring instincts of women, suggesting that there was "something women have that's different, and that is that they really care intensely about life."

In her presentations Caldicott used an intense, direct, and deeply personal approach. She presented factual material about nuclear weapons, but in a less systematic format than in the standard bombing run speeches and with what one observer called a "rather cavalier attitude toward the facts."

Caldicott was not gentle with her audiences. She often began her presentations with the film *Hiroshima/Nagasaki 1945*, A short film of the aftermath of the bombings (Hiroshima/Nagasaki 1945, 1980). Most physicians felt the film was too overwhelming, leading more to apathy than to action in that it depressed people to the point of immobilization. Caldicott talked about the need to make this knowledge personal:

> Think of everything you hold most dear in your life—your children; parents; spouse; friends; home; the beauties of nature in spring as she unfolds the lilacs, dogwood, wisteria, roses, magnolias and daffodils. Then transpose the following facts into your own life. [You] . . . may find the prospect terrifying, but this experience is essential to the emotional adaptation necessary for effective political action (1981d:3).

Conclusions:
The Human Facts of Nuclear War

The physicians personalized the threat of nuclear war by addressing the human facts of nuclear weapons. In the technical language of nuclear strategy, "Human death simply is collateral damage—collateral to the real subject, which is nuclear weapons" (Cohn 1987:23). The technical language of medicine added a new subject to the debate, shifting attention "from the means of destruction and the nature of the physical damage to the indescribable human tragedy" (Kistiakovsky, n.d.).

Debates about how to balance scientific reason and moral passion in describing this tragedy generated much contention. Helen Caldicott's impatience with professional propriety put her at odds with many of her PSR colleagues, although according to one observer, many of the physicians who objected to Caldicott's style may very well have been brought into the issue by her work and only later felt the need for rational justification.

On the other hand, technically oriented activists maintained their professional approach in ways that sometimes seemed arrogant and offensive to others. For example, a speakers' training manual stated that audiences "need to know we're not made up of crazies but respectable professional people and legitimate government sources" (PSR/San Francisco Bay Area 1983:20).

Despite these conflicts, the physicians provided a scientific specification of the apocalypse of nuclear war that served the movement well. By the mid-1980s, the public had indeed been alerted to the dangers of nuclear weapons.

CHAPTER 12

Congress and the Campaign to Stop the MX Missile

JOHN MACDOUGALL

The goal of this chapter is to analyze the resource mobilization strategies used by the arms-control movement in the U.S. Congress in the 1980s. I chose the MX issue because it was one of the few on which the peace movement of the Eighties was relatively successful in Congress, and on which diverse segments of the movement not only agreed but worked hard.

This study should be of interest to readers with a general interest in peace movements or resource mobilization. Most social movement studies using the resource mobilization approach analyze movements' origins, but neglect impact. This research concerns a major movement's impact and its interactions with mainstream institutions like legislatures (studies of movements' impacts include Gamson 1975 and Tarrow 1982). My study should also complement other work on the politics of the MX, such as Holland and Hoover 1985, and Rothenberg 1989.

I define the arms-control movement as all organizations and individuals that sought as a primary goal major steps toward significant arms control by the U.S., and were willing to devote substantial resources to that goal. Thus, the arms-control movement was more or less a subset of the larger peace movement. The former movement includes both new organizations (founded after 1980) and old ones, both more radical and more mainstream ones.

A brief history of the MX debate will provide orientation to the analysis that follows (for more details see MacDougall, forthcoming).

The MX missile was intended to be a successor of the Minuteman, a multiple-warhead ICBM capable of destroying enemy missile silos. A key problem with the MX was to find a basing mode that would make the missile both invulnerable and politically acceptable. This problem was temporarily solved by the so-called Scowcroft Commisssion which, in April 1983, recommended deployment of the MX in hardened Minuteman silos, the development of a new single-warhead ICBM (dubbed Midgetman), and serious efforts at arms control.

The Scowcroft approach appealed to wavering members of Congress, and in May the House voted, by a fifty-three-vote margin, to fund the MX. This stood in striking contrast to the House's vote, a few weeks earlier, in favor of a nuclear freeze resolution. However, the administration lost ground on the MX between the summer of 1983 and the spring of 1985. There were several reasons for this, including the perception by many legislators that the administration was not serious about arms control and the decision by the House Democratic party leadership to make defeat of the MX a top priority. Despite these difficulties, a group of influential centrists, led by Representative Les Aspin, sought support for a series of compromises.

The issue was essentially closed at the end of the 1985 session, when Congress and the administration agreed that fifty would be the maximum number of deployed MXs. This was very different from the two hundred missiles the Carter Administration wanted to deploy and posed much less of a first-strike threat to the Soviet Union.

This chapter primarily concerns the behavior of seven swing Representatives, resources mobilized by the arms-control movement to sway their votes, and the impact of these mobilization efforts. The swing-member study was based primarily on interviews with over sixty congressional aides, administration officials, arms-control lobbyists, and activists.

Impression Management by Legislators

To better understand typical members' of Congress behavior, we can usefully draw on the work of Richard Fenno (1978). After closely observing a diverse group of representatives and drawing heavily on Goffman (1959), Fenno concluded that representatives' behavior can be explained largely by two variables. The first variable is the heterogenenity of the district's voters: the more diverse the major voting blocs among the voters, the more free the members are to vote as they choose, since these blocs are less likely to coalesce into a large and hostile "super-bloc." The second variable is attentiveness; the more attentive a bloc, the more important it is for a member to vote in a way that at least earns the bloc's respect. Thus, members with homogeneous and attentive voters are under especially strong pressure to cast what Fenno calls consistent "strings" of votes, and to come up with plausible explanations for those votes.

Fenno's analysis is particularly appropriate to the 1980s. This was a decade in which extra-congressional party organizations' impact on members has lessened and the potential influence of interest groups increased. In the 1980s, compared to previous decades, individual members were typically more independent in their thinking (Morrison 1986). In addition, the media became important channels of influence (Roberts 1982). In this situation, when there were attentive groups in a member's district, impression management and the creation of "explainable" strings of votes were important goals for members.

Mobilizable Resources for
the Arms-Control Movement

Some of the key resources available to, and exploited by, the arms-control organizations in their dealings with Congress were structural, i.e., they derived from patterns of social relationships (cf. Freeman 1979; McCarthy and Zald 1977). During the 1980s important structural resources forged by the movement were close and enduring alliances with various important institutions, such as the mainstream churches, schools, colleges, foundations, state and local governments, and environmental organizations. It was especially easy to build alliances for the MX struggle, since it was seen as winnable (Pertschuck 1986, Chapters 8-9; Solo 1988: 61-66; cf. Klandermans 1986: 27). In addition, the decline of local party organizations in the 1980s left some political space for grass-roots arms-control groups (cf. Roberts 1982: 65-66). National arms-control organizations became increasingly skillful at lobbying on Capitol Hill, and developed lasting relationships with some important legislators.

On the other hand, the movement generally failed to build significant ties to labor, women's and civil-rights organizations, or to the
media, nonmilitary business, and establishment think-tanks. The administration also succeeded in creating some coalitions on the other
side of the debate, particularly with powerful legislators like Aspin (cf.
Walker and Mendlowitz 1987).

Other major resources a social movement can mobilize are symbols
and culture. A resource the arms-control movement exploited fully
was the legitimacy of the nuclear freeze in the 1980s. The movement
took advantage of public dissatisfaction with the huge federal deficit
and successfully countered the administration's attempts at Red-bait-
ing.[1] However, the movement had limited success in overcoming most
legislators' and voters' belief that the president should be the one to
take the initiative on foreign and military issues. This belief was actively fostered by the Reagan Administration when it took decisive
actions in the international arena and complained of being hamstrung
by Congress. Another potential liability for the movement arose out of
its very success in congressional lobbying. National staff members of
arms-control organizations tended to become overly oriented to the
pragmatic, short-run mentality of Washington politicians, and to forget the more visionary and long-term aspirations that motivated many
(perhaps most) grass-roots movement supporters (cf. Schlozman and
Tierney 1986, chap. 5; Szegedy-Maszak 1989). After the 1983 House
freeze vote, arms-control lobbyists seemed to forget how much citizen
energy they could mobilize if they framed issues in more visionary
terms than those used in Washington.

Resource Mobilization in
Seven Congressional Districts

The seven representatives in this study were all swing members,
i.e., legislators who were considered by arms-control lobbyists likely
to change to an anti-MX position after voting for the missile in May
1983. These members were lobbied hard on the MX later in 1983, and
in some cases in 1984 and/or 1985.

Of the seven legislators, three were consistent supporters of the MX
after the May 1983 vote. One was Representative Glenn Anderson (D-
California). Anderson, who represented a largely blue-collar district,

was a socioeconomic liberal but a foreign-policy conservative. The second MX supporter was Claude Pepper (D-Florida), the congressional standard-bearer for the elderly and chairman of the influential House Rules Committee.[2] The third MX supporter was Olympia Snowe (R-Maine). She is deputy Republican whip in the House, but has shown some independence from her party.

Three members switched in May 1983 from support of the MX to opposition. The first was Lee Hamilton (D-Indiana), a foreign-affairs specialist with a towering reputation for integrity and conscientiousness. Second was Marge Roukema of New Jersey, a recently-elected Republican moderate. The third MX opponent was Robin Tallon (D-South Carolina). He hailed from a rural district that was 40 percent black, and was first elected in 1982.

Finally, there was a special case: Representative Melvyn Dymally, a Democrat from Los Angeles who cast an inconsistent set of votes on the MX. He was black and had liberal impulses, but his district was largely white and blue-collar, and also contained many defense plants (as did Anderson's).

Public Education

In the seven districts I studied, arms-control organizations worked hard to educate the public, both on the specifics of the MX and on arms control in general. For instance, in Representative Hamilton's district much was done in 1983 in schools, churches, and community groups (Sanders 1984). Hamilton's position on the MX received fairly wide support in the district, despite the generally conservative nature of the electorate. Thus, there may have occurred an increase in the attentiveness (in Fenn's terms) of some voting blocs to the MX, and a neutralization of potentially opposing blocs.[3]

Grassroots Lobbying

Lobbying can be defined as conscious efforts to ensure that legislators support particular policies or bills. This was attempted in all the seven districts. Anderson received thousands of anti-MX cards in 1983, and was visited by many delegations of missile opponents. However, a congressional source reported he also received two hundred letters supporting the MX, which was a "pretty respectable" number.

Many of these letters were said to come from employees of military contractors. According to this source, Anderson said he wanted to hear from a more diverse group of MX opponents. This was consistent with Fenno's model: in Anderson's case one bloc of voters was attentive, and he supported it unless opposing blocs became significantly more attentive or more heterogeneous. For anti-MX blocs to succeed, they had to be much more attentive and/or heterogeneous, since the efforts of local MX supporters were reinforced by pressure from the Reagan Administration and from local military contractors.

Anderson also provided an interesting example of how grassroots activists can lobby a legislator in indirect ways. Thanks in part to arms-control groups' efforts, in 1983 Anderson was sent a letter by the state Democratic party urging him to oppose the MX. In 1985 he received a letter of censure from the party chairperson for his support of the missile. Thus, the pressure on Anderson was greater in 1985 than 1983, but on the other hand, arms-control groups in the district were in a weaker position in 1985. In that year they were encountering financial problems, and also the public was less critical of the administration than in 1983-84 because U.S.-Soviet talks had begun in Geneva (Carpenter 1985; Seidita 1985). In any event, home district cross-pressure were sufficient to make Anderson ignore intraparty pressure.

Dymally presented a somewhat different picture. He was philosophically opposed to the MX, and seemed to like explaining his votes in terms of helping the poor and creating jobs for his constituents. Dymally was under some grassroots pressure to oppose the MX. In a poor part of the district, 70 percent of the people contacted signed a petition urging a shift of resources from the MX to social programs. In 1983 he asked SANE (a major arms-control organization) for mail opposed to the MX (Duker 1985). He was no doubt pleased when this resulted in personal letters to him, which he showed to military contractors lobbying him in favor of the MX.

However, strenuous efforts were also made by local military contractors to lobby Dymally to support the MX. These sometimes succeeded: according to a congressional source Dymally voted *for* the MX in May 1983 because twenty-four hundred jobs were at stake at a Northrup military plant in the district, even though this was a "hard vote to live with." This episode suggests a member's general sympathy to arms control can be neutralized when the electorate is attentive and/or heterogeneous on the other side, when there is vigorous lobbying by pro-MX forces.

Snowe was lobbied exceptionally hard by local arms-control groups and their allies. Thousands of petition signatures reached her, according to a Capitol Hill source. The anti-MX constituency was exceptionally diverse and attentive: it included many churches, lawyers' organizations, eighty-five cities and towns, some farmers groups, and many labor unions—all of which took formal stances for arms control. Much was also done to mobilize symbolic resources, through local newspapers, for instance (Derouche 1985; Moore 1985).

This being the case, the question arises: why did Snowe vote *for* the MX? Part of the answer lay in her loyalty to her party and her perception that she had to "balance" her antiadministration votes (for instance, on aid to the Nicaraguan Contras) by a major proadministration vote. Snowe also partially neutralized the anti-MX bloc by supporting segments of the bloc on other issues. For instance, no doubt many of the female opponents of the MX were pro-choice on abortion, and Snowe had a good pro-choice record. She also supported protectionism for ailing Maine farmers and shoe factories. She was thus protected in her pro-MX votes from opponents' backlash by her other favorably viewed votes.

DIRECT LOBBYING IN WASHINGTON

Roukema was heavily lobbied in Washington on the MX by Common Cause and Council for a Livable World (CLW), two respected mainstream arms-control organizations. She was also an active opponent of chemical weapons, an issue on which CLW worked hard. According to a congressional source, she was more involved in the chemical-weapons issue than in the MX one. Roukema was concerned that the Reagan Administration had failed to set proper priorities in its defense policies, and was spending too much on military hardware—on what Roukema called "defense entitlements." She was also heavily lobbied at the grassroots level on the MX (Hedlund 1985; Isaacs 1985; Thomas 1985).

Congressional sources and Barone and Ujifusa (1985: 847) described Roukema's district as socially heterogeneous. Therefore, on the MX it was relatively easy for her to ignore local conservatives and support attentive, dovish voters. In addition, arms-control organizations in

Washington and at the grass roots carefully coordinated their mobilization efforts. No doubt it was easy for Roukema to incorporate her opposition to the MX into a "string" of votes against "defense entitlements."

INDIRECT LOBBYING IN WASHINGTON

Indirect lobbying was an important avenue of influence for arms-control groups in Washington, particularly when it took the form of sympathetic members talking to their colleagues. MX opponents especially benefited from the "Moffett group," a set of aides, members, and lobbyists who met regularly to share information and ideas on arms control (Duncan 1985; cf. Solo 1988:73).

Pepper presented an interesting case of indirect lobbying. Members of the Moffett group pressed him before the November 1983 vote on the MX. Pepper was also lobbied by two other important colleagues: Representative Bennett, another Florida Democrat, and then House Majority Leader Jim Wright. Common Cause got Wright to approach Pepper fifteen minutes before the vote on the MX.

However, according to an arms-control lobbyist, "incredible pressure" was exerted on Pepper by Aspin, by some of his hawkish, congressional colleagues, and by the administration. It is also reported in Ehrenhalt et al. (1985) that Pepper, since his elevation to the chairpersonship of the Rules Committee, felt like "an insider" and considered himself uninformed on foreign and military issues. Accordingly, Pepper was inclined to vote on these issues the way his friends did. To be sure, some of his friends wanted Pepper to oppose the MX, but more important was his loyalty to the commander-in-chief, reinforced by the arguments of congressional "defense experts" like Aspin. Further, in 1984 the administration let Pepper know he should support the MX if he wanted the administration to support his programs for the elderly. Finally, there was strong right-wing pressure at the grass roots, especially from Cubans who constituted the largest ethnic group in the district (Daggett 1985; Duker 1985; Meyerson 1985).

This instance suggests the degree to which the movement's substantial resources, including its congressional ones, can be neutralized by its opponents' resources. In Pepper's case the latter included not only major actors in Washington but a highly attentive and homogeneous bloc of right-wing voters in the district.

The case of Congressman Tallon provides a contrasting example of indirect pressure on Capitol Hill. A congressional source indicated that Tallon was lobbied by fellow members including Representative Spratt, also a Democrat from South Carolina and a highly respected moderate defense expert, who was a solid opponent of the MX (Hedlund 1985; Towell 1983).

This peer pressure was in part attributable to arms-control lobbyists. Tallon was a freshman in 1983, and as such likely to be less influenced by the dynamics of legislators' behavior explained above. Freshmen were paid special attention by arms-control organizations. Tallon also set high store by military preparedness and reducing the deficit, and these priorities no doubt helped him explain his anti-MX votes. Activists both in Washington and South Carolina exploited these factors.

Some Lessons of the MX Case

It is of course hazardous to make statements that go beyond the seven members studied here, but this analysis permits some tentative generalizations. First, *net* resources can be decisive. If arms-control organizations are to be effective, they must make a careful reckoning not only of their own resources but also the strength of their adversaries (congressional hawks, the Pentagon, and so on). They must also anticipate as best they can how and where their adversaries will mobilize.

Second, however, many arms-control and peace groups may possess more resources than might at first be apparent. Particularly valuable, but sometimes neglected, is the potential for arms-control groups to exert indirect pressure through friendly legislators. Such pressure tends to be hard to orchestrate—probably harder than citizens' letters and phone calls—but national organizations became increasingly skilled at indirect lobbying and increasingly close to sympathetic members and their aides.

Third, sometimes resource mobilization efforts have little impact on their own, but cumulatively their effect is substantial. Roukema belonged to the "wrong" party, yet arms-control groups couched their appeals to her in terms of themes that mattered to her, and also carefully coordinated their work in Washington and the district. In Tallon's case national organizations worked hard at indirect lobbying, and although local groups had few resources, they skillfully utilized what they had.

Fourth, it is very helpful if the resources used by the movement are varied in nature. Mobilization efforts can more easily have a cumulative impact. For instance, a member is more likely to be swayed when Washington lobbyists can work in concert with energetic local activists. To use Fenno's (1978) terminology, in such a situation a member will be faced by pro-arms-control blocs that are both attentive and homogeneous—as happened in Snowe's district.

Fifth, although arms-control organizations and congresspersons share a willingness to be flexible and pragmatic, there are still major differences between the goals and values of typical legislators and those of most arms-control activists. If these differences are neglected by national arms-control organizations, the latter are likely to lose touch with the world of grassroots activists and get caught up in the very pragmatic and short-term orientation characteristic of Washington politics. Washington professionals as well as local organizers also have to be very clear about the differences between incremental/pragmatic actions and utopian/transformative ones. Everyone in the movement realized that the MX struggle fell into the first category, but some activists and Washington staff members seem to have forgotten that the MX battle was waged in part to enhance the movement's prospects of winning more utopian battles. Unless these distinctions are made clear, activists are prone to see their inability to move legislators like Snowe as abject failures, or to view the legislative compromise of fifty MXs as a sellout.

Acknowledgments

An earlier version of this chapter was presented at the Center for Conflict Resolution at George Mason University. I am most grateful to Frank Blechman, David Cohen, Mary Anna Colwell, and Richard Healey for their comments.

Notes

1. The struggle against the MX benefited from the rising concern with the budget deficit and with the explosive growth of military spending. However, the movement to reform military procurement procedures and shift priorities towards

readiness and away from hardware had no direct connection to arms-control efforts. Nor did revelations of such things as purchases of eight hundred dollar toilet seats by the Pentagon, although they added to the public's general opposition to military spending (Morrison 1986).

2. Representative Pepper died on May 30, 1989.

3. Boundaries were redrawn in Hamilton's district in 1980, which reduced the size of the liberal voting bloc. He had no prospects of being elected to statewide office, and decided to make membership on the Intelligence Committee a key goal in the early 1980s (Blechman 1988). All of these developments made Hamilton less inclined to support the arms-control movement.

CHAPTER 13

The Meaning of Civil Disobedience: The Case of the Honeywell Project

LEAH ROGNE AND BRADLEY D. HARPER

In the Eighties, members of the Honeywell Project, based in Minneapolis and St. Paul, Minnesota, differed greatly among themselves on the meaning of civil disobedience and nonviolence in their lives and on the role of civil disobedience in the peace movement. For some of these movement activists, nonviolence was a way of life and an end in itself. For them, the Honeywell Project served as a collective effort to express a moral or spiritual vision. For others, civil disobedience was a strategy to be utilized at times to achieve larger movement goals.

In this chapter we explore the meaning of civil disobedience for activists who saw civil disobedience as a tactic and activists who saw civil disobedience as a matter of moral witness. We examine the complex character of moral witness, exploring the consequences of and relationship between the activists' philosophical framework and their behavior in a peace organization. We relate these findings to organizational dynamics and use a dialectical framework to look at the construction of consciousness and praxis by the militant civil disobeyer.

Our discussion is based on the results of a Honeywell Project-sponsored self-study which included a mail-out questionnaire, a series of focus group meetings, and our own participant observation with the Project during 1987-88.[1] As participants in the peace movement, we feel that the ideas we explore here are important for activists to consider as they take steps toward strengthening their resistance. As researchers of the peace movement, we feel this study provides a helpful perspective on the relationship between organizational dynamics and issues of conscience and consciousness.

Background

According to its leadership, the Honeywell Project is the country's oldest peace organization that specifically targets weapons research and production. Nationally, it is regarded as a highly credible and respected voice among groups that engage in civil disobedience. It plays a key role in the state's strong and diverse peace movement.

The Honeywell Project began in 1968 when local peace activists discovered that the Honeywell corporation, known most prominently for its thermostats, was producing antipersonnel fragmentation bombs that were being used in Vietnam. Its initial focus was on mass legal demonstrations at shareholders' meetings and direct discussions with Honeywell management. This early period of strong activism culminated in 1970 when three thousand Project supporters had a tumultuous confrontation with Honeywell security and local police, resulting in the premature adjournment of the annual shareholders' meeting. Activity was sporadic during the subsequent years, and by the late 1970s the Project was essentially dormant.

In the early 1980s, as worldwide protest against deployment of nuclear missiles in Europe mounted and as antiwar activists in the U.S. began to engage in symbolic destruction of nuclear weapons, local peace activists renewed their commitment to resist Honeywell's weapons production. Former activists and new recruits joined together to revive the Project. This time, the Project's efforts focused on the use of nonviolent civil disobedience. Between 1982 and the end of the decade, the Project's resistance resulted in over two thousand arrests for sit-ins, blockades, vigils, and various other forms of symbolic protest and trespass on Honeywell property.

The revived project employed a two- or three-person, full-time paid staff whose activities were guidied by the Core Group, a loosely structured association of six to ten people. The Core Group made broad financial and policy decisions and generated ideas for strategies and tactics. Affinity groups, patterned after those affiliated with the Livermore Action Group (Epstein 1985), were a key element of the Project's structure as emotional support groups and sources of new ideas. Affinity groups were loosely connected to Project decision making through participation by some Core Group members and staff in the monthly affinity group meetings.

In practice, decision making in the Honeywell Project was far from clear-cut. Indeed, many members prided themselves on the Project's relative lack of structure and ambiguous decision-making process. There were no by-laws or constitution, no written guidelines for decision making, and, thus, no routine or clear-cut ways to resolve conflicts when they occurred.

For the most part, Core Group members based their decisions on their personal viewpoints and on speculation about what the membership might want or support. A large number of supporters had no interest in being involved in the decision-making process, although they did feel they had a stake in decisions. Core Group members felt accountable to these supporters, but there was no structure to assure they would be represented. This anarchistic style was functional but sometimes led to confusion and conflict.

The Meaning of Civil Disobedience

The Project's self-study arose out of a need to resolve a potentially debilitating struggle over the future role of civil disobedience in the Honeywell Project. In the fall of 1987, some Core Group members' commitment to civil disobedience as the primary strategy for the Project had waned, and they questioned the wisdom of continuing to place such heavy emphasis on major civil disobedience actions. They speculated that many supporters shared their view and that the Project needed to make significant changes in order to continue to reflect the views of the membership and in order to be more effective, particularly through smaller actions and new strategies which could generate immediate successes.

In contrast, other Core Group members saw civil disobedience as essential to the Project. They cited the views of a core of deeply committed individuals for whom civil disobedience was a moral witness—a personal statement that individuals make regardless of questions of effectiveness. Although not opposing the inclusion of other stategies, this group felt morally constrained to continue planning major civil disobedience actions so that Project supporters would have ongoing opportunities for witnessing and consciousness raising.

In this section we explore varied definitions of the role of civil disobedience for Honeywell Project supporters. We place particular emphasis on the character of the moral witness because of the strength of that position in the organization and because of the intriguing philosophical and organizational questions that are raised by considering the actions of the moral witness. The dimensions of civil disobedience we discuss are: (1) the role of effectiveness; (2) short-term versus long-term change; (3) individual versus social change; (4) individual control over consequences; (5) the relationship between means and ends; and (6) personal versus organizational goals.

For a significant minority of supporters, effectiveness was a major issue. One survey respondent stated, "I have to think about being effective. I can't live without feeling it can change. . . . I want change to happen before my own eyes." For a strong majority, however, the effectiveness of the Project and of civil disobedience was not a critical issue. One supporter stated, "Whether anyone's affected or not, it's something you have to do. Persistence makes a difference." Over half of all supporters who had been arrested expressed the feeling that the significance of civil disobedience was its strong moral statement, compared to only one quarter who saw raising societal awareness as most significant.

Some of the supporters who emphasized effectiveness wanted the Project to shift its focus to include short-term strategies and tactics that could realize immediate results. For example, one respondent questioned whether he would continue to be arrested for civil disobedience:

> I realize civil disobedience is good for media attention and outreach, but I feel we are reaching a saturation level, less media attention. I am leaning towards low key economic *sabotage* as a more effective and spiritualizing tool for social change. I feel that in order for civil disobedience to be effective, which I feel it can be very effective, the repression has to be more direct on the disobeyers (us). Such as in civil rights movement. Since the defense industry is so profitable I feel we have to concentrate on making it *less* profitable, boycotts, *economic sabotage*.

Another respondent considered the consequences of civil disobedience on the organization: "Depending on other strategies used to replace C.D., it [stopping C.D.] could possibly strengthen the organization. The tactic of C.D. seems maybe to have peaked for this city at this time." It was often perplexing to be in dialogue with a strong moral witness about his or her motivations because of an apparent lack of interest in discussing consequences. As one of the respondents argued: "[C.D. is] what I do best—I don't need a rationale. . . . C.D. is the choice of a few. The clearest statement is to put oneself apart from violence. What I say is 'If that's legal, then I want to be a criminal.' It's not complicated for me." Plowshares activists Arthur Laffin and Anne Montgomery have speculated that people continue to raise this issue due to an "American obsession with efficiency and effectiveness" and that the real question is:

> By whose standards are we judging effectiveness—or can we judge it at all? We must be responsible and do our homework, research and choose our site with care, reflect and pray over the pros and cons of the action and symbols, and open up channels of support and communication. But in the end there is always a gap between faith and feasibility and the moment of speaking the truth becomes a leap of faith that opens us to the power of that truth (1987:28).

Cynthia Eller (1988) has "deconstructed" the moral and religious arguments of World War II conscientious objectors and presented an analysis that takes into account varying definitions of effectiveness as well as varying conceptions of the relationship between ends and means and varying visions of time as it relates to the evaluation of the outcomes of one's action. Eller explains that one can better understand pacifists' personal definitions of effectiveness through a careful examination of their moral and ethical reasoning:

> Because pacifists have their own way of evaluating consequences, what a non-pacifist might term a success, a pacifist will term a failure, and vice versa. There are two major emphases at work in pacifist evaluation of consequences: first, pacifists tend to prefer long-range consequences over short-term ones, and second, they value deep individual change above large-scale but shallow social change (1988:121–122).

Tied to the preference for long-term consequences is the belief that "lasting change is the result of many individual transformations" (1988: 123). Moral witnesses did not suffer from the impatience of strategically oriented protestors, who measured success by such external indicators as the numbers attending a demonstration, the quality and quantity of media coverage, and by immediate political results. The following supporter's comment conveys a belief in the need for change at the level of individual consciousness:

> I believe that practicing civil disobedience in support of the peace movement is a process of personal and political development which is challenging, difficult, and results in developing stronger commitment to the cause. At each step of being involved in civil disobedience, I have been challenged to face fears, examine my beliefs, open myself to others in the same process. This has made me stronger and more committed. I believe the same is true for others. We must change ourselves if we expect change in the system. Civil disobedience changes people and confronts those who refused to change.

Further, witnesses often tended to distance themselves from any notion that they had direct control over the course of history. For many, their peace activity was guided by their spiritual beliefs, as in the case of one Project supporter who said, "The outcome is not up to me; it's up to God." According to Eller (1988:128), "The central point is that God is in charge of history and that God will produce good consequences. . . . Responsible Christians can then do their part to bring in Christ's kingdom (the penultimate in good social consequences) by being representatives of it."

Their statements often indicated a sense that the consequences of one's actions may be beyond one's own ability to assess. This does not necessarily mean that they disregarded consequences; rather, traditional measures of the value of accomplishments may be fallacious. Long-time pacifist and political theorist Mulford Q. Sibley (1988) has stated, "Don't be disappointed even if you're greatly disappointed by most standards. . . . I shudder to think what I would be if it weren't for this transcendental ideal that we sometimes forget."

An understanding of the "means/end question" is also necessary to appreciate fully the complexities of the pacifist approach. For many peace activists in the Honeywell Project, a special quality of civil disobedience was the folding together of means and ends. The idea that a nonviolent society could arise through the use of violent means was to them a myth, an anathema to their understanding. The only acceptable means were those that incorporate the ends themselves. This lack of distinction between means and ends colored their conceptualization of effectiveness.

Those concerned about the possibility of the corruption of just ends by unjust means were least likely to become dismayed over issues of tactics and effectiveness when their efforts seemed to be for naught. That spirit, coupled with a view toward long-term as opposed to short-term gains and a focus on transformation of an individual's consciousness, appeared to account more fully for what some viewed as a self-righteous disregard for outcomes.

Many people in the Project evaluated organizational and personal goals separately. Although many supporters, especially those who had been heavily involved in the past, were reevaluating the role of civil disobedience in their own lives and may indeed have shifted a good deal of their peace activity to other groups, a strong majority of all supporters felt the Project should continue its direction. They felt that the Project had a unique role in the peace community as a clear voice for nonviolence and that the Project's mass demonstrations played a critical part in making that voice heard.

Many Project supporters were also involved in other social causes, such as working with AIDS patients or running shelters for battered women, where at least limited tangible results were realizable. One supporter stated that in her work she worried about her effectiveness but she came to the Project for her spirituality. The Project was seen by these people as an arena for reinforcing one's commitment to nonviolence, for publicly practicing one's philosophy, for regularly ritualizing and acting out symbolically one's noncooperation with the war machine. Personal growth and empowerment were seen as major reasons for engaging in civil disobedience. Realization of these goals was not strictly contingent upon organizational success as defined by stopping Honeywell weapons production.

Organizational Dynamics

We see, then, that the Project was made up of a diverse group of people whose reasons for involvement and/or their views on the role of civil disobedience varied widely. The challenge for the Project was to operate in a way that acknowledged the differences but did not allow them to cripple the organization with endless sectarian disputes such as those that have frequently led to the disintegration of social movements on the Left.

In the following discussion, we explore the impact of this contention among forces upon the organizational dynamics of the Honeywell Project. Organizational dimensions affected by the differences in philosophy and style among Project members included (1) short- and long-range planning ability; (2) intragroup member relations; and (3) organizational maintenance and membership retention.

Although both "strategists" and "witnesses" in the Honeywell Project tended to disdain formal structure, members who used civil disobedience as a strategy were more interested than witnesses in engaging in discussions of short- and long-range planning for the organization and more concerned over lack of structure. It was the strategists in the Core Group who originally pushed for some kind of evaluation process that would determine the members' sentiments about the role of civil disobedience in the Project.

In contrast, Core Group members advocating civil disobedience as personal witness initially had no interest in surveying the members and were satisfied to proceed based on their own interpretation of the views of people they considered to be opinion leaders. They were suspicious of the validity of a study group process because they believed these opinion leaders were not interested in participating in a lengthy evaluation and planning process. They consented to the process only after it was agreed to conduct separate discussions at affinity group meetings where the voices of these critical opinion leaders would be heard.

The first study group meeting was attended by both strategists and witnesses. After the first meeting, witnesses ceased attendance. Strategists persisted longer in the apparent belief that they could direct the Project toward a more systematic examination of goals, strategies, and tactics. However, after two or three additional meetings with fewer and fewer in attendance, the study group process was abandoned. The strategists were unable to muster enough support for ongoing study meetings. The inability to reach agreement on the need for planning resulted in the failure of the organization to establish long-term goals.

The organizational effect of the tension between contending forces within the Project was particularly manifested in the relationship between the oldest affinity group and the Project. This affinity group was composed of probably the most experienced, nonviolent resistors in the community, with members having had multiple civil disobedience arrests at a variety of public and private war related facilities. In this group's discussions, the question of whether the group should be involved in civil disobedience would not be seriously considered; rather, discussion centered on what it meant to live with civil disobedience as an integral part of a nonviolent lifestyle.

Some members of this group denied that the group was affiliated with the Project, preferring instead to describe themselves as a support group for people in the community who did civil disobedience. One member explained that the group had distanced itself from the Project because of an impatience with its organizing style and an unwillingness to take any direction from Project staff. Some of these strong moral witnesses found even the limited structure of the Honeywell Project confining. However, members of this affinity group still considered themselves part of the Project as individuals, and they did participate in Project-sponsored activities.

People with widely varying views about the issue of the effectiveness of civil disobedience were able to work with one another in the Honeywell Project, but those for whom measurable success was very important did not tend to sustain their activity over the long-term. For these people, the pay-offs necessary to keep them heavily involved for extended periods of time were not there, and they tended to shift their energies to other peace groups which they saw as having the potential for more immediate, tangible results.

So, a sorting process occurred. Strategy-oriented people became active in the Project, spent considerable energy in planning and executing Project activities, and then moved on to some other segment of the peace movement. Witnesses stayed with the Project because of their more long-term view but, as we have pointed out, many of them had little interest in being involved in day-to-day decision making or in planning. The problem for the Project is obvious: it could not maintain the active involvement of individuals from either of these contingents in the nitty-gritty tasks of organizational maintenance over a long period of time.

The continued life of the organization was dependent on a symbiotic relationship between the strategists and the witnesses. Strategists provided their planning and organizational skills only as long as a minimum of their effectiveness needs were met; witnesses provided their bodies and spirits only as long as their moral needs were met and their tolerance for structure not exceeded. There was over time, an ebb and flow of types of organizational activity and degrees of structure depending on the relative prominence of strategists or witnesses in Project leadership positions.

Because continued involvement of witnesses depended on minimal structure, when conflict occurred there was no formal mechanism to assure that mitigating dialogue would take place. Project leadership was caught in a continual struggle to predict and interpret the response of witnesses to decisions that engendered conflict. The challenge was to find creative ways to engage the witnesses in successful dialogue to resolve conflict and advance Project goals and organizational strength.

Although members of the Honeywell Project did strongly disagree with one another over the role of nonviolent civil disobedience, and although at times these conflicts created significant tension within the organization, the supporters of the Project were generally comfortable with the Project's direction and its place in the larger peace community. Few questionnaire respondents, when asked directly if they had any dissatisfaction with the direction, organization, or operation of the Honeywell Project, expressed any criticism. As stated earlier, Project members did not demand that the Project meet all of their personal goals or all of their goals for the peace movement as a whole.

Civil Disobedience and Consciousness

We believe that the special dynamics of civil disobedience and consciousness are best captured by a dialectical imagery of social life. Two factors are critical to an understanding of dialectics in this context. The first is the conception of reality as comprising both positive and negative elements which are inherently contradictory and which coexist without canceling one another. The ability for one to act in opposition or in negation to the status quo exists coterminously with the alienating forces of the status quo but is obscured by the overwhelming power of the positive. If the positive remains unquestioned, the reality "remains unchanged: stable and inert. A positive—for example, an uncontested society, a force without counterforce, a man without dialogue, an unchallenged teacher, a church with no heretics, a single party with no rivals—will be shut up in the indefinite repetition of its own image" (Ellul 1981:295). The second critical factor is the need for human agency, or praxis. Agency is predicated on an understanding of the contradictory nature of the social order. Change occurs by individuals acting upon these perceived contradictions through freedom, choice, and intentionality.

Lieberson (1985:74) states that "irreversible processes . . . occur when a given causal sequence leads to a fundamental alteration of the dependent variable such that it will not respond in the same way to a reversal in the independent variable. In many respects the committing of civil disobedience is such an irreversible process. Civil disobeyers have at one time undertaken an evaluative process that brought into question fundamental social realities. We speculate that the processes of questioning and negative thinking that lead up to one's consideration of and the actual committing of civil disobedience have a lasting effect on the individual, even if the person later denies the efficacy of civil disobedience. They have been willing to place themselves publicly in opposition to the legal system and to take responsibility for the consequences; this fact affects future life decisions and long-term perceptions of the social order.

Members of the Honeywell Project who risked arrest for civil disobedience were saying "no" to the violent, legal-military "yes" of the established order. Those who used civil disobedience as a strategy were willing to act in opposition to some aspects of the system in order to have a measurable effect. Moral witnesses, however, moved beyond a limited instrumental conception of civil disobedience. Their awareness of the depth of the contradictions led them to a more fundamentally contrary stance where effectiveness was seen as something other than immediate results, where means and ends were held as inseparable, and where lasting change was conceived as resulting from the accumulated transformations of many individual consciousnesses.

The "negative" that moral witnesses presented to the system was not only a suspension of militarism but a suspension of the use of violent means to achieve any ends. In this conception, the means by which the given order is questioned has a critical bearing on the new order that will be created. Human initiative, invention, and imagination are of vital importance both in the dialectical process of revealing the contradictions of the existing order and in the development of actions from which a new social order will emerge. If they are not present in the questioning, they will not be present in the new order.

Indeed, one of the strongest self-critiques among witnesses in the Project was a desire to be more creative and imaginative with civil disobedience actions.

The negativity embodied in nonviolent civil disobedience should not be construed as a manifestation of pessimism or an act of despair. For the civil disobeyers we studied, civil disobedience was a potent, active statement of hope. Inherent in their view of civil disobedience was a vision of alternative community, an alternative conceptualization of power, and alternative possibilities for the structure of society.

Civil disobedience constitutes the transformation of a negation into an affirmation of the freedom of the individual to act in a way unprescribed by the established social order. Nonviolent disobeyers engaged in creative actions in which they took responsibility as a way of asking the keepers of the social order to take responsibility for their actions. They opposed force and militarism with creative nonviolent acts of resistance as a way of laying the groundwork for a creative nonviolent resolution to the question of weapons and war.

A dialectical perspective enables one to grasp some of the special qualities of civil disobedience for many members of the Honeywell Project. Civil disobedience is an affirmation of personal liberation and an acknowledgement of responsibility for the human condition. The hope of the moral witness was (and is) that individual acts of negation and opposition will lead toward a fundamental transformation of self, of others, and of society as a whole.

Conclusion

The meaning of civil disobedience for members of the Honeywell Project eludes simple description and explanation. The issue of effectiveness can be expected to be raised by new people who enter the movement and explore alternatives for nonviolent resistance. So, too, can tension be expected to continue among people who have varying perspectives on the meaning of nonviolent resistance in the peace movement and in their own lives.

The moral witnesses are the figures around whom many of the most interesting and provocative questions revolve. What appears on the surface to be a radical disdain for effectiveness becomes, on deeper exploration, a tenacious devotion to radically redefined outcomes.

Their focus on individual transformations of consciousness locates them on a dimension that is incompatible with many others in the peace movement. Although they sometimes perplex and offend their movement colleagues, they also energize and provoke the imagination of persons at various stages of involvement in peace activity. "Witnesses" supplied the project its special character. Decisions about directions of peace organizations that engage in civil disobedience must take into consideration the critical role that moral witnesses play.

Notes

1.   The questionnaire was sent to a disproportionately stratified random sample of people on the Honeywell Project's 2600-member mailing list. Members of the Core Group were especially concerned that there be adequate representation of the views of 200 to 300 identified Project opinion leaders who make up a relatively small proportion of the total mailing list. Questionnaires were sent to 60 of these opinion leaders and to 140 less involved supporters with response rates of 70 percent and 43 percent respectively.

PART IV

PARTICIPANTS:
Mobilization,
Self-conception,
Participation

CHAPTER 14

Historical Generations in Freeze Member Mobilization

H. Edward Price, Jr.

Who were the activists in the Nuclear Weapons Freeze Campaign? What attitudes did they share, and what demographic characteristics or life experiences did they have in common that shaped their viewpoints? Did factors such as their age, education, and gender make them more likely than other citizens to join the campaign? Why?

Previous Theory and Research

Recent sociological work has found a consistent pattern of such characteristics and experiences among the participants and sympathizers of historical and contemporary movements for social change. In the first half of this chapter I will review the theoretical and empirical literature on this question, and in the second half I will present the data from two surveys on freeze activists that I had the opportunity to study as a result of my involvement in the campaign.

Generational Theory

Generational theory presumes that a person's point of view is most profoundly affected by experiences during youth, that is, during the ages of the late teens and early twenties, and tends to remain relatively constant throughout the rest of the life cycle. Under certain circumstances a large segment of a birth cohort will share youthful experiences that are very different from those of older and younger cohorts. This has tended to occur in periods when "the more rapid increases in the numbers of youth going to colleges and universities, which have long been centers of criticism and unrest, provided a critical mass of young students responsive to the quick spread of ideas and easily mobilized for social and political change" (Braungart 1984a; Braungart and Braungart 1986). When such mobilization actually takes place, a youth movement develops, which may come into conflict with segments of the older generation or even with other segments of its own generation. The members of the cohort who have experienced the youth movement form a historical generation which continues to be a force for social change in later years (Braungart 1984a, 1984b; Braungart and Braungart 1980, 1986; Mannheim 1952).

The Generation of the Sixties

An outstanding example is the historical generation that was in college during the 1960s and early 1970s, when the anti-Vietnam war, civil rights, and feminist movements were influential on large campuses (Braungart 1984, 1984b). As a shorthand expression, I will call this the generation of the Sixties. Insofar as they are college-educated and upper middle class, their disproportionate contribution of time and money to collective action is predicted by mainstream sociological theory (McCarthy and Zald 1973, 1977). What is unexpected is that they show a much greater degree of commitment to movements for social change than the upper middle classes of other generations.

Continued Political Participation. Research on former Sixties activists has found them to be liberal to radical in their political identifications and to have a high level of participation in both conventional and protest politics (Braungart and Braungart 1980; Fendrick and Turner 1989; Fendrich and Lovoy 1988; DeMartini 1983; Weiner and Stillman 1979:135-158, 197; McAdam 1988). Studies of the movement against nuclear power have indicated that the individual's decision to participate in such collective action was influenced by internalized values, principles, and ideologies (Ladd et al. 1983; Walsh and Warland 1983), and have shown that such participation was correlated with a personal history of activism and with membership in the generation of the Sixties (Cable et al. 1988). The same has been found in research on the neighborhood movement (Oliver 1983). Other studies have established the facts that rational and moral judgments favoring citizen action (Tyler and McGraw 1983) and prior participation in Democratic party organizations and the anti-Vietnam war movement (Tygart 1987) were characteristic of people involved in the Nuclear Weapons Freeze Campaign.

The Generation of the Sixties and the Freeze. The freeze campaign's political action strategy of petitions, referenda, electioneering, and lobbying was an expression of the American ideal of grassroots democracy. Why were members of the Sixties generation so responsive to this strategy and the ideal behind it? Participation in the institutionalized political system was a major strategy used in the movement against the Vietnam War, alongside violent and nonviolent demonstrations. In the long run, these strategies were successful (Powers 1984; Katz 1986:93–125). The radicals of the Sixties may have become alienated from the American political system at the height of the war, but this was not true of the Sixties cohort as a whole (Hunt 1982). Further, former Sixties activists have been inclined to continue engaging more in conventional political behavior than in demonstrations (Braungart and Braungart 1980; DeMartini 1983; Fendrich and Lovoy 1988). The generation of the Sixties may have been temporarily demobilized and alienated politically by the events of the mid-1970s, such as Watergate, but they did not abandon American political ideas.

Analysts of public opinion data have discovered that citizens who favored the bilateral freeze proposal were also less likely than opponents to fear and distrust the Soviet Union (Feshback and White 1986). According to a survey done for the Public Agenda Foundation (Yankelovich et al. 1984:38–42), 21 percent of eligible voters saw the Soviet threat as minimal. They were the youngest segment of the public defined by a cluster analysis, the most likely to have graduated from college, and the most likely to have professional occupations. This group clearly includes a disproportionate number of people from the Sixties generation. Significantly, the detailed tables in the *Technical Appendix* to the Public Agenda Foundation's report indicated that those aged thirty-one to forty-five in 1984 were even more likely than younger respondents to advocate arms-control agreements and to reject both the build-up of U.S. military strength to deter the Soviet Union and the use of U.S. forces to stop Communist revolutions

(Belsky and Doble 1984). Why? The movement against the war in Vietnam during the late 1960s and early 1970s rejected the anti-Communist ideology and pro-military feelings that were prevalent both during the Cold War of the 1950s and during the late 1970s and the early 1980s. Thus, the Sixties generation tended to develop different attitudes regarding these issues than did people who became politically conscious in earlier and later years.

Gender Differences

A disproportionate number of the participants in the Nuclear Weapons Freeze Campaign were women (Marullo 1989), but those who saw the Soviet threat as minimal in the Public Agenda survey were predominantly male. Women were more numerous among the voters who perceived Communism as a threat to Americans' basic values but did not think that the Soviet Union was a military enemy and who favored avoiding a nuclear arms race (Yankelovich 1984; Belsky and Doble 1984; cf. Goertzel 1983). Another review of public opinion poll data further revealed that women were more inclined than men to accept total nuclear disarmament and to reject war as a means of settling differences (Smith 1984).

Methods and Results

As a participant observer at the local, state, and national levels of the Nuclear Weapons Freeze Campaign, I was able to do two surveys that can be used to test the predictions and replicate the findings of the sociological work reviewed above. The first survey was done in 1985 of the members of my local freeze group, and the second was done in 1987 of the National Committee of the Freeze Campaign. The findings from both surveys support generational theory and confirm the outcome of previous research.

Membership in a Local Freeze Group

Many activists in the Nuclear Weapons Freeze Campaign were drawn directly from the national organizations that formed the original freeze coalition in the early 1980s, but increasingly, mobilization became centered in spontaneously formed, autonomous local groups, which were guided by the campaign's local organizers' mailings. The local freeze group that served as the basis of this study was founded at the end of 1982 in Jackson County, North Carolina. Jackson County is located in the mountainous western part of the state. The county seat, Sylva, is a small mercantile and industrial center, and the county is also the site of Western Carolina University, a regional campus of the University of North Carolina.

Formation of the Group.   The local freeze group was established by participants in a Fall 1982 campus conference on the nuclear arms race, which was one of many sponsored at colleges across the country by the Union of Concerned Scientists. This conference had brought together experts from both the campus and the local community to give panel presentations on aspects of the nuclear issue.

The founders of the freeze group, nearly all of whom were professional men and women, constituted themselves as a steering committee. General membership in the group was open to the public, with annual dues of ten dollars for an individual or fifteen dollars for a family. The steering committee mobilized the members through a telephone tree and periodic newsletters, which included reprints of articles from national magazines. An education committee offered books and pamphlets on the issues and organized regular educational meetings for members and potential members. The group's leaders also held occasional potluck dinners or house parties to promote social solidarity among the members.

Method of Research.   In the Summer of 1985 the steering committee agreed to help me to do a survey of the members, both for use in planning the future of the group and for my own sociological work. The questionnaire that was mailed to the locally resident members included attitude items on nuclear arms control and related political issues, attitudinal and behavioral items about the local freeze group and its activities, background and demographic items, and items regarding media attention. There were eighty-one questions. Most were closed-ended, but there were some opportunities for open-ended responses. Ninety-nine questionnaires were distributed, and as a result of follow-up telephone calls, seventy-one were returned in time to be included in the data analysis.

Characteristics of the Members.   Most of the respondents in my survey of the local group were clearly from the generation of the Sixties. Fifty-six percent were between the ages of thirty-five and forty-four in 1985. The same percentage had a postgraduate degree, and 90 percent had at least a bachelor's degree. Furthermore, nearly two-thirds of the respondents were female, although women were not as large a majority of the actual members of the group.

Another notable characteristic of the respondents was that they were not highly integrated into the local community. Only 6 percent grew up in the county, and a majority were from out of state. Sixty-two percent had lived in the county for less than ten years. Half were active in no other local clubs or organizations, and 70 percent did not attend religious services regularly.

What incentives did they have for joining the freeze group? Wilson (1973) distinguishes three types of incentives for participation in such a group: material, purposive, and solidary. Certainly the most important incentives that they perceived were purposive—to achieve the goals of the group. First, they saw collective action as necessary (Fireman and Gamson 1979). Ninety-four percent doubted that the Strategic Arms Reduction Talks then underway in Geneva would reverse the arms race. Second, they believed that the freeze campaign presented them with an opportunity for collective action that would be effective (Fireman and Gamson 1979). Its goal was seen as instrumental in reducing the chances that a nuclear war would occur by three-fourths of the respondents, and all agreed that a freeze was needed during the negotiations. They also continued to believe in the possibility of attaining the goal of a freeze through collective action: 83 percent denied that the movement had been defeated, but three-quarters believed that achieving a freeze would require the election of a new president and 60 percent felt it would require civil disobedience. Most importantly, 75 percent thought that there was something they could do to contribute to the success of the campaign. Even larger percentages felt that the local group's petitions and letters to public officials were increasing the movement's chances of success.

Clearly, the viewpoint of the respondents was aligned with the ideology of the freeze campaign (Snow et al. 1986). To what extent that was true before they joined the local group is unknown, but 55 percent indicated that they had learned a great deal about the issues from the group's meetings and literature. There was a correlation of .60

between respondent's participation in the group's activities and how much they thought they had learned about the issues from the group (cf. Sandman and Valenti 1986).

In addition to the purposive incentives for joining the local group, there were solidary or social incentives. As is usually the case in social movements (Snow et al. 1980), recruitment took place primarily through existing networks. Seventy percent of the respondents were invited to the first meeting they attended by a relative or friend, and 53 percent were asked by a relative or friend to become members. Solidary incentives for participation continued after they had joined: 80 percent felt that the group had brought like-minded people together in friendship, and three-quarters indicated that they had enjoyed this. Such incentives were of course most available to those who were most involved in the group's activities, and the gamma correlation of participation with enjoyment was .60.

THE NATIONAL COMMITTEE AS REPRESENTATIVES OF THE MEMBERSHIP

The Jackson County freeze group may or may not be typical of local groups around the country. Fortunately, I had a chance to study what amounted to a national "sample" of freeze activists as a consequence of volunteering to be the North Carolina member of the National Committee of the Nuclear Weapons Freeze Campaign beginning in 1985. In that year the National Committee was reconstituted to reduce the number of members representing the national organizations that had formed the original freeze coalition and to grant each state freeze organization the right to select its own member. In the merger with SANE in 1987, the National Committee became half of the new board of directors of SANE/Freeze.

Method of Research. At the first meeting of the new board in June of that year I distributed a questionnaire to all of its members. That survey instrument consisted of two pages of open-ended items concerning the respondent's socioeconomic background, organizational and resistance activity in social movements, and political identification. I later followed up with two mail-outs of the questionnaire to improve the response rate. Forty-three of the fifty freeze members of the board returned completed questionnaires.

Results.   As was true of the Jackson County freeze group, the most striking things about the freeze board members were their age and educational distributions. Seventy-two percent of the respondents were born during the ten years following World War II, and the median year of birth was 1947. Eighty-one percent had at least a bachelor's degree, and 40 percent also had master's or Ph.D. degrees. Again, they would have been college or university students during the late 1960s and early 1970s, at the time of the anti-Vietnam war movement and other campus protests. (Under the organization's affirmative action rules, half of the members of the board were required to be women, so the gender distribution is artificially constrained.)

Did they have a background of political activism? The questionnaire asked them to list the social movement organizations in which they had been volunteers. In response, nearly all noted at least one in addition to SANE/Freeze and its state and local affiliates, and four of the six who had not been volunteers were full-time career staff employees in such an organization. The median number of organizations listed was five. Sixty-five percent of the respondents included peace groups other than SANE/Freeze. Twenty-one percent mentioned their volunteer work in Vietnam era antiwar organizations or noted their resistance actions during that period, and no doubt more of the respondents were actually involved to some extent in the anti-Vietnam war movement (cf. Weiner and Stillman 1979:135-158). Furthermore, 55 percent had worked as volunteers for the Democratic party.

However, they were not typical of Democratic party voters in their political orientations. Only 22 percent simply called themselves liberals in their answers to an open-ended question on their preferred political label. A more popular term was "progressive," which was chosen by 37 percent. This is a term commonly used in the peace and justice community, and it refers to adherence to movements for social change. A total of 68 percent of the respondents chose this and other leftist self-identifications, including 12 percent who said they were socialists. Another indication of the board members' politics came in a straw poll of their presidential preferences that was conducted at the end of their meeting in January 1988: nearly all of those present personally favored Jesse Jackson, even though the board refused to endorse him officially.

Even more distinctively, 53 percent of the respondents to my questionnaire indicated that they considered themselves to be pacifists.

Notably, all of the plain liberals did so. Pacifist identification was related to the respondent's gender: 60 percent of the women as compared with 40 percent of the men accepted the term.

The values of the respondents were reflected in their careers as well as in their politics. Fifty-eight percent were "social movement professionals" (McCarthy and Zaid 1973), including staff employees and former employees of social movement organizations, progressive foundations, and politicians, as well as independent political consultants whose clients were progressive organizations. On the other hand, only 6 percent of the freeze board were employed by profit-making corporations, and some of these were in manual jobs. A similar pattern of careers outside the corporate establishment has been found in studies of former activists of the Sixties (Braungart 1980; DeMartini 1983; Weiner and Stillman 1979:25).

Conclusion

Can SANE/Freeze count on the commitment of the members of the Sixties generation in the future? Only if political events stimulate their belief in the necessity and opportunity for citizen action to promote peace and disarmament (Fireman and Gamson 1979). If the Bush Administration continues to emphasize the use of international negotiations to achieve such goals, but does not encourage the contributions of popular movements, many former or potential activists may decide not to make any efforts of their own (cf. Boyer 1984). SANE/Freeze President William Sloan Coffin and other peace movement leaders are correct in seeking to maintain commitment by stressing the minimal effects of the INF treaty and the need to continue the grassroots political pressure for further arms reductions.

On the other hand, if the Bush Administration backs away from arms control and Mikhail Gorbachev succeeds in his effort to make the Soviet Union seem less threatening, organizations such as SANE/Freeze may be able to extend their appeal beyond the Sixties generation, to people who were hesitant about the freeze campaign because of their preconceptions regarding the Communists. Coffin, with his age, his personal involvement in citizen diplomacy in Russia, and his earlier Cold War service in the CIA, seems to be an ideal spokesman for the message that the U.S. can cooperate with the Soviet Union to achieve common security.

At the local level, the Sixties generation may themselves create an obstacle to the expansion of participation in the peace movement. If the activists are unable to reach beyond existing friendship networks of people with similar ages and values, local groups can stagnate. This has been called "old timers' disease" (Ayvazian 1986). Conscious efforts must be made to reach out to new groups and to welcome newcomers.

CHAPTER 15

Becoming a Peace Activist: A Life Course Perspective

JAMES HANNON

One of the central and enduring topics in the study of social movements is the motivation of movement participants, particularly movement activists who commit a great deal of time and effort to movement activities. This has been an especially compelling question when asked of conscience-constituents, such as activists in peace movements, who do not stand to personally benefit in any specialized way from the achievement of movement goals.

Recent research gives evidence of a renewed interest in the gradual development of an activist identity and the process of commitment to a particular movement.[1] In a study of micromobilization within several movements, Snow and his colleagues (1986) examine the processes of frame-bridging and frame-amplification whereby movement organizers seek to align the activities and ideology of a movement organization with the values, interests, and beliefs of bystanders and adherents as well as current members (see also Snow and Benford 1988). Ferree and Miller (1985) argue that a movement's ideology is an ongoing social process and that individual commitment to a movement is based on how well that ideology continues to resonate with the individual's values and personal identity.

The clear implication of this and related research (Marullo 1988; Oliver 1983) is that the peace movement must seek to align movement culture and the movement's public persona with the values and personal identities of supporters and bystanders if it is to mobilize a greater number to more active participation. Ferree and Miller

(1985:41) point to another task in the mobilization of peace activists—
the only candidates for mobilization into a peace movement organization are those individuals who have already developed values compatible with the basic message of that organization as well as a sense of
personal efficacy and an identity as a potential activist. An understanding of how contemporary peace activists developed these attributes
can highlight the educational and other interventions that expand the
pool of supporters from which the peace movement recruits activists.

The issue is essentially one of personal development in the context
of political, moral, and religious socialization. One approach to the
study of such development is life course analysis. This chapter takes a
life course approach to the topical life histories of twenty-one peace
activists who have been among the informal leaders of the Boston-area
Pledge of Resistance. The topical life histories have been constructed
from in-depth interviews and from the author's field research as a par-
ticipant-observer.

The Boston-area Pledge
of Resistance

The Boston-area Pledge of Resistance is an autonomous local within
the national network of the Pledge of Resistance. The Pledge, as it is
called, has operated since 1984 as a national peace movement organization opposed to U.S. military involvement in Central America.
Pledge members have organized a variety of civil disobedience direct
actions that have led to the arrest of thousands of participants.

The Boston-area Pledge has been one of the most active local
groups, starting with an occupation of the Federal Office Building in
Boston on May 7, 1985, in protest of President Reagan's declaration of
a trade embargo against Nicaragua. This action led to the arrest of over
five hundred participants. Over the next two years, more than three
thousand members of the Boston Pledge, organized in nearly two hundred affinity groups, conducted a series of direct action protests, as
well as numerous and various forms of educational, theatrical, direct
service, lobbying, and fund-raising activities designed to assist local
groups in Central America and Central American refugees in the Boston area.

The Boston Pledge began to disintegrate as a vital network in 1987 and by the end of 1988 existed only as an elaborate phone-tree to be reactivated in the event of a significant escalation of U.S. military involvement in Central America. However, for Pledge activists the decline of the Pledge as a vital network has not meant the end of their involvement in the peace movement. All of my informants have long-term commitments to various specialized movements within the larger peace movement and they have continued these activities, often within the same affinity groups that were active components of the Pledge network.

Characteristics of the Sample

I selected my informants from two strata within the Pledge. Based on my own observation of the informal power structure of this collectivist organization, I chose ten of the most influential members of the coordinating committee, an all-volunteer, self-selected core group who met on a weekly basis during the most active period in the life of the Pledge. The coordinators set the agenda for spokes meetings, the deliberative body of the Boston Pledge, and provided the facilitators for the tortuous process of consensus decision making, thus functioning as an executive committee.

The spokes who attended spokes meetings were spokespersons for their affinity groups. All Pledge members were encouraged to attend spokes meetings, which were occasions of celebration and solidarity building as well as decision making. However, only the designated spoke was allowed to participate in the final stage of policy decisions, i.e., to endorse, amend, or block consensus in regard to a specific proposal.

Many affinity groups rotated the spoke's responsibility among group members; others had a designated spoke who regularly attended the spokes meetings. For this research, I utilized a list of contact persons for each affinity group the Boston Pledge compiled in June 1985. These contact persons were either designated spokes or affinity group members who had attended the spokes meeting prior to the establishment of the contact list. I chose a random sample of ten spokes from this contact list of 176 affinity groups. Eight of the ten agreed to interviews. I replaced the two who were unavailable with the next name on the list.[2]

The total sample consisted of twenty-one white, native-born U.S. citizens, of whom thirteen were women and eight were men. They ranged in age from twenty-seven to seventy. The median age was thirty- eight. All twenty-one were college educated and all but one were college graduates. They attended and graduated from some of the nation's most prestigious colleges and universities. Ten had graduate degrees.

Fourteen were from Protestant families; four from Jewish and three from Catholic families. Only three were natives of the Boston area. Nine of the other eighteen were from the East Coast. The rest were evenly distributed as to origin among the West, South, and Midwest. Nine were from politically conservative families; seven were from families of liberal political opinion, and the families of the other five were apolitical or very centrist. Not one could be called a "red diaper baby."

Their class status was generally middle class. However, all but six were from upper-middle-class or upper-class families.Consequently, most were less affluent than their family of origin. For most, their downward mobility has been a conscious choice as part of a chosen lifestyle. Although many have professional careers, they organized their work life so that it was consistent with their political commitments and/or provided sufficient time for political activities. Participation in the Pledge was one aspect of a lifestyle that was shaped around political commitments.

The Structural-Developmental Paradigm

The analysis of the life histories is informed by theories of psychosocial, moral, and faith development generated within the structural-developmental paradigm (Erikson 1963, 1968, 1975; Kohlberg 1969, 1973; Fowler 1981; Gilligan 1982). These theories focus on life crises as the critical moments in the development of moral and religious reasoning. In the resolution of these crises, individuals draw upon previous understandings of the world, which are acquired through the typical agencies of socialization, such as family, church, and schools. When these previous understandings are inadequate for resolving a particular crisis, the individual is open to influence from the environment and may be enabled to advance to a higher stage of moral reasoning (Kohlberg 1973) and faith development (Fowler 1981).

The identity crisis, the fifth of Erikson's (1963) eight crises of psychosocial development, is central to the development of political commitments. It is typically a crisis of adolescence. Erikson describes the adolescent mind as "an ideological mind" and suggests that it is "the ideological outlook of a society that speaks most clearly to the adolescent who is eager to be affirmed by his peers, and is ready to be confirmed by rituals, creeds, and programs which at the same time define what is evil, uncanny, and inimical" (1963:263).

The timing of the identity crisis corresponds for many individuals with the development of what Kohlberg has characterized as postconventional moral reasoning, more specifically, a transition from Kohlberg's stage four, social order reasoning, to stage five, social contract reasoning. In the terms of Fowler's stages of faith development, the resolution of the identity crisis and the development of postconventional moral reasoning often coincide with a transition from stage three, synthetic/conventional faith, to stage four, individuative/reflective faith.

These developmental theories underscore the significance of adolescence and the adolescent setting in the adoption of nonconventional political commitments and the development of an activist identity. They also suggest the importance of religious and political socialization in childhood. Such socialization provides the foundation upon which the individual adolescent draws in negotiating a new but not autochthonous identity at the time of the identity crisis.

Dimensions of Development

The life histories of Pledge activists resonate with the concepts of developmental stages and life crises that are central to structural- developmental theories. Four common themes emerge from these life histories. They are not universal experiences but each is shared by a majority and they represent collectively an ideal-typical pattern of development. In general terms these four common themes are:

1. Religious socialization, typically in childhood, in the context of a comfortable and supportive faith community.

2. A radicalizing experience as a college student—in terms of classes, internships, extracurricular activities, or exposure to persua-

sive fellow students in a variety of settings. Whatever the form of the experience, it includes exposure to a radical critique of the social system of the U.S., particularly in terms of economic injustice, racial and gender discrimination, militarism, and imperialism.

3. The influence of one or more sponsors who assist the individual's reconstruction of personal identity as he or she resolves the crisis engendered by the exposure to a radical critique and new world views and/or by the transition to a new role.

4. Participation in a network of like-minded peers, particularly at the time of the reconstruction of personal identity, but also, in a less intense manner, over the life course.

RELIGIOUS SOCIALIZATION

The influence of religious socialization has operated in one or more of the following ways in the lives of my informants.

Visionary Influence.   Religious ideas and values provide a utopian vision of the just society. To the degree that the society falls short of this vision, the individual who has internalized this vision has the raw material for constructing radical political commitments.

Cheyenne, a woman in her mid-thirties, was the charismatic leader of the Boston Pledge during the period of greatest activity. She described the importance of the moral orientation she received in church.

> (I) was raised Catholic, which had a very significant effect on my development. Although I no longer feel any connection to Catholicism as a religion, it was where my worldview was formed, through the stories and the experience of being in church. It was like—this is the way the world is supposed to be and this is the way people are supposed to be with one another.

Countercultural Influence.   In the United States, religious communities constitute one of the areas most nurturant of alternative cultures because they enjoy protection from the state and retain a relative autonomy from the hegemonic ideology of state institutions (see Hannon 1984; Williams 1973).

Even in churches that do not emphasize the visionary and prophetic elements of Judeo-Christian teaching, the traditions of the denomination often shape the corporate culture in directions that are alternative to the mainstream culture. This corporate culture may be conformist in all but a few areas, but the latter may be quite important in the formation of an individual's social consciousness.

Caroline was a recently ordained minister in her early forties and the spoke of an affinity group based at a divinity school in a Boston suburb. As a young reporter in Charlotte, North Carolina, in the mid-1960s, she was troubled by the segregation of the local churches within her own denomination, the Presbyterian Church in the United States. By joining an American Baptist congregation in Charlotte, Caroline placed herself in a church where congregational polity and a determined minister had combined to produce an integrated environment in the midst of a segregated society. Later, when she was informally sanctioned by the journalism community for a friendship with an African-American man, this congregation gave her strong support. Her commitment to church and civil rights, and a willingness to "rock the boat" in the future were all strengthened by the integrationist counterculture of that church.

Communitarian Influence. The subjective experience of religious community is as important as the content of religious teachings. If one's first experiences as a member of a community are positive, one is more likely to be open to new groups as potentially rewarding communities later in life. Even more than a condition of openness, the desire to replicate the experience of a supportive and purposeful community can also motivate individuals to seek political organizations that will perform the same function as the religious communities of their youth.

Cheyenne's positive experience of community in her parish church was lost when she could no longer accept Church teaching. At the age of twenty-four she left her job as a high school English teacher and traveled around the country, seeking a home in one of the alternative communities established in the 1960s and 1970s. Finally, in what she described as "*the* life-changing experience for me," she attended a two-week training program at the Movement for a New Society headquarters in Philadelphia. "I walked into MNS and in two weeks knew I wanted to spend the rest of my life working with those kinds of people. It was like coming home and all of a sudden having the words."

Political Influence. Religious communities are important locations for moral education and for the development of a sense of "how the world should be." Less frequently, they are also the setting for a more specific political education that emphasizes the shortcomings of the political order and proposes an agenda for social reform. For members of the traditional peace churches or liberal denominations that maintain a critical stance toward the state and hegemonic ideologies, the religious community is a school for radicals, as well as the source of a more general prophetic impulse.

Such a radical political agenda is also provided by quasi-religious philosophies such as co-counseling, or reevaluation counseling (RC). David, the spoke for the Democractic Socialists of America affinity group, was in his early twenties. He began to develop his radical potential as a seven-year-old practitioner of RC.

> "Co-counseling has a lot of very interesting ideas. . . . It has strong opinions about oppression, and it validates peoples' experiences of oppression. . . . And although I haven't done RC in quite a while, that was sort of an early exposure to what is oppression. . . . It's not an abstraction, it's something that a seven-year-old can very easily deal with . . . it talks about oppression as being a result of and part of people's emotional make-up and part of the way that people work, and that you have to deal with it on a personal basis."

College as a Developmental Setting

Matriculation at a college or university, particularly as a resident student, is a propitious moment for the development of a new identity, particularly in terms of political activism (see Coles 1969). Regardless of the historical period, college matriculation is a major step in the process of individuation, coinciding with the achievement of adult status, legally conferred at the age of eighteen. As in the case of military service, college students in residence at the college have truly left home, usually for the first time. For many, it is also a final break from their families of origin in terms of primary residence.

After matriculation the primary locus for students' political socialization is likely to switch from family to campus community. Prior to matriculation, the political beliefs and prejudices of one's family are usually reinforced by neighborhood, church, and school. At college many students are exposed for the first time to peers and authority figures who hold political views radically different from those of the students' parents. For some of the Pledge activists, this experience was an intellectual crisis, an exposure to new information and a critical perspective that challenged radically the political values of their families and communities.

Bill, a housing policy analyst and activist in the sanctuary movement as well as the Pledge, was in his early fifties. He grew up in a fundamentalist and politically conservative household in North Carolina and experienced a major developmental crisis at North Carolina State in the 1950s.

> I can remember taking a contemporary issues course, where all of us had a subscription to the *New York Times* . . . and we were dealing with a lot of stuff . . . the McCarthy hearings . . . a lot of material about that, about what an outrage that was to civil liberties. I feel really lucky. I can't remember the guy's name who was teaching that course but it seemed real clear that that was just pretty outrageous stuff that was going on.

For Elizabeth, a Quaker activist and college administrator in her late fifties, matriculation at Bryn Mawr enabled her to break from the political conservatism of her family.

> My political formation was there. I took political science as a freshman and became a Democrat. . . . This was a secret conversion. (Professor) David Bachrach talked to us about labor conditions at the A&P supermarket chain. Questions were raised that had never been spoken about at all [in her family]. . . . So when Stevenson ran for the first time I rooted passionately for him. . . . My emergence as owner of my own thoughts was in school.

The radical experience of college was not limited to the classroom. For many, the greater influence was the commitment to liberal values within a college community and the exposure to a way of life quite different from that of their family and hometown. For Ellen, an early commitment to gospel values led to matriculation at Meredith College, a Methodist women's college, where the social justice dimension of the gospels was consistently emphasized.

Meredith was a wonderful place for me because it reinforced a kind of liberal possibility. . . . It was a good environment, a supportive environment for that. . . . We were all sort of working-class, lower-middle-class simple people but whenever they had a speaker or whenever they had a play or concert there, it was open to everyone in Raleigh and black people could come and didn't have to sit in the balcony and I was seeing that, that you could live differently in the midst of all this [segregation].

College also provides the opportunity for experiences outside the classroom that are difficult to obtain in other settings. For Susan, a program in her junior year took her to Guatemala where she spent six months, including three months in a remote Indian village where she was the only one who spoke English. Her exposure to the hardships of village life and the genocidal campaign of Guatemala's military government proved to be a life-altering experience.

Intervention by a Sponsor

A crisis of some sort is the harbinger of development to a more mature stage of faith or moral reasoning. However, the individual in the process of transition is at risk for an unsuccessful resolution of the crisis in the form of regression or despair which can lead to a variety of maladaptive behaviors. Gilligan emphasizes these risks when she describes a life crisis as "a dangerous opportunity for growth, a turning-point for better or worse" (1982:108).

In trying to resolve crises in the direction of growth, individuals, particularly adolescents, benefit from the intervention of a sponsor.[3] For Cheyenne, an important sponsor was her professor of education at Rutgers who intervened to assist her during her identity crisis which coincided with her exposure to radical critiques of the educational system.

Her first reaction to these radical books was discouragment and fear that she would never be able to work effectively in educational institutions designed for social reproduction. At this point she was in danger of the role diffusion and despair that Erikson describes as the risk of the identity crisis. However, Cheyenne was challenged by her professor to undertake a rigorous analysis of the progressive possibilities for educators in the 1970s. She recalls the paper that she wrote as a result of a summer's intensive study. "It was, it still is, the most exciting thing I ever wrote. . . . It's the emotional and intellectual process I went through as I read each one of those books. . . . Finally, I came to a place of knowing that . . . I'll always be a teacher and I know I have to find ways to teach the things that have change in them."

Teachers and clergy are particularly likely to function as sponsors because of the nature of their positions and because of self-selection to professions that provide the opportunity for being a nurturant sponsor. Nevertheless, sponsors appeared in a variety of roles for my informants, including colleagues, supervisors, parents, fellow students, and the parents of fellow students.

These sponsors generally shared several attributes. These included as unusual, occasionally persistent interest in the lives of those they assisted, superior knowledge of the intellectual and emotional issues central to the developmental crisis, and a balance between empathic support for the difficulties experienced by those in developmental transition and a demand that these individuals not shrink from the self-reflection, study, and other personal challenges that were required for successful development. In every case the sponsor was older than my informant, although the age difference varied from two years in the case of fellow students and colleagues to forty years in the case of one student-teacher relationship.

In a few cases, sponsors functioned as such without the direct intervention typical of the majority of cases. For example, some professors and ministers operated as sponsors without full awareness of their effects on students and parishioners. Leaders of peace movement organizations exercised the influence of sponsors by serving as role models for those who were struggling to determine whether it was possible to live happily in attunement with their new information and world views. In this sense, public figures and authors such as Daniel Berrigan and Barbara Deming were also identified as sponsors.

PARTICIPATION IN GROUPS AND NETWORKS OF LIKEMINDED PEERS

Much of the sociological literature on conversion emphasizes the importance for converts of finding a role within a community of the converted if they are to complete a conversion process and maintain a commitment to the new philosophy, religion, and/or movement

(Lofland 1978). For some Pledge activists, the personal changes in identity and world view that accompanied their initial involvement in political activity constituted a true conversion. For others, becoming a peace activist was a gradual development that included no dramatic transformations. Regardless of the degree of personal transformation involved in their first efforts as political activists, participation in a group committed to social change efforts was an important dimension in the maintenance of their activist identities and the broadening and deepening of their political commitments.

For young adults who have always "felt different" because of their interests in social change efforts, participation in a group of fellow activists is a reassuring experience. They no longer feel isolated and unsure whether their interests are some sort of madness. This was one of the important features of Cheyenne's participation with Movement for a New Society, where "it was like coming home and suddenly having the words," i.e., a basis of communication with others who would understand and validate her "heartfelt sense that there was something wrong with the world."

The influence of peers at a college campus and the close proximity of those peers makes college an optimal environment for the development of such peer groups. Following her exposure to a Marxist analysis in the classroom, Alice's participation in such a peer group at Brown simultaneously strengthened and broadened her political commitment in a direction that led her toward a career as a feminist peace activist.

> In my last year of college women's liberation movement stuff . . . blossomed and the group of women I got involved with to do political work was a group of socialist women and I think had they only been feminists I probably wouldn't have gotten involved with them but since they were also left-thinking, and that was sort of where the activism was, that propelled me into feminism.

For other Pledge activists, important peer groups and networks have included formal organizations such as the Democratic Socialists of America, Clergy and Laity Concerned, Amnesty International, anti-nuclear groups such as New England's Clamshell Alliance, and a variety of affinity groups organized around particular issues such as women's rights, gay and lesbian rights, and environmental issues. In

addition to these groups and networks formally committed to social change, other important peer groups include housing collectives, collegial networks, and religious fellowships—even at the level of an entire congregation in the case of Quaker meetings and other peace churches.

Political activists of any age are subject to discouragement and burnout. Participation in a peer group, or affinity group, is often the most effective means of establishing mutual support in the face of defeats and the inevitable questions concerning the merit of political work which requires so much personal and familial scarifice. The mutual support may be more than emotional. For example, several Pledge activists describe collective living arrangements as shaping their political development because of the economic flexibility they encourage as well as the mutual socialization and support.

Political networks as well as affinity groups also contributed to the broadening of political commitments. In the process of intragroup and intergroup interactions, individual commitments evolved to include a larger set of issues and a holistic appraisal of the interconnectedness of these issues. This is the most important political legacy of antinuclear networks, e.g., the Clamshell Alliance, which united affinity groups with dissimilar styles and political identities.

Another value of affinity groups is that they constitute one form of the preexisting networks that have been identified as critically important in the mobilization of participants into social movements (Oberschall 1973; Freeman, 1975).[4] Movement organizers within the Pledge network are fully aware of the importance of such groups. They view the affinity group structure as critical to the success of the Pledge, however short-lived, and consider the creation of many of the Pledge's affinity groups to be among the Pledge's most important accomplishments.

Conclusions and Implications

The small sample size and the sample characteristics set limits on the generalizability of these findings. For example, it is obvious that there are activists in the peace movement who developed the relevant commitments and identity without attending college. Nevertheless, there are some implications to be drawn from the life histories of these

Pledge activists who are representative of at least one important segment of the peace movement.

Adolescence and young adulthood were the critical periods in their development as peace activists. Churches and colleges were important settings for that development. Therefore, the peace movement should make major commitments to these settings. In one sense, this has always been the case—peace movements recruit and program heavily in churches and colleges. However, long-range planning could focus more on the quality of the young adult's experience in those settings. For example, peace studies programs on many college campuses now offer students an intellectual home as well as peers who share their interests. Such academic programs often allow and may even require student participation in an internship with a peace-related organization. A peace studies program also signifies to the campus and larger community that a concern with peace issues and a commitment to social change is not deviant. The identity of peace activist is easier to acquire and maintain in such a setting.

Sponsors played an important role in the development of an activist identity. Adults in a variety of settings can serve as sponsors. However, college provides an unequaled possibility for the sponsor relationship. This possibility extends to campus ministers, academic staff, and internship supervisors, but faculty have the best opportunity to get to know at least some of their students in classes, during office hours, and at campus events. Over the course of even one semester and in the context of coursework, a professor can act as sponsor for a student who is negotiating an identity crisis or a postpsychic numbing emotional crisis.

For many college faculty, the concept of sponsorship may create some anxiety. The professional role encourages an emotional distance from students. In some academic institutions, to be nurturant is to be marginal and may be damaging to one's career. Nevertheless, there are structured opportunities that enhance the possibility of empowering students in a nurturant fashion. In part, this is a cultural struggle within the university. Faculty who have a commitment to empowering students as potential activists empower themselves by joining together in programs that evaluate positively close collaboration between faculty and students.

If college is an important setting for the development of peace activists, then the peace movement should also advocate policies that in-

crease access to college education for those currently excluded for financial reasons. Demands can be made at the federal level for an increase in student loan programs. In an era of cutbacks at state universities, state legislatures can be lobbied to resist raising tuitions and to increase scholarship programs for state residents. The tendency of state legislatures to cut educational budgets by raising nonresident tuitions should also be resisted because the experience of being a college student in residence at the campus seems particularly important in promoting individuation. Diverse student bodies also increase exposure to different philosophies and lifestyles, thus providing the raw material for personal changes as well as peer networks that can promote more lasting transformations.

Finally, the development of an activist identity requires experience of participation in some form of social movement organization. The heuristic value of participation underlines the importance of movement organizing in various settings where potential activists live and work. Therefore, the success of particular movement organizations and strategies should be evaluated not strictly in terms of goal attainment but also in terms of how many participants are mobilized, educated on the issues, and encouraged to join future social change efforts.

Acknowledgments

This research was supported by a grant from the Clark University Faculty Development Fund. I thank Shelly Tenenbaum, Robert J.S. Ross, James Castonguay, and the editors for their assistance and comments on an earlier draft.

Notes

1.   These are also the foci of the commitment models of movement participation that were generated in the arly 1970s (Gerlach and Hine 1970; Turner and Killian 1987; Wilson 1973). In part, this recent return to the study of commitment processes has resulted from dissatisfaction with the overly rationalistic assumptions of the collective action model that is central to resource-mobilization theories of movement participation (McCarthy and Zald 1973, 1977; Oberschall 1973). For a critique of the collective action paradigm and resource mobilization theories, see Oliver (1983) and Cohen (1985).

2. The twenty-first informant is the spouse of one of the coordinators and was interviewed at the same time as her husband. She was also a designated spoke for her affinity group.

3. Although "mentor" is a more familiar term, Fowler (1981:287), following Erikson, uses the term "sponsor" "in the context of preparation of children and adults for Christian baptism and church membership." Although progression to a more mature stage of moral or faith development does not share all the characteristics of conversion (see Lofland 1978; Lofland and Skonovd 1981; Snow and Machalak 1983), they are often fairly similar phenomena in regard to issues of personal identity and the adoption of new roles (see Gordon 1974; Jones 1978; Shaffir 1978).

4. In the sociological literature, mobilization is often equated implicitly with recruitment. It is more useful to consider mobilization as divided into three parts: recruitment, deployment, and retention. Affinity groups are beneficial in recruitment but may be even more important in deployment and retention. Interpersonal solidarity bonds promote faithful attendance at movement activities, particularly at events that involve some personal risk. Also, the pleasure associated with affinity group participation and the group's identity as an activist collective are likely to prolong individual and group participation in the activities of a larger movement.

CHAPTER 16

Self-conceptions of Peace Activists

Carmen Knudson-Ptacek

Previous studies of the personal lives of people involved in political action have shown a relationship between images of self and images of the ideal society (Elms 1986; Erikson 1975; Keniston 1968; Stewart and Healy 1986). The purpose of this chapter is to determine how peace activists view themselves and their relationships to the social world and how those perceptions are translated into social action.

Peace activists were interviewed about themselves, their families, and the social world. All were involved with PEACE—a group dedicated to changing the way people think about war. (The name of the group has been changed to protect the anonymity of the respondents.) According to Lofland, Colwell, and Johnson's typology (Chapter 6) they would be considered transcenders. This group was particularly interesting to me because they were mainstream Americans who were careful to define themselves as an educational organization, not a protest group. Yet there was something different about how they viewed the world and why they believed they could change a social pattern of warring that has existed for centuries.

The activists could be distinguished from the nonactivists in the study through their language, which expressed a view of self that was connected to others at the public and private levels. This way of viewing the self contrasted with the individualistic stance held by most Americans (Bellah et al. 1985; Clecak 1983; Etzioni 1983). This chapter explores (1) how the connected self was constructed among PEACE activists, (2) how connection was experienced by various types of PEACE activists, and (3) how the connected self was translated into social action.

Self and Society

According to Mead (1934) the self develops as an individual distinguishes him- or herself as an object interacting with others and stores perceptions about the nature of self and the social world. The self, for purposes of this study, was defined as stored images about the nature of one's relationship to others which give meaning to current behavior. It includes three concurrent aspects: images of oneself, images of the rest of the social world, and images of how one is linked to it. Perceptions of how one is separate from and connected to others are particularly salient (Cohler and Geyer 1982; Kegan 1982).

Recent studies of female development suggest that women tend to perceive themselves as being more connected to others than do most men (Belenky, Clinchy, Goldberger, and Tarule 1986; Lyons 1983; Gilligan 1982). Gilligan and Lyons related the connected view of self to an ethic of care and responsibility that resolves moral dilemmas by determining what will make the best outcome for all. They contrasted the connected morality with a more separated ethic emphasizing justice and the balancing of individual rights and resolving of moral dilemmas on the basis of principle (see Kolberg 1969). This study relates the connected view of self to a morality of care and predispositions to cooperative behavior regardless of gender.

Social movements are often collective attempts to resolve moral problems by integrating images of self and society. Just as religion provides a shared moral code (Kehoe 1986), efforts to change society proselytize a new moral ideal. When perceptions of self and society are not parallel, disillusionment and anomie occur. When feelings of disillusionment and lack of meaning are not accompanied by a perception that society can be changed, people may turn to religion to resolve their dilemmas (Lofland 1985; Tipton 1982).

For most activists in earlier studies, commitment to peace work shifted almost every aspect of their lives, including home, work, religion, and ethics. Sustained activity became embedded in a larger belief system consistent with its principles, and influenced the perspectives of other family members (Frank and Nash 1961; Keniston 1968). Similarly, PEACE activism was part of developing a connected self. As images of their relationships between self and others changed, so did their judgments of appropriate moral behavior.

The Research Process

Forty-one PEACE activists were interviewed about themselves, their families, and their social worlds. To help distinguish aspects unique to the activists, a comparison sample of fifteen nonactivist siblings, friends, and spouses of the activists were also interviewed.

All the activists were volunteers in PEACE. The sample was selected for the purpose of generating theory (Glaser and Strauss 1967). Particular attention was paid to expanding the sample to include a variety of ages and socioeconomic and marital statuses. The activist sample consisted of 19 men and 22 women, ranging in age from 26 to 79. All were white middle- and upper-middle-class persons. All but 4 had college degrees, and 13 had advanced degrees. Although participants were purposefully selected to include a range of ages and socioeconomic backgrounds, the sample appears to be fairly representative of persons involved in the group.

The nonactivists were selected because of their close association with the activists (siblings, friends, or spouses). They included 7 men and 8 women, and ranged in age from 38 to 72. There was more diversity of educational background in the nonactivist sample, with 8 holding advanced degrees, 2 with bachelor's degrees, and 7 with no college degrees. They were a diverse group in terms of occupations and income, and represented a wide range of political beliefs.

The interview format was flexible, allowing the respondents to speak freely in their own terms about themselves and their social worlds. The three-hour interviews were taped and transcribed. A content analysis identifying key themes for each individual was done after each interview. As analysis revealed patterns characterizing the group, hypotheses were inductively formulated and tested in subsequent interviews.

The Language of Connection

The PEACE activists in this study perceived themselves to be inexorably connected to others. They saw fulfillment and success coming through relationships with others and believed that self-development required orienting oneself to the larger whole. In the words of activist Diane:

I am not in this family for myself—so I can get what I want in life. . . . It's like learning what it means to be for another person and to be for the family unit, and then to be for the world. The irony and beauty of it is that developmentally I have grown tremendously as a person in ways that never would have emerged when I was my own goal.

The activists defined a morality based on concerns for the connections they experienced and responsibility toward the common good. The keys to their PEACE activity were (1) perceptions of interdependence, (2) beliefs that a connected way of living was possible, and (3) perceptions of personal connection to the problem.

INTERDEPENDENCE

The sense of affecting—and being affected by—others contributed to the activists' sense of responsibility. George discovered this interdependence personally when he went to Nepal: "It was just about the time of the embargo. The price of oil skyrocketed. . . . They were trying to make a conversion to kerosene. The rest of the world catapults the prices of oil and there was nothing they could do . . . totally interdependent!"

Since they saw themselves embedded in an interdependent global system, they felt a moral responsibility for their part of it. Their commitment to the whole was not necessarily altruistic. For example, "Either we die together or we survive together," was a common comment demonstrating that they saw their own fates tied to that of the collective.

POSSIBILITY

Their images of themselves as connected to others in an interdependent global system allowed PEACE activists to believe that changing from a moral order based on competing self-interests to one based on the cooperation for the common good was both possible and necessary. Their belief in the possibility of change frequently resulted from their personal experiences of change. Elaine explained this view: "I know it's possible to change. I've done it myself . . . [My husband and I have different personalities and backgrounds] and yet we actually worked it out! We live well together. So I know it is possible." Becoming involved in PEACE gave other activists a vision of connection as a possibility. Indeed, modeling that possibility appears to have been an important function of PEACE.

The belief that change was possible was also associated with a view of self and society as being on a developmental path toward connection. The activists equated developmental change with moving toward connection and away from self. Their sense was that movement toward cooperation is in the natural order of things. Margaret expressed this image: "[Development is] people growing and changing and gaining greater perspective—moving from being ego-centric. . . . It seems to be that that's the way it's supposed to be. People are supposed to develop. People are supposed to get along."

Because their views of themselves and society suggested that change was possible, the activists felt a moral responsibility to discover how to move society beyond self-interest.

Personal Connection

Because the activists defined society interdependently, they saw themselves as part of the problem. They were, therefore, also part of the solution. Moral commitment to and responsibility for the public good generally involved experiencing personal connection between self and social issues. Most of the activists I interviewed shared stories pinpointing their awareness of this connection.

Michelle, for example, experienced personal connection between herself and world events because she was physically present where news was happening:

> I was flying to Harrisburg, Pennsylvania, and the people behind me lived at Three Mile Island. They were talking about how concerned they were living there. I remembered reading about it and all, but it seemed so far away. And there I was. And I go to my hotel room that night and I turned on the news and the Falkland crisis was happening. It was just too much. I felt like if it weren't one thing it would be another. I cried myself to sleep that night and I also made a commitment to myself that I would try to change something.

Commitment in the public realm was new to Michelle. On the other hand, Elizabeth, who had been active in the peace movement in the sixties, was reconnected with what she "already knew" when her niece and nephew began having dreams about nuclear war. In a different fashion, Patricia and Sean were connected to public issues concerning life and death by transferring their work experience with children who had cancer and their personal experiences of the birth of a new baby and the death of his father.

VIEWS OF NONACTIVISTS

In contrast to the personal connection to public issues experienced by the activists, the nonactivists separated the self from society. Although some saw themselves connected to a whole at the family level, they—like the persons described by Bellah et al. (1985)—tended to view society as a collective of autonomous individuals arbitrating competitive self-interests. Though some of the nonactivists shared some of the activists' concerns for the world, they did not envision the possibility of change or the personal responsibility for finding solutions.

For example, nonactivists Delores and Ben shared most of the political views of their activist friends, but she expressed concerns for relief from responsibility to others: "I think I've gotten to the stage in my life where I'm not doing all the 'I shoulds.' I'm doing what I want to do. I deserve this portion of my life. I gave enough to kids and family and friends years ago."

Though Ben had been very involved in political aspects of his dental association, they saw themselves as separate from public issues: "We're willing to listen, but we're not involved. . . . The dental political association was something different. That was my profession. It was my livelihood. I was interested in what was being done."

Types of Moral Connection

Though the activists shared images of a moral order based on a sense of self connected to a larger whole, they experienced four different (though interrelated) types of connection. Prophets experienced spiritual connection; that is, a thread uniting all of life and providing personal meaning and direction. Wisemen experienced a political connection, which was focused on the processes that make a political system work. Friends experienced relational connection; that is, a sense that personal satisfactions come through connections and commitments to others. At the periphery of PEACE were the Watchdogs. They experienced a defensive connection based on the need to band together for self-protection.

The Prophets

Moral responsibility for the group known as Prophets was based on a sense of spiritual connection. Some defined spirituality as God; others as common humanity or nature. Some were involved in organized religions. PEACE provided a spiritual community for others. To these activists moral authority lay in a system uniting all life spiritually. Their moral responsibility was to do what was right for that system. These people felt they had access to special knowledge or truths that they were obligated to share with others. The truth they experienced was that all life on the planet is interconnected.

Sandra, 38, was representative of the Prophets. She was the mother of two young children and a former school administrator who had decided to devote all her spare time to PEACE. Her concerns had been aroused by a sense of personal connection to a global life system that she felt she had a responsibility to preserve: "When I became pregnant with my kids, to see how the fetus grows and how that reproduces itself through the whole cycle. . . . I feel very responsible about the earth—about how things are. . . . I think when my kids were born I had a real sense that I was responsible for more than my life."

Sandra saw God in the life system and in herself as a part of it. She experienced a sense of spiritual connection to all of life and the moral obligation of one who bears knowledge that is necessary for survival of the whole:

> I guess I would say it has to do with our souls. . . . It has to do with the whole organic system . . . I believe we are the consciousness of it. And because of that we have an incredible responsibility to preserve it and to allow it to continue. . . . [T]here's nothing that's going to rescue us except the part of God that's in us and the knowledge that we have been given.

Sandra perceived that the world was in a crisis that demanded a response from her. When asked to explain why she needed to respond, she used the word "blessed" to describe her position and described a spiritual connection to the life system. Moral authority, to Prophets like Sandra, lay in that system.

THE WISEMEN

Wisemen, a mostly male group, experienced a political connection that was more pragmatic and rational than a spiritual connection. Politics, for these activists, was based on concern for what makes the system they are embedded in work. Political reality was that all are connected and must learn to live together harmoniously. The moral challenge was to develop a clear picture of that connectedness and accept that reality. Political astuteness lay in what works for the whole, therefore responsibility was to move beyond self-interest to see how the system works and what is necessary for survival.

Wes, 50, was representative of the Wisemen. He was the father of two adult children and a retired corporate vice-president who worked fulltime as a PEACE volunteer. He reported a lifetime interest in understanding how to make the system work—which he equated with power. Learning to see himself as part of a whole shifted Wes's perceptions of power from something he personally possessed and controlled to an understanding of the system and his part in it: "I think power 30 years ago was defined in terms of not being pushed around. . . . I considered myself this little rock against the tide. Now what is needed is to perceive where the river is and where it is going."

Wes saw authority outside himself in the flow of life itself. His morality was based on doing the right thing as defined by what was necessary for life. "Put me in a boat in the river. I can work to influence which way the boat goes, but there is something bigger than the boat—life itself—that I don't have to fight or dam up or divert. . . . We're all in the same boat together . . . and I'm saying let's respond to what life is asking us."

Wes recognized that he needed people, but he understood that connection primarily in terms of the integration of knowledge and history. Only at the end of the interview did he voice a personal connection to real people outside his family.

THE FRIENDS

In contrast to Wes, the Friends understood connection primarily in terms of commitment to lifelong relationships. They were less inclined than either Wes or Sandra to speak of the "life system." Their concerns were more personally focused. They did not separate being an individual from responsibility to the larger good. Since satisfactions were perceived through connections to others, their moral responsibility was to make life better for everyone.

Bill and Nancy were characteristic of the Friends. Bill, 39, was president of a family corporation. Nancy taught science part time in the local elementary school. They had three school-age children and were involved in a variety of civic activities. Their relational connection was expressed primarily through family and business ties in which they were committed to the good of their relationships before satisfaction of personal desires. This commitment helped their family system find workable solutions: "There has been mostly mutual respect that if one of us felt more strongly than the other, usually that person would give in . . . ultimately we're going in the same direction. It's just not worth it not to have both of us happy."

For Bill, commitment to relationships extended to work: "The president of [the family corporation] has an interesting focus for the family. There's emotional ties to it. My grandfather started it. I feel an obligation to how it impacts on the other family members and how it impacts on the employees."

Their sense of relational connection and moral responsibility to others extended to humanity and had grown out of experiences connecting them to people and places in other parts of the world. Bill, for example, described "the feeling always of not being separate" when he lived in Japan and traveled in other parts of the world. His reaction to visiting Poland and Auschwitz illustrates his sense of moral responsibility to other people and commitment to making relationships better: "I feel such a sense of loss . . . each of these things is in relation to people behaving inhumanly to other people. . . . If I can't bring witness to the fact that this was inhuman to have done and demonstrate that somehow, then I'm in some way not creating a positive out of a negative."

Friends did not experience interpersonal ties as confining and were willing to set aside self-interests to benefit the whole. Their relational connection translated into the belief that it is "right" to define one's own interests in the context of finding a solution that is best for everyone involved.

WATCHDOGS

A fourth kind of connection, Watchdogs, was demonstrated by a spouse who was marginally involved in PEACE. This connection was not based on a sense of self as part of a whole, but rather on the belief that individuals face common threats. Connection to others was experienced as a need to band together for self-protection. Moral authority lay in what was best for oneself and one's own, and responsibility was to take action on one's own behalf and for one's own good. Such action was only perceived to be effective when people work together against forces that threaten them all. By doing so, everyone could have better lives. Therefore, it was "right" to work for the common good.

Tim, 42, was one of the few PEACE activists who experienced a defensive connection. He and his wife Jeannette, 33, owned a heavy-machine business and had one child. The interview began with his concern about a proposed new housing development disrupting traffic on his street. This mirrored the individualistic concerns he expressed for protecting the life system: "Right now the people in charge of our government are playing with our lives. It may cause that little boy over there [his son] to have cancer or his children to be born with one leg."

Moral dilemmas, to Tim, had to do with individual rights. His understanding of contributing to the larger community was to make individual lives better, to return an obligation, and to give before you can get. Like other PEACE activists, Tim rejected war because it doesn't work. Unlike most activists who saw that it doesn't work because it is bad for the whole, Tim saw that it doesn't work because it is bad for individual people:

> Look at Viet Nam. I saw all my friends go off to war. And when it was all over I watched the president prolong the war . . . so that a certain man could get reelected; ended the war thirty days before the election. And how many boys died in the last nine months? When it was all over they negotiated and they still had to talk about it, so why not talk about it and stop killing people. They could have saved sixty thousand lives.

Though Tim did not view himself as embedded in a larger system and did not share the concern for connections expressed by most PEACE activists, he shared a sense that he needed others in order to survive.

Translating Connection into
Social Action

The PEACE activists I interviewed described turning from the Protestant ethic prescribing success in the marketplace (Weber [1904] 1958) to a morality based on concern for the whole. Their "conversion" was, in part, because they saw their own survival as contingent on the survival of the whole. In addition, they perceived themselves as holding a privileged position in society. Their senses of moral responsibility and the possibility of a different way of living were derived from their prior experiences of accomplishment and their freedom from financial struggle.

Although participation in the antiwar movement of the Sixties was characterized as an identity crisis before making adult commitments (Flacks 1971; Keniston 1968), PEACE activism in this study was the *result* of adult commitment. Such activism would more aptly be termed a crisis of generativity (Erikson 1963; Greenwald and Zeitlin 1987), that is, concern for the next generations. In contrast to the youth of the Sixties, the PEACE activists I interviewed felt connected to the world in which they lived. Their activism was the result of their perceptions of themselves as parts of a global system. Their social action grew, not from alienation or isolation, but from perceiving themselves connected to the problem and, therefore, also part of the solution.

How to be social activists desiring to convert others to their way of thinking and still maintain connection was difficult for most of the PEACE activists in this study. They perceived that living consistently with connection required openness to differences and not imposing their will on others. At the same time, they were convinced that survival of the planet and their own survival were at risk. Sandra expressed the conflict inherent in these dual purposes: "I think I can influence a certain number of people—hopefully I convince them—or I mean that they will be convinced on their own. I don't try to convince them. I just present the material, but through the way I present it and the knowledge that I can give them, they will be able to move on also."

The activists emphasized that discovering how to work together and modeling that process were more important that selling people on an idea. Yet their belief that the planet was in crisis meant that, in practice, maintaining open dialogue was often very difficult. Pauline dropped out of involvement with PEACE in part because she felt that instead of modeling openness to different perspectives, the leaders sometimes imposed their ideas on everyone: "It seemed like they welcomed individual opinions to a certain degree, but if you strayed too far off it, it wasn't really accepted, and that bothered me."

Living consistently with connection was a goal the PEACE activists tried hard to achieve. Trying to be open and accommodating differences at the time they evangelized their version of the truth tested the limits of their vision of the possibility of connection.

Continued involvement in PEACE activity required the development of a shared world (see also, Berger and Kellner 1970; Hess and Handel 1959; Reiss 1981). Their ability to live consistently with their images depended on support for those images in their personal environment. In addition, contact with other PEACE activists provided a community validating their images of the possibility of global connection and sustained their belief that peace was a more rational alternative than war.

Conclusions

For the activists in this study, participation in the peace movement depended on holding a view of the self as connected to others on the personal and public levels. Three factors were significant in explaining their involvement:

1. They perceived themselves as interdependent within a system and responsible for changing it.
2. They believed that change was possible, based on their own personal experience.
3. They experienced their connections to others in a very personal manner and felt responsible to become involved.

The activists experienced several distinct types of connections, thus each type responded to different calls for involvement in the peace movement. Balancing their sense of connection with their desire to make social changes challenged most. Their continued involvement required support of the connected view of self in their personal and social network.

PEACE activism was associated with a view of self as personally connected to the whole. This change from the individualistic perspective—which, according to Bellah et al. (1985), is based on the perception of an autonomous self and the rules of the competitive marketplace—appears to change the definition of a relationship from a competitive one to a cooperative one and facilitates willingness to work for the common good. This suggests that developing a view of self as part of a system is an important part of the ability to resolve problems at the interpersonal and societal levels.

Imagining a moral order based on connection depended heavily on the activists' idealism (i.e., imagining something they had not experienced) and their belief in the possibility of change. Their idealism, however, was accompanied by a rational judgment that nations could not war and continue to survive. Without those beliefs, nations will probably persist in viewing war as more rational than peace.

CHAPTER 17

Patterns of Peacemaking in the Local Freeze Campaign

Sam Marullo

One of the difficulties confronting the freeze campaign was how to mobilize a social movement at the grassroots level on an issue in which decisions were made by a national elite that was well-insulated from the public. The campaign chose a strategy and set of tactics that consisted of mobilizing a large number of middle-class citizens to demand of their elected officials that they halt the arms race through a bilateral nuclear weapons freeze. This strategy was squarely in the political mainstream, relying on a pluralist model of democratic participation through which large numbers of citizens would force their elected representatives to discuss and debate the issue, ultimately assent to the wisdom of halting the superpower arms race, and take the political actions necessary to implement the freeze ("National Strategy for a NUCLEAR WEAPONS FREEZE" 1981).

How this strategy was to be translated into action at the local level was deliberately never specified by the national campaign for both principled and pragmatic reasons.[1] This enabled the local groups to devise their own strategies and tactics in pursuit of a nuclear freeze. The local freeze organizations thus had to find means of mobilizing support in their own communities and devising tactics that would sustain them while nationally "adding up" to be an adequate pressure to get the executive, military, and congressional leadership to agree to take steps to halt the arms race. Across the nation, these strategies took on a great variety of forms. As Lofland, Colwell, and Johnson discuss (Chapter 6), these strategies reflect the organizations' models of creating social change. The analysis contained in this chapter illustrates how these images of social change varied even at the local level within a single metropolitan area freeze campaign.

The Greater Cleveland Nuclear Weapons Freeze Campaign (GCNWFC) serves as the case study for this analysis of individual models of social change at the local level. The particular focus is on the variety of actions undertaken by participants in the local freeze campaign. Specifically, I examine models of movement involvement as a reflection of the individual's conceptualization of "doing" social change. That is, the types of activities an individual chooses to undertake are presumed to be caused by the individual's perception of how he or she can change the system. There appear to be eight such models of peacemaking operationalized by the members of the Cleveland Freeze Campaign.

The eight types are determined by combinations of four dimensions found among the specific actions that individuals undertook. These dimensions are: individual participatory actions, freeze organizational actions, actions to confront nonmovement individuals, and actions to confront the system directly. Through this analysis, we see that these activities appealed differently to movement members, with some members preferring some types of activities over others. Combinations of positions along the four dimensions are used to create the eight ideal-types of local movement participants described below.

Types of Activities and
Models of Change within the Freeze

There are several ways one can analyze an individual's participation in a social movement. For example, one could consider the skills or resources that are required to undertake a particular type of activity, producing a classification scheme that reflects the various types and levels of resources available to movement participants. Similarly, one could consider the institutional spheres with which the activities take place, thereby reflecting the movement's strategy concerning how change should occur as well as the opportunities available to act within particular spheres. The approach that I find to be most useful, however, and the one that is used in this chapter, is based on the individual's model of engaging in social change. Individuals' perceptions of doing social change are influenced not only by their political attitudes and beliefs, but also by their past organizational experiences, current movement organizations' goals, strategies, and operations, and the larger social context within which they belong.

Four Types of Activities

The conceptualization underlying this approach is that individuals involved in SMOs are purposive actors attempting social change within a more or less constrained environment (Fireman and Gamson 1979). For individuals involved in the peace movement at the local level during the 1980s, this translated into four readily available modes of action: acting as an individual through widely available, relatively low-cost political means; acting through freeze or other peace movement organizations in order to create alternative interest groups to compete in the political system; taking actions to confront individuals in other institutional settings with the peace movement's message; or directly confronting the major institutions of the government through illegal action as a means of challenging its authority.

These four modes of action are not the only activities that members could undertake, but they do cover the major participation forms as well as the largest portion of time that members spent on peace activism. The first set of actions undertaken within the local freeze campaign were those that the individual did by him- or herself, outside of freeze organizations, that were readily available to most (middle-class) individuals. This included the activities of: attending public lectures or films about the arms race, voting for elective officials based on their positions on weapons-related issues, attending church peace-group meetings, donating money to peace groups, attending peace rallies or demonstrations, and writing or phoning their representatives regarding peace issues. I will refer to these six activities as individual level actions. This type of activity reflects the individual's faith in a participatory model of democratic change. As I argue later, this model of social change is overly simplistic and fairly easily resisted by entrenched institutional actors, yet it underlies the strategy of mass, middle-class mobilization utilized by many recent movements.

The second set of activities includes participation in freeze organizational operations, such as: volunteering in the GCNWFC office, attending meetings, serving on committees, attending national rallies such as the June 12, 1982, rally in New York, and organizing local events. By engaging in these freeze organizational actions, individuals are expressing their faith in a pluralist model that interest groups are needed to influence the political decision-making process to achieve change. Although this image of social change is more sophisticated than the participatory model, it is likely to fall victim to the tendency to displace movement goals with organizational goals and turn inward on itself (Solo 1988).

The third type of activity undertaken at the local level was more directly confrontative of those outside the movement. Whereas the first set of actions was done individually and more or less privately, and the second set was undertaken with those who were known to feel supportive about peace issues, the third set placed the individual in contact with at least some people who were opposed to the movement. These confrontational actions were deliberate in the sense of trying to win new converts to the movement or obtaining new vehicles for spreading the movement's message. These activities including working on petition drives, doing door-to-door canvassing, phone-banking, or voter registration, or working with school officials or labor leaders to win support for freeze activities. Success in these efforts reflected a real growth of the movement. However, there were often failures and rebuffs at such efforts of proselytizing and conversion, making them more risky at the individual level. Such actions reflect a more aggressive power-building pluralist model and appear to be an essential component of successful contemporary movements' strategies.

The fourth type of action undertaken at the local level were those intended to directly challenge the legitimacy of the political system. By definition these activities are illegal and activists undertake them for precisely this reason. They were meant to be dramatic symbolic protests to awaken the public to the seriousness of the nuclear threat as well as challenges to the legitimacy of the system that produced the current danger. These actions include withholding federal taxes, illegal trespass, and other forms of civil disobedience. These civil disobedience actions pose an even greater level of risk to the individual and pose a potentially revolutionary challenge to the system because the participants refuse to accept the authority of the legal and political institutions.

Underlying Models of Change

From the discussion thus far, we see that several analytical concepts are incorporated in these four modes of movement activities. The first is the level of risk or confrontation the individual is willing to undertake in pursuit of his or her goals of making peace. The four modes are presented in order of increasing risk, with the individual actions involving the least risk to the individual and the civil disobedience actions the most. When a movement is vibrant and expanding, individuals are increasingly likely to undertake greater risk activities, and unless the government acts repressively, the costs of undertaking such activities decrease. Note, however, that even within a given mode there are varying levels of risk involved.

A second dimension embedded in this conceptualization of modes of action is the institutional realm in which the activities take place. For the peace movement, the political realm is of utmost importance, so many of the activities would be focused there, or so it would seem. At first glance, it appears that the individual level actions do indeed take place primarily in political institutions, the organizational activities obviously occur within the peace movement, the confrontational actions occur primarily in other institutions, and the civil disobedience actions are in opposition to the political system. However, since most peace groups operate at the local level, exerting influence on the national political bodies responsible for military and foreign policy is an extremely difficult undertaking. Local institutions such as churches, schools, businesses, local city councils, state legislatures, local police departments, and the local media thus become the target for all four types of activities. Furthermore, many actions are designed explicitly to affect targets in several institutional spheres, so the prospect of using the institutional nexus of action only tends to complicate rather than clarify an understanding of the actions.

Similarly, but in a more tempting fashion, the function of an activity may serve as another dimension of classifying movement actions. Some of the more common purposes of undertaking particular actions include whether the activity is designed to educate the public, raise revenues for the organization, recruit new members, sway political leaders' opinions, build coalitions with allies, or boost solidarity of members. However, as any good organizer will say, an action should always be planned with as many as possible of these purposes in mind.

To try to classify activities along dimensions that are intentionally intermingled by the actors would only lead to analytical nightmares.

Finally, there is not a simple monotonic relationship between the four types of actions and the amount of resources needed to undertake them. Indeed, there is nearly as much variability of required resources to undertake various activities within each type as there is among the four types. For example, relatively few resources are needed to vote appropriately for a candidate, attend meetings, do door-to-door canvassing, or get arrested for trespassing. Considerably more are needed to organize events, to donate money, to do labor outreach, and to undertake tax resistance. However, there is an overall increase of resources required as one moves from individual level actions to civil disobedience. Thus, although this dimension may demonstrate an aggregate level difference in requisite resources, there is also a great deal of variability within the four modes of action.

Given this lack of conceptual clarity, I suggest that it is most helpful to conceive of the modes of action as reflections of the individual's image of doing social change—i.e., of making peace. This can vary from a simplistic image of voters expressing their preferences through the electoral process and their elected officials representing their views (a representative democracy model), to a classical pluralist model of differentially powerful interest groups competing to have their positions implemented, to a more critical view of a firmly entrenched elite within the military-industrial complex that refuses to sacrifice its interests unless forced to do so by either a comparatively powerful institutional actor or the threatened or actual breakdown of public order. Yet another conceptualization would see social change occurring as a result of deep individual moral transformations that have to occur throughout the population. These images of political change are not perfectly operationalized by the four action modes, however, but require combining them into logical sets (from the actor's point of view).

The factor analysis presented in the next section illustrates that these modes are empirically consistent with the way freeze members participated in movement activities. Following this, the local freeze participants' actions are examined through a cluster analysis to demonstrate the coherence of particular sets of activities and their pursuit of only a limited number of combinations of them. The ability to distinguish between these modes of activity and the appearance of only select combinations of them is taken as evidence of the purposive nature of these actions and the meaningfulness of the ideal-types of movement participation described below.

Factor Analysis of Movement Actions

The four modes of activity not only make sense conceptually as dimensions of models of change, but are also well grounded empirically, as demonstrated through a factor analysis of local freeze members' actions.[2] A factor analysis based on eighteen possible activities included in the survey produces four factors that capture 48 percent of their total variation.

The eighteen action items included in the factor analysis are listed in Table 17.1. Each of these items is dichotomous, asking the respondent whether she or he has taken part in that particular activity in the previous two years. The results shown in Table 17.1 are the rotated factor pattern matrix coefficients for the items and the first four factors.[3] The initial eigenvalues provide support for the existence of four dimensions.[4]

As can be seen in Table 17.1, the first factor has the individual action items loaded most highly on it. The coefficients in the table represent the correlation coefficients between the particular action items and the rotated factor, which range from .54 to .75. The second factor contains the freeze organizational items loaded most highly, with correlations ranging from .45 to .73. The third factor consists of the confrontational action items, with correlations ranging from .41 to .73. The fourth factor consists of the two civil disobedience action items with correlations of .63 and .80. An oblique rotation of the axes demonstrates that the factors are moderately correlated with each other—a finding consistent with the clustering of individuals into a select number of combinations of these indexes.[5] These four action indexes form the conceptual basis for the typology of individuals that follows.

Typology of Actions

It should be obvious that not all individuals who took part in the movement participated in all types of actions. The median number of

Table 17.1. Factor Analysis of Eighteen Action Items Used in Creating Modes of Action Indexes (*N*=325)

	Varimax Rotated Factor Pattern			
Item	Individual action (FACTOR 1)	Freeze organization (FACTOR 2)	Confron-tational (FACTOR 3)	Civil disobedience (FACTOR 4)
Issue voting	0.75	−0.05	0.14	−0.07
Write/phone rep.	0.69	0.04	0.17	0.02
Films or lectures	0.03	0.31	0.00	0.19
Donate money	0.61	0.02	0.17	0.09
Church peace gp.	0.58	0.35	−0.02	0.11
Demonstration	0.54	0.35	0.16	0.19
Freeze committee	−0.02	0.73	0.20	0.03
Office volunteer	0.05	0.64	0.05	−0.00
Attend meeting	0.38	0.53	0.23	−0.17
Organize event	0.36	0.47	0.14	0.18
Attend nat'l rally	0.21	0.45	0.19	0.18
Petition drive	0.32	−0.01	0.73	0.05
Labor outreach	−0.04	0.20	0.63	0.08
Voter registration	0.22	0.17	0.57	0.06
Canvass or phonebank	0.16	0.40	0.56	−0.10
Education issue	0.05	0.38	0.41	0.23
Tax resistance	0.02	0.04	−0.03	0.80
Civil disobedience	0.20	0.05	0.21	0.63

Initial Eigenvalues and Proportion of Variation Explained by Four Factors

Eigenvalue	4.85	1.52	1.16	1.06
Proportion	0.27	0.08	0.07	0.06
Cumulative	0.27	0.35	0.42	0.48

	Inter-Factor Correlation Matrix			
	Individual action (FACTOR 1)	Freeze organization (FACTOR 2)	Confron-tational (FACTOR 3)	Civil disobedience (FACTOR 4)
Individual action	1.00	0.53	0.37	0.41
Freeze organization	0.53	1.00	0.37	0.45
Confrontational	0.37	0.37	1.00	0.18
Civil disobedience	0.41	0.45	0.18	1.00

activities undertaken was five for the randomly selected members and twelve for the purposively chosen activists. It is also clear that participation in these activities was not randomly distributed among the movement participants. If participation in each of the four modes of action is considered as a dichotomous event, there are sixteen (2^4) combinations of actions that the individual could have undertaken. However, not all of these combinations were likely nor do they all make sense from the actor's point of view. Conversely, some combinations were very likely and can be identified as ideal-types of participation in the freeze campaign. This section explores these ideal-types of participation based on a cluster analysis of movement participants.

Cluster analysis is a data simplification technique that combines cases based on their similarities on a predesignated set of characteristics. The cluster analysis that produced the typology reported on here aggregated cases on the basis of their standardized scores on the four action indexes.[6] The resulting clusters are indicated in Figure 17.1, which also illustrates the sixteen theoretical types of participants based on the dichotomized action indexes. The names I have assigned to these ideal types of participants and the number of cases in each type are also given in Table 17.2.

These eight types of participation are characterized by various combinations of the four modes of action and the intensity level on them. At the lowest level of freeze movement participation are those who are only nominally members of the movement—the adherents who express support for the movement's goals but who do not undertake any action in support of it. In the membership sample, 10 percent of the respondents participated in no activities whatsoever. Another 20 percent undertook one or two actions that were invisible to the movement—voting for a candidate depending on his or her position on weapons issues or contacting their elected officials about the arms race. At the other extreme are those who are fully engaged in all types of action, including civil disobedience. These fully engaged civil disobedients make up roughly one-tenth of the combined membership and activist samples (only 7 percent of the membership sample). In between these two extremes are various types of participants whose activities reflect the several models of change inherent in the movement.

Adherents: The adherents are those who express support for the movement's goals but do not undertake any visible action in support of

Table 17.2. Ideal-Types of Freeze Movement Participants[a]

| | **No civil disobedience actions** | | | |
| | *No confrontation action* | | *Confrontation action* | |
	No freeze	*Freeze*	*No freeze*	*Freeze*
Limited individual action	*Adherents* 97[b] 29.8%[c]	— 0 0%	— 0 0%	— 0 0%
Many individual actions	*Weak supporter* 47 14.2%	*Peripheral member* 43 12.6%	*Strong supporter* 28 8.0%	*Active member* 65 16.0%
				Core member 50 6.8%

| | **Civil disobedience actions** | | | |
| | *No confrontation action* | | *Confrontation action* | |
	No freeze	*Freeze*	*No freeze*	*Freeze*
Limited individual action	— 0 0%	— 2 0.6%	— 1 0.3%	— 0 0%
Many individual actions	*Partially engaged CD* 13 3.4%	— 3 0.9%	— 0 0%	*Fully engaged CD* 34 7.4%

[a]Table is set up according to hypothetical dichotomization of the four action indexes. The names in the cells correspond to those given in the text. Cells with no names (—) are either empty or nearly so, indicating the combination does not exist as an ideal type. The numbers in the cells reflect the number of cases in the clusters produced by the cluster analysis.

[b]The numbers include both the random and purposive samples; $N = 383$.

[c]The numerator and denominator used in computing percentages are based only on the random sample; $N = 325$.

their feelings. They are the individuals that activists and organizers always try to get to turn out to events or otherwise find ways to register their sentiments so that their numbers can be used when lobbying elected officials. One strategy that organizers use is to find indicators of support that are very low in cost so that the adherents may easily undertake them. Ennis and Schreuer (1987) discuss a local referendum for a nuclear free zone as one such means of mobilizing weak support for the movement. In the case of the freeze, opinion polls repeatedly found 70-80 percent of the public supported a freeze, but only a miniscule fraction of them ever took positive action in support of it. Given a countywide population of 1.9 million, even if only 60 percent of the local population supported the freeze, the GCNWFC could conceivably have claimed the support of some 1.1 million adherents. The mailing list of ten thousand names represents tapping less than .09 percent of these potential supporters, and at best only two thirds of these are actually undertaking any visible actions in support of their sentiment.

Weak Supporters: These individuals do not participate in freeze organization activities, but they do undertake several individual actions indicating their support. The weak supporters have engaged in three to five individual acts (in addition to voting for candidates based on their positions on weapons issues and contacting their elected officials, they are likely to donate money to peace groups, attend films or lectures on the arms race, or attend a demonstration) and perhaps they have undertaken one confrontational action (either working on a petition drive or doing voter registration), but they do not engage in organizational activities. This pattern of action, undertaken by one-seventh of the random sample, is consistent with the participatory model of social change—that individuals' actions by themselves can aggregate to create change.

Strong Supporters: Eight percent of the respondents are strong supporters who engage in many individual actions, from four to six (of the possible six) actions on this index, and also engage in two or three confrontational actions. The strong supporter not only does nearly all that he or she can do as an individual, but also takes the freeze message to others in their institutional settings to convince them that they too should support the freeze. The strong supporter thus expends more resources and assumes greater risks than the weak supporter in working for peace. Like the weak supporter, however, the strong supporter does not undertake any freeze organizational activities.

The model of change most consistent with this type of behavior is a mass-market approach to the participatory model. The strong supporters realize the importance of spreading the freeze message, but for one reason or another they do not feel that working on organizational activities is a valuable use of their time. I use the term "mass market participatory model" because the strong supporter appears to act on the assumption that convincing large numbers of people to support the freeze is important and then he or she makes a judgment regarding how to accomplish this goal most effectively. In the strong supporter's opinion, spending time on organizational activities is not as important as actually getting out there and doing the work.

Peripheral Movement Members: Like the weak and strong supporters, the peripheral movement members have undertaken several individual actions. However, they have also participated in a small number of freeze organization actions. They make up roughly 13 percent of the random sample. The three types of movement members (peripheral, active, and core) have undertaken several individual actions, but they vary in their degree of freeze actions as well as the number of confrontational actions. The peripheral movement members have engaged in one to three actions directly related to the freeze campaign, such as attending meetings, helping to organize events, or volunteering at the freeze office, but they have not engaged in any confrontational actions. The key distinction between the members and supporters is that the members act as though the freeze organization matters—they are willing to expend some of their energy doing organizational work. The movement members' actions reflect an interest group model of change that gives some weight to the importance of organization.

Active Movement Members: The active movement members engage in more freeze organization activities than do the peripheral members, typically undertaking from three to five organization actions. They make up roughly 16 percent of the respondents. Like the peripheral movement members and both types of supporters, the active movement members have also engaged in numerous individual activities. In addition to these, most have also done a moderate amount of confrontational activity. This may result from simply being active in all types of organization-sponsored activities or through genuinely accepting the movement's image of how social change will happen. These actions reflect the belief that peace groups have to be made stronger by making them larger and more representative of the mass of middle-class voters. This reflects a power-building pluralist interest group model.

Core Movement Members: The core movement members (7 percent of the sample) are fully active in each of the three spheres of activity—individual, freeze organization, and confrontational—but they draw the line at civil disobedience. They expend greater resources on behalf of the movement and engage in greater risk-taking than do the active or peripheral members and the supporters. Over half (56 percent) of the individuals who appeared in this cluster were from the purposive sample of leaders in the local movement. The core movement members are typically known as group leaders, although many of the leaders are also found in the fully engaged civil disobedient category discussed below.

The model of change reflected in this pattern of behavior is the power-building pluralist model. However, the core members are themselves fully empowered as they assume greater responsibility for operationalizing, implementing, and even designing the movement's strategy than do the active members.

Partially Engaged Civil Disobedients: The partially engaged civil disobedients have undertaken at least one act of civil disobedience (usually illegal trespass) and a large number of individual actions, but no freeze or confrontational activities. This pattern suggests that one path to civil disobedience may result from a development process whereby supporters who adhere to a participatory model become disenchanted with the apparent lack of effectiveness of their actions and carry their individual protest to its logical extreme. They apparently eschew power politics altogether, as indicated by their lack of confrontational or freeze organizational activities. Their civil disobedience is quite likely to be rooted in a religious framework, although in general they are not pacifists. Their actions are a direct challenge to the policies of a corrupt or unjust government, and their goal is to change those policies and the individuals who make them. They do not, however, see the entire system as illegitimate, nor do they see the utility of creating alternative interest groups. They see change coming about as a result of an individually based moral revolution to which their actions provide witness.

Fully Engaged Civil Disobedients: The fully engaged civil disobedients undertake high levels of all four types of action. They are actively involved in the local freeze campaign (a third of them are from the activist sample), they engage in nearly all of the individual and confrontational activities enumerated, and have undertaken illegal activities on behalf of the peace movement. They represent the extreme end of those who pursue the power-building interest group model. However, not only do they see the need to build powerful interest groups representing their desire for peace, but they also seek to challenge the legitimacy of the current system and contribute to the perception of its illegitimacy. They feel fully empowered in their actions, complete with a well-developed rationale (usually religious) for their total resistance to the arms race. Both types of civil disobedients see their actions as symbolic statements of protests and hope that others will be "awakened" by their actions. However, the fully engaged disobedients' participation in organized groups helps accomplish several other things as well: it facilitates the spread of the protest message, it leads to a greater challenge or crisis of the system in confronting it, and it offers an alternative vision of a form of social organization that it hopes to substitute for the unjust system now in place.

Conclusion

The dual objectives of a social movement are that it effectively press its demands for change on the state and that it mobilize sufficient resources to do so. In order to achieve the former, a successful movement must engage the state on a large number of fronts, employ a variety of tactics, and pose an actual or potential threat to its stability. In terms of mobilizing sufficient resources, movements must create the opportunities and enticements for individuals to express their demands, find the means to sustain these demands, and develop the channels to target its mobilized resources at the state. In postindustrial, Western democracies, social movements typically take on the form of voluntary organizations as a means of mobilizing support and focusing claims at the government. This is done when there exists widespread sentiment that the government is not being responsive to the wishes of the populace. However, the lack of consensus over the alternative goals and the lack of a commonly shared model of how social change should occur usually leads to the emergence of a movement that pursues a number of goals through a variety of means. Even when there is a momentary consensus on the policy goals of the movement, as was the case with the emergence of the nuclear freeze campaign in the early 1980s, the movement still exhibits a great diversity in the manner in which it pursues its goals. As Lofland, Colwell, and Johnson discuss in Chapter six, this diversity can be seen at the level of movement segments and SMOs that engage in various strategies, employ diverse tactics, and develop alternative frameworks of analysis. This chapter demonstrates that this variability is found at the individual level as well, even within a single organization.

The Cleveland Freeze Campaign accepted as its primary goal the implementation of a bilateral nuclear weapons freeze. In order to achieve this goal, a wide number of tactics were employed and the organization was structured so as to accommodate as large a number of supporters as possible. This resulted in freeze members undertaking a wide variety of activities in pursuit of the freeze, guided by their own images of how to implement change. This varied considerably, as individuals sought change through individual participatory actions, through the operations of local freeze groups, by attempting to spread the freeze message through other institutions, and by directly challenging the authority of the state at the local level. These activities were undertaken in such a way as to illustrate a small number of social change models held by individuals.

For movement organizers, a discouraging finding presented here is that nearly one-third of those on the organizational membership list do not undertake any actions in support of the movement that are visible to the public or the peace movement leaders. These adherents believe their participation via official means of expressing opinion is a sufficient method of pursuing change.

Movement supporters believe that more than mere electoral participation action is needed and engage in individual efforts at educating themselves and those around them. They are willing to give symbolic support to movement objectives, and give varying amounts of money or time toward movement goals, but they do not make commitments to peace groups. The strong supporters are distinguished from the weak supporters in that they are willing to engage in peace activism in the other institutional spheres of their lives in order to spread the message. Whereas the weak supporter adopts a participatory model of change, the strong supporter assumes a responsibility for mass marketing the movement's ideals.

The movement members adopt a pluralist interest group model of social change that requires the building of stronger peace movement challenging groups. The members not only undertake individual participatory actions, but also devote time to organizational activities. They vary in their commitment to organization building, with peripheral movement members undertaking fewer freeze movement activities and few, if any, confrontational activities, whereas the active movement supporters undertake substantial amounts of both. At the highest levels of movement building are the core movement members who feel empowered to assume responsibility for creating and carrying out the movement's strategy.

Those undertaking civil disobedience envision a different mechanism of social change—one requiring the explicit denial of current institutional arrangements. There is often little agreement as to what the replacement for the status quo should be, or even how their withdrawal of support will affect the system, but they share the image that the arms race will not stop until the current set of relations is denounced as illegitimate. Civil disobedience is usually based on values (often religious) that give greater weight to the symbolic acts of denouncing the system rather than pragmatic, short-term rewards. The partially engaged disobedient does not accept the importance of building challenging groups or operating within their framework. In contrast, the fully engaged disobedient does value the existence of these challenging groups along one of two lines. The first function of these groups is that they serve the needs of movement supporters by providing a challenge to the state. The second is that PMOs may serve as models for alternative institutional relations that will ultimately replace the state's institutions once true social change is achieved.

The empirical evidence from this local freeze group provides support for the claim that individual's actions reflect several models of social change. Social movement researchers would do well to use this as another organizing concept in explaining SMO participation at the individual level. Social movement activists would also benefit from understanding the implications of this finding. For example, a great deal of internal conflict arises over tactics often because the conflicting parties are operating under different (unspoken) assumptions about the importance of specific actions for achieving change. Similarly, strategy sessions often seem to go nowhere not because individuals don't listen or don't care what others have to say, but because they interpret the proposed strategies in light of their own internal change model. And finally, the interconnectedness of movement parts, or the importance of coalition building, is often debated in terms of its benefits or costs to a particular PMO, whereas the role of movement integration or structure contained in their models of change unknowingly colors the debate.

Even though the national freeze campaign started with a fairly explicit model of change, it was reluctant to elaborate it for a number of reasons. More importantly, however, the national model provided little guidance for organizers at the local level. This enabled a large number of people to participate while operating under a variety of images—which is precisely what many of the original organizers desired. However, it also left unchallenged the images of social change that were ultimately ineffective. The effort to maintain broad support for the freeze resulted in the campaign deliberately leaving undeveloped its opportunity to mount a more effective challenge to the system.

Notes

1. The principle adhered to by the national campaign was to promote grass-roots autonomy and control of the campaign. The pragmatic reason for not trying to determine local strategy and tactics was that there was simply too much diversity across local contexts and among local groups to try to reach agreements on specific goals, strategies, and tactics.

2. A survey conducted on a random sample of the GCNWFC mailing list in 1984 provided information on the activities undertaken by 325 members. The survey instrument was a lengthy questionnaire inserted in the newsletter of the GCN-WFC. The response rate was 33 percent—a very respectable return considering the length of the questionnaire and the method of distribution. An additional 58 surveys (61 percent response rate) were obtained from a purposive sample of the

core activists of the local freeze campaign, based on a reputational method selected by a panel of three organizational leaders and myself. The results reported on here are based on the randomly selected membership survey unless otherwise noted. For a more complete description of the method and instrument, see Marullo (1988).

3.   The analysis was done through a principal components analysis using squared multiple correlations on the main diagonal. The factors presented here have been rotated using a varimax rotation. Although factor analysis presumes interval level data, the technique is robust and unbiased for use with dichotomous level variables (Tabachnick and Fidell 1983). The results presented in Table 17.1 are correlation coefficients between each action item and four hypothetical scales (factor one through factor four) created from linear combinations of the action items.

4.   The conventional criteria used to determine how many factors to retain is that their eigenvalues should be greater than one (Kaiser 1960).

5.   The oblique rotation was done by using a promax rotation in SAS. After a varimax rotation, promax performs an oblique rotation that targets the strongest item on each factor as having a maximum correlation (1.00) with the factor and rotates the factors accordingly. The correlations given in the bottom panel of Table 17.1 represent the pairwise correlations among the four factors.

6.   This statistical technique operates by iteratively placing cases into fewer clusters based on the similarity of the designated variables. At first, each case is considered to be a separate cluster and those with identical scores on the indexes are combined into clusters. These clusters are then combined on the basis of collapsing together those clusters with the least differences between them. Eventually, all the cases are collapsed into one all-inclusive cluster with all of the differences among cases being within the cluster. Before getting to that point, however, the cases are divided into a handful of clusters that may provide insights into meaningful types. For this data, meaningful ideal-types can be seen to fit into eight good-sized clusters. Although there are actually more than eight clusters at this point in the analysis, several have only a few cases in them with outlying values or strange combination of values. These are indicated in Table 17.2, but they are ignored in the remainder of the discussion.

Bibliography

Adams, Ruth and Susan Cullen, eds. 1981. *The Final Epidemic: Physicians and Scientists on Nuclear War*. Chicago: Educational Foundation for Nuclear Science. Distributed by University of Chicago Press.

Alinsky, Saul D. 1972. *Rules for Radicals: A Practical Primer for Realistic Radicals*. New York: Vintage Books.

_____. [1946] 1969. *Reveille For Radicals*. New York: Vintage Books.

American Peace Test. 1988. *Reclaim the Test Site Action Handbook*. Salem, OR: American Peace Test National Clearing House.

Archibald, Kathleen. 1963. "Social Science Approches to Peace: Problems and Issues." *Social Problems* 11:91–104.

Ayvazian, Andrea. 1986. *Organizational Development: The Seven Deadly Sins*. Amherst, MA: Peace Development Fund.

Ball, George. 1985. "The War for Stars Wars." *New York Review of Books*. April 11.

Barash, David P. and Judith Eve Lipton. 1982. *Stop Nuclear War! A Handbook*. New York: Grove Press.

Barkan, Steven E. 1979. "Strategic, Tactical and Organizational Dilemmas of the Protest Movement Against Nuclear Power." *Social Problems* 27:19–37.

Barone, Michael and Grant Ujifusa. 1985. *The Almanac of American Politics 1986*. Washington: National Journal.

Belenky, Mary F., Blythe Clinchy, Nancy Goldberger, and Jill Tarule. 1986. *Women's Way of Knowing: The Development of Self, Voice and Mind*. New York: Basic Books.

Bellah, Robert N. 1976. "New Religious Consciousness and the Crisis in Modernity." Pp. 333–352 in A. Glock and R. Bellah, eds., *The New Religious Consciousness*. Berkeley: University of California.

Bellah, Robert N., Richard Madsen, William Sullivan, Ann Swidler, and Steve Tipton. 1985. *Habits of the Heart: Individualism and Commitment in American Life*. Berkeley: University of California Press.

Belsky, Lisa and John Doble, eds. 1984. *Technical Appendix to Voter Options on Nuclear Arms Policy: A Briefing Book for the 1984 Elections*. New York: The Public Agenda Foundation.

Benford, Robert D. 1988. "The Nuclear Disarmament Movement." Pp. 237–265 in Lester R. Kurtz, *The Nuclear Cage*. Englewood Cliffs: Prentice Hall.

_____. 1987. *Framing Activity, Meaning, and Social Movement Participation: The Nuclear Disarmament Movement*. Ph.D. diss., University of Texas. Ann Arbor, MI: University Microfilms.

_____. 1984. *The Interorganizational Dynamics of the Austin Peace Movement*. M.A. thesis, University of Texas.

Berger, Peter and Hansfried Kellner. 1970. "Marriage and the Construction of Reality." Pp. 50-61 in H. P. Dreitzel, ed., *Recent Sociology* (No.2). New York: Macmillan.

Beyond War. 1987a. "Beyond War: A New Way of Thinking," (Informational Booklet). Palo Alto, CA. March.

————. 1987b. "Working Together We Can Build A World Beyond War" (Informational Booklet). Palo Alto, CA. April.

————. 1987c. *On Beyond War*, No. 33. Palo Alto, CA. October.

————. 1986. *On Beyond War—Special Report*. Palo Alto, CA. October.

————. 1984. *On Beyond War*, vol. 1, no. 4. Palo Alto, CA. October.

Blechman, Frank. 1988. Personal communication.

Blow, Richard. 1988. "Moronic Convergence: The Moral and Spiritual Emptiness of New Age." *New Republic* January 25:24–27.

Blumer, Herbert. 1939. "Collective Behavior." Pp. 25–45 in Robert Park, ed., *An Outline of the Principles of Sociology*. New York: Barnes & Noble.

Bolton, Charles D. 1972. "Alienation and Action: A Study of Peace Group Members." *American Journal of Sociology* 78:537–561.

Bordewich, Fergus M. 1988. "Colorado's Thriving Cults." *New York Times Magazine* May 1:37–43.

Bouchier, David. 1978. *Idealism and Revolution: New Ideologies of Liberation in Britain and the United States*. New York: St. Martins Press.

Boulding, Elise. 1984. "The Participation of Sociologists in the Nuclear Debate." Paper presented at the American Sociological Association Annual Meetings, San Antonio.

Boyer, Paul. 1984. "From Activism to Apathy: The American People and Nuclear Weapons, 1963-1980." *Journal of American History* 70:821–843.

Bradley, David. [1948] 1983. *No Place to Hide: 1946–1984*. Hanover: University Press of New England.

Braungart, Richard G. 1984a. "Historical Generations and Generational Units: A Global Pattern of Youth Movements." *Journal of Political and Military Sociology* 12:113–135.

————. 1984b. "Historical Generations and Youth Movements: A Theoretical Perspective." *Research in Social Movements, Conflicts, and Change* 6:95–142.

Braungart, Richard G. and Margaret M. Braungart. 1986. "Life Course and Generational Politics." *Annual Review of Sociology* 12:205–231.

————. 1980. "Political Career Patterns of Radical Activists in the 1960s and 1970s: Some Historical Comparisons." *Sociological Focus* 13:237–254.

Bromley, David G. and Anson D. Shupe, Jr. 1979. *"Moonies" in America: Cult, Church, and Crusade*. Beverly Hills: Sage Publications.

Butts, David. 1983. "Fighting the Nuclear Threat." *Images* [Supplement to *Daily Texan*] July 15 :12–13.

Cable, Sherry, Edward J. Walsh, and Rex H. Warland. 1988. "Differential Paths to Political Activism: Comparisons of Four Mobilization Processes After the Three Mile Island Accident." *Social Forces* 66:951–969.

Caldicott, Helen. 1984. *Missile Envy: The Arms Race and Nuclear War*. New York: Bantam Books.

_____. 1981a. "Dr. Helen Caldicott, M.D.: On the Medical Consequences of Nuclear War." Speech presented in Berkeley, April 20, 1981. Watertown, MA: Women's Party for Survival. Brochure, 11 pp.

_____. 1981b. "A Physician's View of Nuclear War: An Interview with Helen Caldicott." Berkeley: Conservation Press. Newspaper folio reprint, 4 pp.

_____. 1981c. "Nuclear War: This May Be Your Last Christmas" (Interview). *U.S. Catholic* 46:18–24.

_____. 1981d. "Introduction." Pp. 1-3 in Ruth Adams and Susan Cullen, eds., *The Final Epidemic: Physicians and Scientists on Nuclear War*. Chicago: Educational Foundation for Nuclear Science.

_____. [1978] 1980. *Nuclear Madness: What You Can Do!* New York: Bantam Books.

_____. 1979. "At the Crossroads." Excerpts from a speech originally given for a Mobilization for Survival event, originally in December 1977 issue of *New Age*. San Francisco: Abalone Alliance. Brochure, 13 pp.

Californians for a Bilateral Nuclear Weapons Freeze. 1982. "The Last Epidemic and the Californians for a Bilateral Nuclear Weapons Freeze." Packet for people showing the film, *The Last Epidemic*. San Francisco: Californians for a Bilateral Nuclear Weapons Freeze.

Cantril, Hadley. 1941. *The Psychology of Social Movements*. New York: John Wiley & Sons.

Carpenter, Tim. 1985. Personal communication.

Carroll, Berenice and Charles Fink. 1983. *Peace and War: A Guide to Bibliographies*. New York: ABC-CLIO.

Carroll, Eugene. 1985. "Move Toward Test Ban." *New York Times*. January 8.

Caspar, Barry M. 1983. "Like Caldicott in a Can." *Nuclear Times* 2(October):21.

Cassel, Christine, Michael McCally, and Henry Abraham, eds. 1984. *Nuclear Weapons and Nuclear War: A Sourcebook for Health Professionals*. New York: Praeger Scientific.

Celcak, Peter. 1983. *America's Quest of the Ideal Self: Dissent and Fulfillment in the 60s and 70s*. New York: Oxford University Press.

Cevoli, Cathy. 1983. "These Four Women Could Save Your Life." *Mademoiselle* 90(January):104–107.

Chatfield, Charles. 1971. *For Peace and Justice: Pacifism in America, 1914–1941*. Knoxville, TN: University of Tennessee.

Chivian, Eric et al. 1982. *Last Aid: The Medical Dimensions of Nuclear War*. International Physicians for the Prevention of Nuclear War. San Francisco: W. H. Freeman.

Clancy, Frank. 1986. "Showdown at Ground Zero." *Mother Jones*. November.

Clotfelter, James. 1986. "Disarmament Movements in the United States." *Bulletin of Peace Proposals* 23(June):2.

Cohen, Jean. 1985. "Strategy or Identity: New Theoretical Paradigms and Contemporary Social Movements." *Social Research* 52(4): 663–716.

Cohler, Bertram and Scott Geyer. 1982. "Psychological Autonomy and Interdependence within the Family." Pp. 196–223 in F. Walsh, ed., *Normal Family Processes*. New York: Guilford.

Cohn, Carol. 1987. "Slick 'Ems, Glick 'Ems, Christmas Trees and Cookie Cutters:

Nuclear Language and How We Learned to Pat the Bomb." *Bulletin of the Atomic Scientists* 43(5):17–24.

Cole, Nancy. nd. INFACT mail fund and pledge solicitation letter.

Cole, Robert. 1985. "The Freeze: Crusade of the Leisure Class," *Harper's*. March.

Coles, Robert. 1969. "Social Struggle and Weariness." Pp. 311–327 in Barry McLaughlin, ed., *Studies in Social Movements*. New York: Free Press.

Conetta, Carl. 1988. *Peace Resource Book: A Comprehensive Guide to the Issues, Organizations, and Literature 1988–89*. Cambridge, MA: Ballinger Publishing.

Conrad, Peter and Joseph W. Schneider. 1980. *Deviance and Medicalization: From Badness to Sickness*. St. Louis: Mosby.

Cooney, R. and H. Michalowski. 1977. *The Power of the People: Active Nonviolence in the United States*. Culver City, CA: Peace Press.

Coover, Virginia, Ellen Deacon, Charles Esser, and Christopher Moore. 1978. *Resource Manual for Living Revolution*, 2d ed. Philadelphia: New Society Press.

Creative Initiative Foundation. 1984. "Beyond War: A New Way of Thinking ('The Beyond War Statement')." Palo Alto, CA. March.

Curtis, Russell L., Jr., and Louis A. Zurcher. 1974. "Social Movements: An Analytical Exploration of Organizational Forms." *Social Problems* 21:356–370.

———. 1973. "Stable Resources of Protest Movements: The Multi-Organizational Field." *Social Forces* 21: 356–370.

Cushnir, Howard. 1986. "The Great Peace That Couldn't." *Mother Jones*. June.

Daggett, Steve. 1985. Personal communication.

D'Antonio, William V. 1983. "Observing." American Sociological Association *Footnotes*.

DeMartini, Joseph R. 1983. "Social Movement Participation, Generational Consciousness, and Lasting Effects." *Youth & Society*. 15:195–223.

Derouche, Catherine. 1985. Personal communication.

Douglass, James. 1987. "Civil Disobedience As Prayer." Pp. 93–97 in Arthur Laffin and Anne Montgomery, eds., *Swords into Plowshares: Nonviolent Direct Action for Disarmament*. New York: Harper & Row.

———. 1984. "Tracking the White Train: People of Faith Resist the Rolling Threat." *Sojourners* (February):12–16.

Drew, Elizabeth. 1983. "A Political Journal." *New Yorker*. June 20.

Duker, Laurie. 1985. Personal communication.

Duncan, Jeffrey. 1985. Personal communication.

Edsall, Thomas Byrne. 1984. *The New Politics of Inequality*. New York: Norton.

Ehrenhalt, Alan et al. 1985. *Politics in America*. Washington: Congressional Quarterly Press.

Eight Minutes to Midnight. 1981. *Eight Minutes to Midnight: A Portrait of Dr. Helen Caldicott*. 60 minutes, color. Direct Cinema Limited.

Eister, Allan W. 1950. *Drawing-Room Conversation: A Sociological Account of the Oxford Group Movement*. Durham, NC: Duke University Press.

Eitzen, D. Stanley. 1986. *Social Problems: Third Edition*. Boston: Allyn & Bacon.

Eller, Cynthia. C. 1988. Moral and Religious Arguments in Support of Pacifism: Conscientious Objectors and the Second World War. Ph.D. diss., University of Southern California.

Ellul, Jacques. 1981. "On Dialectic." Pp. 291–308 in C. G. Christians and J. M. Van Hook, eds., *Jacques Ellul: Interpretive Essays*. Urbana, IL: University of Illinois Press.

Elms, Alan. 1986. "From House to Haig: Private Life and Public Style in American Foreign Policy Advisors." *Journal of Social Issues* 42(2): 33–53.

Ennis, James and Richard Schreuer. 1987. "Mobilizing Weak Support for Social Movements: The Role of Grievance, Efficacy, and Cost." *Social Forces* 66 (December):390–409.

Epstein, Barbara. 1985. "The Culture of Direct Action: Livermore Action Group and the Peace Movement." *Socialist Review* 82/83:31–61.

Erikson, Erik. 1975. *Life History and the Historical Moment*. New York: Free Press.

———. 1968. *Identity, Youth and Crisis*. New York: Norton.

———. 1963. *Childhood and Society*, 2d ed. New York: Norton.

Ervin, Frank R. et al. 1962. "The Medical Consequences of Nuclear War. II. Human and Ecological Effects in Massachusetts of an Assumed Thermonuclear Attack on the United States." *New England Journal of Medicine* 266(22):1126–1136.

Etzioni, Amitai. 1983. *An Immodest Agenda: Rebuilding America before the Twenty-first Century*. New York: McGraw Hill.

———. 1962. *The Hard Way to Peace*. New York: Collier Books.

Faludi, Susan. 1987. "Inner Peacenik." *Mother Jones* April:20–53.

Fay, Brian. 1987. *Critical Social Science: Liberation and Its Limits*. Ithaca, NY: Cornell University Press.

Fendrich, James Max and Kenneth L. Lovoy. 1989. "Back to the Future: Adult Political Behavior of Former Student Activists." *American Sociological Review* 53:780–784.

Fendrich, James Max and Robert W. Turner. 1989. "The Transition from Student to Adult Politics." *Social Forces* 67:1049–1057.

Fenno, Richard F., Jr. 1978. *Home Style: House Members in their Districts*. Boston: Little Brown.

Ferguson, Marilyn. 1980. *The Aquarian Conspiracy: Personal & Social Transformation in the 1980s*. Los Angeles: J. P. Tarcher.

Ferguson, Thomas and Joel Rogers. 1986. "Big Business Backs the Freeze." *Nation*. July 19/26.

Ferre, Myra M. and Frederick D. Miller, 1985. "Mobilization and Meaning: Toward an Integration of Social Psychological and Resource Perspectives on Social Movements." *Sociological Inquiry* 55:38–62.

Feshback, Seymour and Michael J. White. 1986. "Individual Differences in Attitudes Towards Nuclear Arms Policies: Some Psychological and Social Policy Consideration." *Journal of Peace Research* 23:129–138.

Fine, Melinda and Peter Steven. 1984. *American Peace Directory 1984*. Cambridge, MA: Ballinger.

Fireman, Bruce and William Gamson. 1979. "Utilitarian Logic in Resource Mobilization Perspective." Pp. 8–44 in Mayer N. Zald and John D. McCarthy, eds., *The Dynamics of Social Movements*. Cambridge, MA: Winthrop Publishers.

Flacks, Robert. 1971. *Youth and Social Change*. Chicago: Markham.

Forsberg, Randall. 1984. "The Freeze and Beyond: Confining the Military to Defense as a Route to Disarmament." *World Policy Journal* 1(Winter):287–318.

Forsberg, Randall and David S. Meyer. 1985. "Military Spending: Can We Budge It?" *Defense and Disarmament News* 1(June/July):3–6.

Fowler, James. 1981. *Stages of Faith*. San Francisco: Harper & Row.

Fox, Renee. 1977. "The Medicalization and Demedicalization of American Society." *Daedalus* 106:9–23.

Frank, Jerome and Earl R. Nash. 1965. "Commitment to Peace Work: A Preliminary Study of Determinants and Sustainers of Behavior Change." *American Journal of Orthopsychiatry*, 106–119.

Freeman, Jo. 1983. "A Model for Analyzing the Strategic Options of Social Movement Organizations." Pp. 193–210 in Jo Freeman, ed., *Social Movements of the Sixties and Seventies*. White Plains: Longman.

————. 1979. "Resource Mobilization and Strategy: A Model for Analyzing Social Movement Organization Actions." Pp. 167–189 in Mayer Zald and John D. McCarthy, eds., *The Dynamics of Social Movements*. Cambridge, MA: Winthrop.

————. 1975. *The Politics of Women's Liberation: A Case Study of an Emerging Social Movement and its Relation to the Policy Process*. New York: David McKay.

Freeze Voter Education Fund. 1986. *A Peace Activist's Political Organizing Manual*. Washington, DC: Freeze Voter Education Fund.

Gamson, William A. 1975. *The Strategy of Social Protest*. Homewood, IL: Dorsey Press.

Geiger, H. Jack. 1982. "The Effects on a City in the United States." Pp. 137–150 in Eric Chivian et al., *The Medical Dimensions of Nuclear War*. International Physicians for the Prevention of Nuclear War. San Francisco: W. H. Freeman.

————. 1981a. "The Illusion of Survival." *Bulletin of the Atomic Scientists* 37:116–119.

————. 1981b. "Illusion of Survival." Pp. 173–181 in Ruth Adams and Susan Cullen, eds., *The Final Epidemic: Physicians and Scientists on Nuclear War*. Chicago: Educational Foundation for Nuclear Science.

Gerlach, Luther and Virginia Hine. 1970. *People, Power, and Change: Movements of Social Transformation*. Indianapolis: Bobbs-Merrill.

Geschwender, James A. 1983. "The Social Context of Strategic Success: A Land-Use Struggle in Hawaii." Pp. 235–251 in Jo Freeman, ed., *Social Movements of the Sixties and Seventies*. White Plains: Longman.

Gilligan, Carol. 1982. *In a Different Voice*. Cambridge: Harvard University.

Gitlin, Todd. 1987. *The Sixties: Years of Hope, Days of Rage*. New York: Bantam Books.

_____. 1980. *The Whole World is Watching*. Berkeley: University of California Press.

Glaser, Barney and Anselm Strauss. 1967. *The Discovery of Grounded Theory*. Chicago: Aldine.

Glock, Charles Y. and Robert N. Bellah, eds. 1976. *The New Religious Consciousness*. Berkeley: University of California.

Goffman, Erving. 1959. *The Presentation of Self in Everyday Life*. New York: Doubleday.

Gordon, David. 1974. "The Jesus People: An Identity Synthesis." *Urban Life and Culture* 13:159–178.

Goertzel, Ted George. 1983. "The Gender Gap: Sex, Family, Income and Political Opinions in the Early 1980s." *Journal of Political and Military Sociology* 11:209–222.

Grandmothers for Peace. 1987. "Grandmothers for Peace." Sacramento: Grandmothers for Peace brochure.

Greenwald, David and Steven Zeitlin. 1987. *No Reason to Talk about It: Families Confront the Nuclear Threat*. New York: Norton.

Grimshaw, Allen D. 1983. "Sociologists Must Contribute to World Peace Movement." American Sociological Association *Footnotes*.

Gromyko, Anatolii and Martin E. Hellman. 1988. *Breakthrough: Emerging New Thinking*. New York: Walker & Company.

Grove, Lloyd. 1986a. "Martin Holladay: In Prison. Paying for His Civil Disobedience." *Washington Post*. August 5.

_____. 1986b. "Missile Vandal Freed." *Washington Post*. September 26.

Gusfield, Joseph R. 1981. "Social Movements and Social Change: Perspectives of Linearity and Fluidity." *Research in Social Movements, Conflicts and Change* 4: 317–339.

Gusfield, Joseph R. 1979. "The Modernity of Social Movements: Public Roles and Private Parts." Pp. 290–307 in A. Hawley, ed., *The Future of Societal Growth*. New York: The Free Press.

_____. 1966. "Functional Areas of Social Movement Leadership." *Sociological Quarterly* 7:137–156.

_____. 1963. *Symbolic Crusade: Status Politics and the American Temperance Movement*. Urbana: University of Illinois Press.

_____. 1957. "The Problem of Generation in an Organizational Structure." *Social Forces* 35:323–330.

Hannon, James. 1984. "Religion and Ideology and Praxis: Current Considerations in Marxist Theory." In *Religion: The Cutting Edge*, titled issue of *New England Sociologist* 5:37–57.

Hannon, James T. and Sam Marullo. 1988. "Education for Survival: Using Films to Teach War as a Social Problem." *Teaching Sociology* 16:245–255.

Harrington, Michael. 1968. *Toward a Democratic Left: A Program for a New Majority*. New York: Macmillan.

Hedemann, Ed. 1981. *War Resisters League Organizer's Manual*. New York: War Resisters League.

Hedlund, Jay. 1985. Personal communication.

Henslin, James M. and Paul M. Roesti. 1976. "Trends and Topics in *Social Problem* 1953-1975: A Content Analysis." *Social Problem* 24:54–69.

Hersey, John. [1946] 1981. *Hiroshima*. New York: Bantam.

Hertsgaard, Mark. 1985. "What Became of the Freeze?" *Mother Jones*. June: 44–47.

Hess, Robert and George Handel. 1959. *Family Worlds*. Chicago: University of Chicago.

Hiroshima/Nagasaki 1945. 1980. *Hiroshima/Nagasaki 1945*. 17 minutes, black and white. Produced by Eric Barnouw and Paul Ponder.

Holland, Lauren H. and Robert A. Hoover. 1985. *The MX Decision: a New Direction in U.S. Weapons Procurement Policy*. Boulder: Westview.

Houston, Jean. 1972. *The Possible Human: A Course in Extending Your Physical, Mental & Creative Possibilities*. Los Angeles: Houghton-Mifflin.

Hunt, John P. 1982. "Political Behavior, Political Alienation, and the Sociology of Generations: A Cohort Analysis of Recent Trends." *Sociological Focus* 15:93–106.

If You Love This Planet. 1982. *If You Love this Planet: Dr. Helen Caldicott on Nuclear War*. 26 minutes, color. Produced by the National Film Board of Canada. Direct Cinema Limited.

Institute for Defense and Disarmament Studies. 1988. *1988/89 Peace Resource Book: A Comprehensive Guide to Issues, Groups, and Literature*. Cambridge, MA: Ballinger.

Isaacs, John. 1985. Personal communication.

Isserman, Maurice. 1987. *If I Had A Hammer: The Death of the Old Left and the Birth of the New*. New York: Basic Books.

Jenkins, J. Craig. 1983. "Resource Mobilization Theory and the Study of Social Movements." *Annual Review of Sociology* 9:527–553.

Jenkins, J. Craig and Charles Perrow. 1977. "Insurgency of the Powerless." *American Sociological Review* 42: 242–268.

Jergen, Mary Evelyn. 1985. *How You Can Be a Peacemaker: Catholic Teachings and Practical Suggestions*. Liguouri, Missouri: Liguori Publications.

Jones, R. Kenneth. 1978. "Paradigm Shifts and Identity Theory: Alternation as a Form of Identity Management." Pp. 59–82 in H. Mol, ed., *Identity and Religion*. Beverly Hills: Sage.

Kaiser, Hans B. 1960. "The Application of Electronic Computers to Factor Analysis." *Educational and Psychological Measurement* 20: 141–151.

Kaplan, Fred. 1987. "'Star Wars': The Ultimate Military Industrial Compact." *Boston Globe*. September 14.

Kassebaum, Nancy L. 1985. "Arms Control After the Summit." *Arms Control Today* (November/December):7–9.

Katz, Elihu and Paul Lazarsfeld. 1955. *Personal Influence*. Glenco, IL: The Free Press.

Katz, Milton S. 1986. *Ban the Bomb: A History of SANE, The Committee for a Sane Nuclear Policy, 1957–1985*. Westport, CT: Greenwood Press.

Katz, Neil H. 1974. *Radical Pacifism and the Contemporary American Peace Movement: The Committee for Nonviolent Action, 1957–1967*. Ph.D. diss., University of Maryland.

Keerdoja, Eileen. 1981. "The Hunger Project Feeds Its Coffers." *Newsweek* June 15:18–21.

Kegan, Robert. 1982. *The Evolving Self: Problems and Process in Human Development*. Cambridge: Harvard University.

Kehoe, Alice. 1986. "Revitalization Movements and the Hope of Peace." *Zygon* 21(4) 491–500.

Keniston, Kenneth. 1968. *Young Radicals: Notes on Committed Youth*. New York: Harcourt, Brace, & World.

Keyes, Ken, Jr. 1982. *The Hundredth Monkey*. Coos Bay, OR: Vision Books.

Killian, Lewis M. 1984. "Organization, Rationality and Spontaneity in the Civil Rights Movement." *American Sociological Review* 49: 770–83.

Kistiakovsky, George. n.d. Quote in Physicians for Social Responsibility brochure.

Klandermans, Bert. 1986. "New Social Movements and Resource Mobilization." *International Journal of Mass Emergencies and Disasters* 4:13–38.

Kohlberg, Lawrence. 1973. "Continuities in Childhood and Adult Moral Development Revisited." Pp. 180–204 in P. B. Baltes and K. W. Schaie, eds., *Lifespan Development Psychology*, 2d ed. New York: Academic Press.

———. 1969. *Stages in the Development of Moral Thought and Action*. New York: Holt, Rinehart & Winston.

———. 1969. "Stage and Sequence: The Cognitive-Developmental Approach to Socialization. Pp. 347–380 in D. A. Goslin, ed., *Handbook of Socialization Theory*. Chicago: Rand McNally.

Kramer, Ronald C. and Sam Marullo. 1985. "Toward a Sociology of Nuclear Weapons." *Sociological Quarterly* 26:277–292.

Krauthammer, Charles. 1985. "Who Killed the Freeze?" *Washington Post*. July 26. .

Kreisberg, Louis. 1984. "Where We Are and Where We Could Go in Peace Research." Paper presented at the American Sociological Association annual meetings, San Antonio.

Kurtz, Lester R. 1988. *The Nuclear Cage*. Englewood Cliffs: Prentice Hall.

Ladd, Anthony E., Thomas C. Hood, and Kent D. Van Liere. 1983. "Ideological Themes in the Antinuclear Movement: Consensus and Diversity." *Sociological Inquiry* 53:252–272.

Laffin, Arthur and Anne Montgomery, eds. 1987. *Swords into Plowshares: Nonviolent Direct Action for Disarmament*. San Francisco: Harper & Row.

Lang, Kurt. 1983. "World Conflict Research Needed." American Sociological Association *Footnotes*.

Lauer, Robert H. 1976. "Defining Social Problems: Public Opinion and Textbook Practice." *Social Problems* 24:122–131.

Leaning, Jennifer. 1983. "Civil Defense and Survival." *PSR Newsletter* 4(1):3, 12–14.

Leavitt, Robert. 1983. "Freezing the Arms Race: The Genesis of a Mass Movement." Kennedy School of Government-Case Program, Harvard University, case study.

Lierberson, Stanley. 1985. *Making It Count: The Improvement of Social Research and Theory*. Berkeley: University of California Press.

Loeb, Paul. 1987. *Hope in Hard Times: America's Peace Movement and the Reagan Era*. Lexington, MA: Lexington Books.

Lofland, John. 1988. "Consensus Movements: City-Twinning and Derailed Dissent in the American Eighties." *Research in Social Change, Conflict and Social Movements* 11:163–196.

———. 1985. *Protest: Studies of Collective Behavior and Social Movements*. New Brunswick, NJ: Transaction.

———. 1978. "Becoming a World-saver Revisited." Pp. 10–23 in James T. Richardson, ed., *Conversion Careers: In and Out of the New Religions*. Beverly Hills: Sage.

———. [1966] 1977. *Doomsday Cult: A Study of Conversion, Proselytization, and Maintenance of Faith*. Enlarged Edition. New York: Irvington Publishers.

Lofland, John, Victoria Johnson, and Pamela Kato. In press. "Peace Movement Organizations and Activists: An Analytic Bibliography." *Behavioral and Social Science Librarian*.

Lofland, John and Norman Skonovd. 1981. "Conversion Motifs." *Journal of Scientific Study of Religion* 20:373–385.

Lowi, Theodore J. 1971. *The Politics of Disorder*. New York: Basic Books.

Lyons, Norma. 1983. "Two Perspectives: On Self, Relationships, and Morality." *Harvard Educational Review* 53(2) 126–145.

MacDougall, John. 1985. "The M-X Missile in the House of Representatives: Notes on 7 Swing Representatives." Unpublished manuscript.

MacDougall, John. In press. "The Freeze Movement, Congress and the M-X Missile." In Bert Klandermans, ed., *Peace Movements in International Perspective*.

Mack, John E. 1982. "The Perception of U.S.-Soviet Intentions and Other Psychological Dimensions of the Nuclear Arms Race." *American Journal of Orthopsychiatry* 52:290–599.

Mack, Raymond W. 1969. "The Components of Social Conflict." Pp. 327–37 in R. M. Kramer and H. S. Specht, eds., *Readings in Community Organization Practice*. Englewood Cliffs, NJ: Prentice-Hall.

Mannheim, Karl. 1952. "The Problem of Generations." *Essays on the Sociology of Knowledge*. London: Routledge & Kegan Paul.

Marullo, Sam. 1989. "Gender Differences in Peace Movement Participation." Paper presented at the Eastern Sociological Society meetings, Baltimore, MD.

———. 1988. "Leadership and Membership in the Nuclear Freeze Movement: A Specification of Resource Mobilization Theory." *Sociological Quarterly* 29:407–427.

McAdam, Doug. 1988. *Freedom Summer*. New York: Oxford University Press.

_____. 1982. *Political Process and the Development of Black Insurgency*. Chicago: University of Chicago Press.

McCarthy, John D., David W. Britt, and Mark Wolfson. In press. "The Institutional Channeling of Social Movements by the State in the United States." *Research in Social Movements, Conflicts and Change* 12.

McCarthy, John D. and Mayer N. Zald. 1977. "Resource Mobilization and Social Movements: A Partial Theory." *American Journal of Sociology* 82:1212–1241.

_____. 1973. *The Trend of Social Movements in America: Professionalization and Resource Mobilization*. Morristown, NJ: General Learning Press.

McCrea, Frances B. and Daryl Kelley. 1983. "Thinking the Unthinkable: Toward a Sociology of Nuclear Weapons." Paper presented at the Society for the Study of Social Problems meetings, Detroit, MI.

McGrory, Mary. 1986. "An Unrepentant Mother Imprisoned for Attacking a Missile Site." *Boston Globe*. April 16.

_____. 1985. "Arms Control Gathers Moss." *Washington Post*. May 16.

Mead, George Herbert. 1934. *George Herbert Mead on Social Psychology* (A. Strauss, ed.). Chicago: University of Chicago Press.

Mechling, Elizabeth and Gale Auletta. 1986. "Beyond War: A Socio-Rhetorical Analysis of a New Class Revitalization Movement." *Western Journal of Speech Communication* 50(Fall):388–404.

Mehan, Hugh and John Wills. 1988. "MEND: A Nurturing Voice in the Nuclear Arms Debate." *Social Problems* 35:363–383.

Meyer, David S. 1990. *A Winter of Discontent: The Nuclear Freeze and American Politics*. New York: Praeger.

Meyerson, Brenda. 1985. Personal communication.

Michels, Robert. 1962. *Political Parties*. New York: Collier Books.

Miller, Judith. 1982. ". . . And Now a Disarmament Industry." *New York Times*. June 25.

Mills, C. Wright. 1958. *The Causes of World War III*. New York: Simon & Schuster.

Mogey, Wendy. 1982. "Depolarizing Disarmament Work: Twelve Guidelines to Help Us Reach New People." The New Manhattan Project, American Friends Service Committee.

Molander, Earl A. and Roger C. Molander. 1987. "Social Movement Building in Expert-Dependent Issue Areas." Paper presented at American Political Science Association meetings, Chicago, IL.

Molander, Earl A. and John Parachini. 1988. "From Social Movement Building to Lobbying." Paper presented at International Society for Political Psychology meetings, New York, NY.

Molotch, Harvey. 1979. "Media and Movements." Pp. 71–93 in M. N. Zald and J. D. McCarthy, eds., *The Dynamics of Social Movements*. Cambridge, MA: Winthrop.

Moore, April. 1985. Personal communication.

Morrison, David C. 1986. " Chaos on Capitol Hill." *National Journal*, September 27, pp. 2302–2307.

Moyer, William. 1977. *A Nonviolent Action Manual: How to Organize Nonviolent Demonstrations and Campaigns*. Philadelphia: New Society Press.

National Conference of Catholic Bishops. 1983. *The Challenge of Peace: God's Promise and Our Response*. Washington, DC: U.S. Catholic Conference.

"National Strategy for a NUCLEAR WEAPONS FREEZE." 1981. Institute for Defense and Disarmament Studies mimeograph.

Neal, Mary. 1988. *Balancing Passion and Reason: A Symbolic Analysis of the Communication Strategies of the Physicians' Movement against Nuclear Weapons*. Ph.D. diss., University of California, San Francisco.

Needleman, Jacob. 1970. *The New Religions*. New York: Doubleday & Company.

New York Times. 1985. "Disarmament Groups Seek Rallying Point After Faltering on Atom Freeze." August 19.

Nusbaumer, Michael R. and Judith A. DiIorio. 1985. "The Medicalization of Nuclear Disarmament Claims." *Peace and Change* 1:63–73.

Nusbaumer, Michael R., Daryl Kelley, and Judith A. DiIorio. 1989. "The Discovery of War as a Social Problem: Teaching as Sociological Practice." *Teaching Sociology* 17:316–322.

Oberschall, Anthony. 1973. *Social Conflict and Social Movements*. Englewood Cliffs, NJ: Prentice Hall.

Oliver, Pamela. 1983. "The Mobilization of Paid and Volunteer Activists in the Neighborhood Movement." *Research in Social Movements, Conflicts and Change* 5:133–170.

Olson, Mancur. 1968. *The Logic of Collective Action*. New York: Schocken.

Osgood, Charles. 1962. *An Alternative to War and Surrender*. Urbana: University of Illinois Press.

Panapoulos, Frank. 1986. "Plowshare: Disarmament By Example." *Weapons Facilities Network Bulletin* 1(Winter):1&6.

Pertschuk, Michael. 1986. *Giantkillers*. New York: Norton.

Physicians for Social Responsibility. 1962. "Special Study Section: The Medical Consequences of Nuclear War." *New England Journal of Medicine* 266(22):1126–1154.

Piven, Francis Fox and Richard Cloward. 1979. *Poor People's Movements: Why They Succeed, How They Fail*. New York: Vintage Books.

Plesch, Daniel. 1982. *A Disarmament Action Manual: What Do We Do After We've Shown 'The War Game'?* London: Campaign for Nuclear Disarmament.

Plummer, William 1984. "Separated from her Children, Jailed Nuke Protester Liz McAllister Says She's Serving Prime Time for Peace." *People*. August 27.

Powers, Thomas. 1984. *Vietnam: The War at Home*. Boston: G. K. Hall.

PSR/Greater Boston. 1982. "Speaking Out on the Threat of Nuclear War: A Practical Guide Prepared by the Greater Boston PSR." Cambridge, MA: PSR/Greater Boston.

PSR/San Francisco Bay Area. 1983. "Speakers Training Manual." Edited by Stanley Nudelman. Berkeley: PSR/San Francisco Bay Area. November 10.

———. n.d. "Nuclear Weapons and the Nation's Health: A PSR Primer." Berkeley: PSR/San Francisco Bay Area.

Reiss, David. 1981. *The Family's Construction of Reality*. Cambridge: Harvard University.

Ringler, Dick, ed. 1984. "Nuclear War: A Teaching Guide." *Bulletin of Atomic Scientists*, 40(December): 1s–32s.

Rizzo, Renata. 1983. "Professional Approach to Peace." *Nuclear Times* 1:10–13.

Rizzo, Renata and R. Harris. 1987. "Grass Roots Opt for Unity: Freeze/SANE Merger." *Nuclear Times*. January:29.

Roberts, Steven V. 1982. "Congressmen and their Districts: Free Agents in Fear of the Future." Pp. 65–84 in Dennis Hale, ed., *The U.S. Congress*. New Brunswick: Transaction.

Robinson, Chris. 1982. *Plotting Directions: An Activist's Guide*. Philadelphia, PA: RECON Publications.

Rogers, Everett M. 1983. *Diffusion of Innovations*, 3rd ed. New York: Free Press.

Rose, Peter I. and Jerome Laulicht. 1963. "Editorial Forward." *Social Problems* 11:3–5.

Rosenthal, L. 1982. "Anti-Nuclear Medicine: Interview with Helen Caldicott." *Science Digest* 90:70–71.

Rothenberg, Lawrence S. 1989. "Do Interest Groups Make a Difference? Lobbying, Constituency Influence and Public Policy." Paper presented at the Midwest Political Science Association meeting.

Sanders, Ruth. 1984. Personal communication.

Sandman, Peter M. and Jo Ann M. Valenti. 1986. "Scared Stiff—or Scared into Action." *Bulletin of the Atomic Scientists* 42(Jan)1:12–16.

San Francisco Chronicle. 1984. "Anti-Nuclear Speaker Scares Students." September 28.

Sasson, Ted, Pam Solo, and Paul Walker. 1988. Letter to "Dear IPIS Friend." Institute for Peace and International Security.

Scholzman, Kay L. and Tierney, John T. 1986. *Organized Interests and American Democracy*. New York: Harper & Row.

Schwartz, Jim. 1984. "A Conspiracy of Conscience: Michigan Peace Protests Against Williams International." *Nation*. December 8.

Seidita, Jo. 1985. Personal communication.

Shaffir, William. 1978. "Witnessing as Identity Consolidation: The Case of the Lubavitcher Chassidim." Pp. 39–57 in H. Mol, ed., *Identity and Religion*. Beverly Hills: Sage.

Sibley, M.Q. 1988. Interview with Leah Rogne. February 11.

Sidel, Victor W., Jack Geiger, and Bernard Lown. 1962. "The Medical Consequences of Nuclear War. II. The Physician's Role in the Post Attack Period." *New England Journal of Medicine* 266(22):1137–1144.

Smelser, Neil J. 1962. *Theory of Collective Behavior*. New York: The Free Press.

Smith, Howard. 1982. "Disarming Europeans." *Village Voice*. April 27.

Smith, Tom W. 1984. "The Polls: Gender and Attitudes Toward Violence." *Public Opinion Quarterly* 48:384–396.

Snow, David A. and Robert B. Benford. 1988. "Ideology, Frame Resonance and

Participant Mobilization." *International Social Movements Research* 1:197–217.

Snow, David, E. Burke Rochford, Jr., Steven Worden, and Robert Benford. 1986. "Frame Alignment Process, Micromobilization, and Movement Participation." *American Sociological Review* 51:464–481.

Snow, David A., Louis A. Zurcher, Jr., and Sheldon Ekland-Olson. 1980. "Social Networks and Social Movements: A Microstructural Approach to Differential Recruitment." *American Sociological Review* 45:787–801.

Snow, David and Richard Machalak. 1983. "The Convert As a Social Type." Pp. 259–289 in Randall Collins, ed., *Sociological Theory*. San Francisco: Jossey-Bass.

Solo, Pam. 1988. *From Protest to Policy*. Cambridge, MA: Ballinger.

———. 1985 unpublished. "Interview With Randy Kehler."

Solomon, Frederick and Robert Q. Marston, eds. 1986. *The Medical Implications of Nuclear War*. Based on a symposium held at the National Academy of Sciences, September 20–22, 1985. Washington, DC: National Academy Press.

Sorokin, Pitirim. 1937. *Social and Cultural Dynamics: Fluctuations of Social Relationships, War, and Revolution*, vol. 3. New York: American Books.

———. 1925. *The Sociology of Revolution*. Philadelphia: J. P. Lippincott.

Staples, Lee. 1984. *Roots to Power: A Manual for Grassroots Organizing*. Westport, CT: Praeger.

Stewart, Abigail and Joseph Healy. 1986. "The Role of Personality Development and Experience in Shaping Political Commitment: An Illustrative Case." *Journal of Social Issues* 42(2):11–31.

Stone, Donald. 1976. "The Human Potential Movement." Pp. 93–115 in A. Glock and R. Bellah, eds., *The New Religious Consciousness*. Berkeley: University of California.

Sullivan, William Cuyler, Jr. 1982. *Nuclear Democracy: A History of the Greater St. Louis Citizen's Committee for Nuclear Information, 1957–1967*. Washington University of College Occasional Papers No. 1. St. Louis: Washington University.

Sweeney, Duane, ed. 1984. *The Peace Catalogue*. Seattle, WA: Press for Peace.

Szegedy-Maszak, Marianne. 1989. "The Movement: Rise and Fall of the Washington Peace Industry," *Bulletin of the Atomic Scientists* 45(January-February):18–23.

Tabachnick, Barbara and Linda Fidell. 1983. *Using Multivariate Statistics*. New York: Harper & Row.

Tarrow, Sidney. 1982. *Cycles of Protest*. Ithaca: Cornell University, Center for International Studies.

Taylor, Betsy. 1985 unpublished. "If We Can't Change the Politicians' Minds . . . Let's Change the Politicians." August.

Taylor, Richard J., Phyllis B. Taylor, and Sojourners. 1987. *The Practice of Peace: A Manual and Video for Nonviolence Training [in] Preparation for Actions of Faith and Conscience*. Washington, DC: Sojourners Resource Center.

Thiermann, Ian. 1980. *The Last Epidemic*. 35 minutes, color. Produced by Eric Thiermann. Impact Production.

Thomas, Daniel C. 1987. *Guide to Careers and Graduate Education in Peace Studies*. Amherst, MA: Five College Program in Peace and World Security Studies.

Thomas, Daniel C. and Michael T. Klare, 1989. *Peace and World Order Studies: A Curriculum Guide*. Boulder, CO: Westview.

Thomas, James. 1985. Personal communication.

Tilly, Charles. 1978. *From Mobilization to Revolution*. Reading, MA: Addison-Wesley.

Tipton, Steven M. 1982. *Getting Saved from the Sixties: Moral Meaning in Conversion and Cultural Change*. Berkeley: University of California Press.

Tirman, John. 1983. "Destabilizing Space: Star Wars from Scenario to Fact." *Nation*. October 24.

Towell, Pat. 1983. "M-X Gains Narrow House OK." *Congressional Quarterly Weekly Report* (July 23): 1483–8.

Turk, Herman and Myron J. Lefcowitz. 1962. "Towards a Theory of Representation Between Groups." *Social Forces* 40:337–341.

Turner, Ralph H. 1970. "Determinants of Social Movement Stategies." Pp. 145–164 in T. Shibutani, ed., *Human Nature and Collective Behavior*. Englewood Cliffs, NJ: Prentice Hall.

Turner, Ralph H. and Lewis M. Killian. 1987. *Collective Behavior*. Englewood Cliffs, NJ: Prentice Hall.

Tygart, C. E. 1987. "Participants in the Nuclear Weapons Freeze Movement." *Social Science Journal* 24:393–402.

Tyler, Tom R. and Kathleen M. McGraw. 1983. "The Threat of Nuclear War: Risk Interpretation and Behavioral Response." *Journal of Social Issues* 39:25–40.

Tyrell, R. Emmett, Jr. 1985. "As Star Wars Grows, Interest in Freeze Declines." *Washington Post*. March 4.

U.S. Out of Central America. 1983. *Recipes for Organizing: The USOCA Cookbook*. San Francisco, CA: U.S. Out of Central America.

Walker, Jack L. 1983. "The Origin and Maintenance of Interest Group in America." *American Political Science Review* 77:390–406.

Walker, R.B.J. and Saul H. Mendlovitz. 1987. "Peace, Politics and Contemporary Social Movements." Pp. 3–14 in Saul H. Mendlovitz and R.B.J. Walker, eds., *Towards a Just World Peace*. London: Butterworth.

Waller, Douglas. 1987. *Congress and the Nuclear Freeze: An Inside Look at the Politics of a Mass Movement*. Amherst, MA: University of Massachusetts Press.

Walsh, Edward J. and Rex H. Warland. 1983. "Social Movement Involvement in the Wake of a Nuclear Accident: Activists and Free Riders in the TMI Area." *American Sociological Review* 48:764–780.

Weber, Max. [1904–1905] 1958. *The Protestant Ethic and the Spirit of Capitalism* (T. Parson, trans.). New York: Scribner.

Weiner, Rex and Deanne Stillman. 1979. *Woodstock Census: The Nationwide Survey of the Sixties Generation*. New York: Viking Press.

Williams, Raymond. 1973. "Base and Superstructure in Marxist Cultural Theory." *New Left Review* 82 (Nov.-Dec.):3–16.

Wilson, James Q. 1973. *Political Organizations*. New York: Basic Books.

Wilson, John. 1973. *Introduction to Social Movements*. New York: Basic Books.

Wittner, Lawrence S. [1969] 1984. *Rebels Against War: The American Peace Movements, 1933–1983*. Philadelphia: Temple University Press.

Wollman, Neil. 1985. *Working For Peace: A Handbook of Practical Psychology and Other Tools*. San Luis Obispo, CA: Impact Publisher.

Women's Action for Nuclear Disarmament. 1986. *Turnabout: Emerging New Realism in the Nuclear Age*. Boston: WAND Education Fund.

————. n.d. Direct mail solicitation letter.

Yankelovich, Daniel, Robert Kingston, and Gerald Garvey. 1984. *Voter Options on Nuclear Arms Policy: A Briefing Book for the 1984 Elections*. New York: The Public Agenda Foundation.

Zald, Mayer N. and Robert Ash. 1966. "Social Movement Organizations: Growth, Decay and Change." *Social Forces* 44:327–341.

Zald, Mayer N. and John D. McCarthy, eds. 1987. *Social Movements in an Organizational Society: Collected Essays*. New Brunswick, NJ: Transaction Books.

Zald, Mayer N. and John D. McCarthy. 1980. "Social Movement Industries: Competition and Cooperation Among Movement Organizations." Pp. 1–20 in L. Kriesberg, ed., *Social Movements, Conflict and Change*. Greenwich, CT: JAI Press.

————. 1979. *The Dynamics of Social Movements: Resource Mobilization, Social Control, and Tactics*. Cambridge, MA: Winthrop Publishers.

Zola, Irving K. 1972. "Medicine as an Institution of Social Control." *Sociological Review* 20:487–504.

Zurcher, Louis A. and Russell L. Curtis. 1973. "A Comparative Analysis of Propositions Describing Social Movement Organizations." *Sociological Quarterly* 14:175–188.

Zurcher, Louis A. and R. George Kirkpatrick. 1976. *Citizens for Decency: Antipornography Crusades as Status Defense*. Austin: University of Texas Press.

Zurcher, Louis A. and David A. Snow. 1981. "Collective Behavior: Social Movements." Pp. 447–482 in M. Rosenberg and R. H. Turner, eds., *Social Psychology: Sociological Perspectives*. New York: Basic Books.

Index